RACE AND ETHNIC RELATIONS IN LATIN AMERICA AND THE CARIBBEAN

An Historical Dictionary and Bibliography

by

Robert M. Levine

The Scarecrow Press, Inc.
Metuchen, N.J., & London
1980

Library of Congress Cataloging in Publication Data

Levine, Robert M
    Race and ethnic relations in Latin America and the
Caribbean.

    Includes index.
    1.   Latin America--Race relations--Dictionaries.
2.   Latin America--Ethnic relations--Dictionaries.
3.   Latin America--Race relations--Bibliography.
4.   Latin America--Ethnic relations--Bibliography.
I.   Title.
F1419. A1L48   980'. 004   80-15179
ISBN 0-8108-1324-6

To

Craig & Carol Hendricks,
Antônio & Marília Paixão,
Antônio Augusto & Maria Helena Prates,
e famílias

CONTENTS

INTRODUCTION

The issues of race and ethnicity pervade the history of Latin America and the Caribbean, a vast geographical region given to extensive variation but at the same time subject to common socio-racial experiences. These include slavery, miscegenation, the evolution of racially-determined social strata, the penetration of foreign values and philosophies, and rebelliousness in search of racial or ethnic identity and human dignity.

A dictionary of terms, names, and events related to racial and ethnic questions must necessarily be limited and selective. Some entries are keyed (by authors' names) to books and articles listed in the bibliography, so that readers may consult the original source for further information, especially when the item deals with a concept or interpretation under debate in the historiographical literature.

The amount of coverage given to individual countries and societies to some degree reflects the literature, although I have made an effort to provide information on the entire region, from Mexico and the Bahamas to Patagonia. However, in countries where racial themes have played unusually important roles--Brazil, those in the Caribbean, Mexico, the Andean republics--treatment has been more extensive.

I have interpreted the thematic scope of socio-racial issues as broadly as possible. The dictionary emphasizes relations among races and ethnic groups more than it looks at the individual groups themselves, leaving Amerindian tribal life, then, to the anthropologists. Slavery obviously plays an extremely important role, as do race relations, prejudice and discrimination, and the ramifications of racial themes in formal and popular culture and everyday life.

Entries are arranged in alphabetical order. Spelling follows customary usage. Except where indicated, items refer to Spanish America, although the dictionary includes ex-

vii

tensive material from countries and places where the first language is French, Dutch, English, Portuguese, Aymará, Guarani, and various patois dialects. The rich African heritage of Latin America and the Caribbean is much evident as well.

No dictionary of this kind could have been compiled without access to the path-breaking work of such scholars as Magnus Mörner, Charles Wagley, Roger Bastide, H. Hoetinck, Marvin Harris, Eric C. Williams, Leslie Rout Junior, and Gilberto Freyre. Novelists have also provided important insight into racial and ethnic attitudes, terms, and relations; among the writers of fiction I have consulted I include V. S. Naipaul, Jorge Amado, Graciliano Ramos, Miguel Angel Asturias, and Jorge Luis Borges.

I would especially like to thank Barbara Beresford for her help in typing the manuscript.

Robert M. Levine
July 23, 1979
Port Jefferson, N. Y.

THE DICTIONARY

ABAKUA SOCIETY. A secret sect among Cuban slaves which broadened, by the late nineteenth and early twentieth centuries to form the basis for a series of working-class associations, the abakúa potencias, which in 1920 were courted by one of the presidential candidates (Mendocal) and thereby elevated to legitimate political status.

ABASI. The Efor deity worshipped by the secret Afro-Cuban society of the Nañigos. The society survived its transfer from Africa, and mostly has survived in undiluted form. Goat sacrifices are used as part of the initiation rite and patterned ritual drawings are employed. The drawings seem related to the pontos riscados of the Bantu candomblés in Rio de Janeiro--patterns chalked on the ground to summon spirits, and exploded with small amounts of gunpowder at the conclusion of the ceremony. See also CANDOMBLES; BANTU-YORUBA TRANSFER; EFOR.

ABENG. An instrument fabricated from the horn of a cow, used by maroons in Jamaica to signal their readiness for battle or to warn of danger. The term has been used for the name of a militant student newspaper at the University of the West Indies. See also MAROONS.

ABID. A slave, in Arabic. See also AZENAGUE.

ABOLENGO. A Bolivian term connoting "good lineage," although not equated with "racial purity." Heath notes that in fact miscegenation with Indian noblewomen was an approved custom in the early colonial period.

ABOLICIONISMO, O. An anti-slavery tract written in 1883 by Joaquim Nabuco. The book became the central ideological expression of the moderate wing of abolitionism and stressed humanitarian and moralistic themes. The book was faintly racist, rooted in the premise that if

1

slavery were abolished, Brazil could shift its working class base to free labor, especially European immigrants.

ACABRALHADO. A person with one mulatto and one black parent; a mixed breed. Term used in Brazil.

ACADEMIAS SUPERIORES. Secondary-level schools that were established in Brazil for the first time after Independence (1822). These afforded mixed-bloods the possibility of education beyond the rudimentary primary schools which were scattered through the Brazilian colony, especially those youths who were sponsored by their "natural" fathers or other relatives in the dominant class.

ACCOMPONG. A maroon village in the Jamaican parish of St. Elizabeth, from the word "akropong," which means the residence of a village chief.

ACCULTURATION. The mixture of cultural elements. Mörner shows how, in Latin America, miscegenation became a major vehicle in acculturation, although acculturation may well occur without miscegenation.

ACOBOCLAR. A Brazilian phrase meaning "to behave or appear like a caboclo, or peasant." The word also is defined in Brazilian-Portuguese dictionaries as meaning "rustic, rural, churlish, boorish." See also CABOCLO.

ACTION VANGUARD WORKERS PARTY. A black power, anti-imperialist organization in Guyana allied with the Ratoon and Ascria groups, whose propaganda is considered to have influenced the government of Prime Minister Forbes Burham to assert national control over the nation's foreign-controlled mining industry.

ADE. Spiritist (xangô) emblem of the African divinity Dadá.

ADELANTAR LA FAMILIA; ADELANTAR LA RAZA. "Improving the family; improving the race." A nineteenth-century Cuban phrase that illustrates the view that young women should choose the lightest-skinned available suitor for marriage.

AFFRANCHI. A freed slave holding the legal rights of a French citizen, in the West Indian colonies.

AFONSO ARINOS LAW. An anti-discrimination law passed

by the Brazilian Congress in 1951 and signed by President Vargas. Although considered unnecessary at that
time, the movement to enact such a law was spurred by
an incident in which a leading hotel in São Paulo (the
Othon) refused to register the visiting United States
dancer Katherine Dunham. Most critics point to the
fact that the law has never been enforced.

AFOXE. An Afro-Brazilian Carnival group of the city of
Salvador, Bahia.

AFRICANISING. Defined by Roger Bastide as the passion
among some European intellectuals to popularize and
praise African culture, perhaps as a form of guilt. J.
Jahn's Muntu and Sartre's Orphée Noir (Black Orpheus)
are cited as examples.

AFRICAN SLAVERY, PORTUGUESE see GUIMARÃES

AFRO-CHRISTIANITY. The general term for the syncretistic cults and religions that absorbed Christian, mostly
Catholic, ritual and symbols while retaining local or
tribal deities and practices.

AFRO-CUBAN MOVEMENT. An illegal political organization
led by Evaristo Esteñoz and Pedro Ivonet during the
Gómez administration (1909-1913) to gain better treatment for Cuban blacks and to restore the right to organize political groups based on race or color. Thwarted,
they led an insurrection in 1912 in Oriente province which
was crushed by government troops advised by United
States officers, killing about 3,000 blacks. This was the
last major Afro-Cuban demonstration in Cuban history.

AFRO-INDIAN CONCUBINAGE. Although tolerated during the
early Spanish colonial period (the ladinos who accompanied the Spanish conquistadores faced the same lack
of women within their own group as the Europeans), by
the mid-sixteenth century concubinage between blacks and
Amerindians was frowned upon, and in several munici-
palities blacks were threatened with castration if they
persisted in such liaisons.

AFRO-LATIN AMERICAN DANCE. Sambas, frevos, tangos
and other, even less-inhibited dance forms derived from
African tribal dances are considered sensual, imitating
"the vicissitudes of seduction, right up to its climax in

orgasm" (F. Ortiz). This is contrasted to North American Negro dances, which anthropologists consider "more
'Negro' than 'African.' " These urban dance forms are
characterized by gestures firmly repressed in everyday
life, and even contain elements of anti-white frenzy and
motor violence (R. Bastide).

AGASSIZ, LOUIS. A Swiss-born, Harvard-trained ethno-
grapher of the mid-nineteenth century whose writings of
race popularized the (unscientific) notion that climate af-
fected racial differences, and that the white race, residing in the temperate zone, was therefore superior.
Agassiz's writings were influential in Latin America
among members of the elite seeking confirmation of
their feelings about racial degeneracy and the backwardness of the mixed underpopulation.

AGREGADO. An Andean-region name given to a member of
an Amerindian village community who has been "adopted"
into the group rather than being born into it. Such persons enjoy higher status and are called originários.

AGUIA FUTEBOL CLUBE. A social club in the black district of Vidigal, in Rio de Janeiro, "discovered" in
1970 by avant-garde upper-class whites, who travel to
the club for samba, much in the same way as New York
whites visited Harlem in the 1920's.

AHI TE ESTAS ("Here you are") see SOCIO-RACIAL CLAS-
SIFICATIONS

AIZAN. The Haitian Voodoo deity incorporating the attributes of Jesus Christ. The Brazilian Yoruba version
is Obatala.

A LA CRIOLLA. Meaning "Creole style," this phrase is
used in a pejorative sense to show peninsular disdain
for creole behavior. See CRIOLLO.

ALBINO see SOCIO-RACIAL CLASSIFICATIONS

ALCAÇOVAS, TREATY OF. Signed between Spain and Portugal in 1479, limiting Spain's penetration of Africa to
the Canary Islands and assuring Portugal uncontested
control (for the foreseeable future) of the African coast
for trading purposes. In exchange, the Portuguese sold
slaves directly to Spanish brokers at Cádiz. See also
SARRACENOS NEGROS.

ALEMAN DE MIERDA. Chilean vulgarism for German settlers, meaning "shit-German."

ALEMÃO BATATA. A Brazilian word for a German colono
that literally means "potato-German."

ALBARRAZADO. The offspring of a gibaro male and an Indian woman. See GIBARO.

ALEGRIA, CIRO. The Peruvian author of the Indianist novel,
Wide and Alien Is the World (1941), an eloquent statement on contemporary relations between the surviving
Amerindian communities and the encroaching Hispanic
world. See also INDIGENISMO.

ALGUAZILS. Policemen in early nineteenth-century Port of
Spain, usually free blacks, who were paid for picking
up other blacks after curfew and for rounding up es-
capees.

ALMEIDA, JUAN. The mulatto comandante of the Moncada
barracks attack in Cuba in 1953, praised after 1959 by
Fidel Castro as a symbol of the revolutionary government's concern with the racial discrimination issue.
See also HISTORY WILL ABSOLVE ME.

ALMOJARIFAZGO. A duty charged on imports and exports
by Spanish colonial authorities which extended to slaves
as well as other merchandise. Until 1543 the duty was
7.5 percent of the cost of each slave; thereafter it was
raised to 10 percent. In later years the tax varied from
viceroyalty to viceroyalty.

ALUFAS see BLACK ISLAM

AMA. A Negro nursemaid. See also BABA.

AMANDALA. A black power publication of the United Black
Association for Development of Belize.

AMARAL, RAUL JOVELINO. The head of the military arm
of the short-lived Frente Negra Brasileira in the early
1930's. The Frente Negra militia wore uniforms and
were subject to rigid discipline. The militia, however,
did little more than parade.

AMARELO. 1) "Yellow," the racial/color designation used
on Brazilian work registration forms for Orientals.

Although the federal census since 1950 has omitted race/
color data, in fact, all employees must indicate their
color in their identification papers. 2) A term used to
describe light-skinned mulattos.

AMERICANACCI. Italian slang for someone who has emigrated to North or South America and returned.

AMERIND. A term suggested in 1899 and used for the peoples native to the New World before the European Conquest. It is derived from the term "American Indian."

AMERINDIAN PROTOTYPE. Given that Amerindians lack
the B blood type, and many Asians share that group,
anthropologists assume that although Amerindians are
to a greater or lesser degree Mongoloid, no "pure"
Amerindian prototype may be identified among peoples
now alive.

AMPARO. "Protection," or "shelter," the arrangement
whereby manumitted slaves who could not pay the annual Crown tax were seized and put into the hands of
clergymen or officials, who then could set them to work.
See also SEMI-LIBERATION.

ANDALUS, EL. Moslem Spain, broadly acculturated prior
to the fall of Granada in 1492 although Arabs and Ber-
bers represented only a small minority of the Spanish
population. Ethnic miscegenation occurred more frequently before 1391; after that time segregation and
persecution were the rule.

ANDRESOTE, JUAN (ANDRES LOPEZ DE ROSARIO). A
Venezuelan zambo and leader of a struggle against the
monopoly of the Caracas Company in 1730. Allying with
Dutch ship captains and merchants on Curaçao, his rebel army--comprised of free blacks, escaped slaves,
and Indians--rose in revolt, but his initial successes
frightened the landowners who had supported the movement, and Andresote was forced to flee to Curaçao.
The conflict continued and was ultimately crushed blood-
ily by armed repression after 1733.

ANDROFAGO. A cannibal who eats only male flesh. "An-
drophagy" is allegedly practiced by Brazilian Amerindian
tribes who follow cannibalistic behavior only as a by-
product of warfare, i.e., eating male prisoners taken
in battle.

ANENECUILCO. Zapata's village in Morelos, Mexico, which was the heart of the Amerindian and Mestizo rebellion that flared into a major element of the Mexican Revolution.

ANGOLA see CANDOMBLES; NATIONS

AÑINGOTARSE. To squat, or cower. The verb has been used in Central America with reference to the stereotyped behavior of Amerindians or ladinos.

ANNAMABOE. A Gold Coast slave entrepôt from which the largest quantities of slaves were shipped to Jamaica before 1788. Jamaican slaves generally came from the Gold Coast or from southern Nigeria.

APALENCADO. A slave living in the palenque, the settlement of fugitive runaways. See also CIMARRONES.

APARCERIA. A form of polyandry among La Plata gauchos whereby, in the late eighteenth century, women of all racial backgrounds lived in huts near ranching centers and acted as "wife" to several gauchos who visited from time to time. Children were raised irrespective of the identity of the fathers, who ostensibly worked out mutual agreements over visitation rights.

APIRI. An Indian colono in rural Bolivia who transported goods by mules and horses from the altiplano to urban centers until his function was replaced by trucks.

A QUARTE PIQUETTES. A French form of whipping slaves by which the victim was tied to four stakes or posts.

ARACUANOS. Native peoples indigenous to Chile's coast who were partially absorbed after the Conquest through assimilation and partially driven out of central Chile by military force. In later years, intellectuals began to pay homage to the Aracuanos and their fierce spirit of independence. See also ENCINA, FRANCISCO ANTONIO.

ARANHA, FELIPPA MARIA. A black woman, the leader of a force of fugitive slaves and Amerindians in the Brazilian Amazon (in the region of the Trombates) that successfully resisted Portuguese efforts to crush them. Little, however, is known about the maroon colony itself or about its leader.

ARAWAKAN.   The largest indigenous linguistic group in South America, stretching from Florida through the Caribbean into Argentina, Brazil, and Bolivia.

ARDRA   see   NATIONS

ARGOLO, NILO.   A character in Jorge Amado's Tent of Miracles, based on the Bahian Medical School's mulatto professor of legal medicine, Raimundo Nina Rodrigues.

ARGUEDES, ALCIDES (1879-1946).   Racist Bolivian author who was prominent at the turn of the twentieth century (see PUEBLO ENFERMO).   Arguedes also wrote La Raza de Bronce, published in 1919.   It is thought to be the first great Indianist novel and is sympathetic to the plight of the Amerindians subdued by the conquistadores and the Catholic clergy.   In general, Arguedes considered Bolivians to be lazy, trecherous, and barbarous.

ARM RULE.   In colonial Saint Domingue, the law held that any mulatto or free man of color who struck a white, for any reason, would have his arm hacked off.

ARRENDEROS.   A colonial Peruvian term used in the Southwest for tenant sharecroppers.   On the coast, the term "yanacona" was used instead.   Wages were low, averaging three reales per day, although the right to grow crops for personal consumption was considered an additional form of payment.

ARUAKS.   The original inhabitants of the West Indies, supplanted by the Carib Indians, their traditional enemies. The Caribs killed the Aruak men but kept their wives as concubines.   After the conquest, the Caribs themselves disappeared from the larger islands but survived on such smaller ones as St. Lucia and St. Vincent.

ASASE.   Earth-mother, a Fanti-Ashante spirit adopted by the Bush Negroes in French Guiana and Dutch Guiana (Surinam).

ASHOLA AGUENGE.   The Mayombé (Cuba) Mother of Waters.   See also   MAYOMBE SYNCRETISM.

ASIENTO.   The monopoly granted by the Spanish Crown for the slave trade.   It was first given in 1528, although licenses for the same purpose had been granted annually since 1518.

ASSOCIAÇÃO JOSE DO PATROCINIO. A group linked to the Frente Negra of São Paulo, Brazil, in the late 1920's.

ATAHUALPA (1500-1533). The leader of the Inca Empire, who was captured by Pizarro in 1532 and executed in spite of delivering a roomful of gold as ransom.

ATL. The Nahuatl word for water and a root word of the Nahuatl language. Meyer notes the universal importance of water from a pantheistic and a pragmatic standpoint in Nahuatl culture.

"ATROCIOUS IRONY." The term used by Brazilian statesman Rui Barbosa in 1898 to lament the fate of the ex-slave a decade after legal emancipation, when little real improvement in the lives of blacks could be perceived.

ATTA. The leader of the ill-fated Berbice slave uprising in Dutch Guiana in 1762. See BERBICE SLAVE REBELLION.

AVES SIN NIDO ("Birds Without Nests"). The title of a volume published in 1889 by the Peruvian author Clorinda Matto de Turner. The book was one of the earliest portrayals of the squalid life of non-white Peruvians, although it has been largely forgotten.

AXAYACATL. Aztec ruler from 1469 to 1481, and the builder of the great temple-palace where Cortês and his entourage were lodged when they arrived in Tenochtitlán.

AXE. A candomblé spell.

AYLLU. The ancient form of Amerindian community in Andean region, maintained after the Conquest by the contemporary Aymará and Quechua.

AYMAMON. A cacique of the Taino tribe of Puerto Rico at the time of its conquest by Ponce de León in 1508.

AYMARA. A pre-Incan tribe which preserved its linguistic identity even after its conquest by the Incas in the fifteenth century. Heath notes that anthropologists have always considered the Aymará "dour and unpleasant," although lately some have modified this characterization.

AZENAGUES. Members of an Islamic Berber tribe, part of the Tuareg group, who were first kidnapped by Portuguese sailors in the voyages of exploration along the African coast in the 1440's. They were then used as middlemen in the purchase of slaves, which the azenagues procured from interior regions. Prince Henry of Portugal prohibited the enslavement of the azenagues after 1446, when the trade became formalized.

AZUL. "Blue," as in "blue-blood."

-B-

BABA. A Brazilian nursemaid, typically black and portrayed as the equivalent of the North American "mammy." Proponents of the racial democracy theme point to the role of the baba in raising children of the elite and to the woman's status as "one of the family."

BABALÃO. A candomblé priest and soothsayer. See also AXE.

BABALORISHA. 1) A type of secret religious fraternity in northern Brazil, especially aroung Maranhão, which is exclusively Afro-Brazilian in membership. Also known as BABALÃO. 2) A candomblé priest.

"BABEL RACIAL" ("Racial Babel"). A term coined in 1978 by journalist Antônio Felipe Canoa to describe Brazilian racial reality, in contrast to the official concept of racial democracy.

BACKRA. Corruption of the Ibo word mbakara, meaning "white man."

BAFAN. A Jamaican term for a child or man who suffers from rickets. In Twi language it refers to a child who does not learn to walk during its first seven years.

BAJANS. The name for Barbadians, considered to be the "patricians of the islands," a people apart who are known for their loyalty to Great Britain and to British patterns of behavior. West Indians call the Bajans political reactionaries, and refer to their skill at cricket (Gary Sobers, the greatest cricketer in the world, is a Bajan) as evidence of the Bajan effort to "put life back into the Englishman's dying game." Suffice it to say, Bajans are not strong proponents of the black power movement sweeping the Caribbean.

BALLA. The leader of an uprising of fugitive slaves and Caribs on the island of Dominica in 1785.

BALLANO, KING. A cimarron leader operating from the San Blas Mountains in the Isthmus of Panama who led raids on Spanish mule trains carrying cargo eastward to Porto Bello. He was captured, castrated, and released in 1553, whereupon he returned to his former activities. His ultimate fate is unknown.

BALL-PAN-MAN. A vendor of foods--pindas, jelly-coconuts, booby eggs, snow-balls--in the streets of Kingston, Jamaica.

BAMBOULA. A drum dance popular on St. Thomas, V.I. among nineteenth-century blacks, but replaced after the 1860's by street masquerading.

BANDEIRANTES. Brazilian mestizos from the captaincy of São Vicente (later called São Paulo) who lived off the land, spoke the lingua geral--Tupí-Guaraní--and participated in Indian-hunting expeditions and voyages up the inland rivers in search of gold and diamonds. They were also called mamelucos. In later centuries the bandeirantes acquired a reputation for path-finding and pioneer-like bravery which obscured the fact that most were adventurers and enslavers of the aboriginal population.

BANTU. A term applied by Brazilians to designate slaves from Angola, the Congo, and Mozambique--the majority of slaves in Brazil. More highly regarded were blacks from Gulf of Guinea ports, known as Minas, and from the Cape Verde/Portuguese Guinea region.

BANTU RELIGIOUS INFLUENCE. Strongest in Brazil, especially among followers of the fetish-worship cult macumba. Macumbeiros (practicioners) perform ritual sacrifices of domestic animals to Bantu deities--Ganga-Zumba, Canjira-mungongo, Cubango, Sinhu-renga, Lin-

gongo and others--and engage in ritualistic dancing.
This influence has been actively combatted by the Catholic Church, although in the 1970's macumba ceremonies
have become fashionable among the upper middle classes, and macumba popularity has flourished.

BANTU-YORUBA TRANSFER. In some parts of Latin America, Bantu spirits have merged with or been influenced
by, in syncretistic fashion, Yoruba deities. Thus the
Yoruba thundergod, Changô, is identified by Angolans
as Zazê and by Congolese as Quigongo.

BAPTIST FREE CHURCH. A church founded in 1894 in
Jamaica by a Reverend Bedward. It exhibited features
characteristic later of the Father Divine sect in the
United States. Bedward proclaimed himself the reincarnation of Moses, St. John the Baptist, and Jesus
Christ, and promised destruction of white society by
1920. This message was also proclaimed in rural
Brazil in 1897 by the religious mystic Antoniô Conselheiro, leader of the Canudos insurrection.

BARACOONS. Temporary stockades used to hold African
slaves during auctions in Cartagena and elsewhere. The
baracoons were surrounded by caldrons of boiling water
to be used in case of an uprising of the chained slaves,
who were also fed potions to increase the gloss of their
skins, rubbed with gun powder, oil, and lemon juice,
and stripped of all garments, in order to show their
bodies.

"BARÃO DO CHOCOLATE." A Brazilian landowner of somewhat dark moreno hue who was elevated by Emperor
Pedro II to the nobility, and who other members of the
elite, according to Gilberto Freyre, dubbed "the Baron
of Chocolate."

BARBARO. A pejorative term used in the Bolivian Oriente
for tribal Indians, labelling them "barbarous."

BARBOSA, JOSE CELSO (1857-1921). A middle-class Puerto
Rican mulatto and a leading supporter of separatism
from Spain and, ultimately, statehood, with English as
Puerto Rico's official language. Barbosa studied at the
University of Michigan, and was granted an honorary
Master of Arts degree in 1903.

BARBUDA. A small Caribbean island almost exclusively Negro in population.

BARCLAY, ARTHUR. A Barbadian black who emigrated to Liberia and in 1904 became its President.

BARRACONES. Slave quarters within the city limits to which new arrivals, or bozales, were taken to be housed and viewed for resale.

BARRIADAS. Squatter settlements.

BASTIAAN see Carpata

BASUNDI see NATIONS

BATA-COTO. A Yoruba war drum which produced such stirring effects on Brazilian slaves that it was banned after 1835, when its use figured prominently in a slave revolt of that year.

BATOULA see MARAN, RENE

BEAN-EATER. United States border-area pejorative term for a Mexican.

BEAST-LICK. A heavy blow dealt to a Negro or slave, brutal enough to stun a donkey.

BEBIAN, AUGUSTE (1789-1839). A Guadelupean educator whose school for black and mulatto children founded in 1837 was the first of its kind in the Antilles.

BECKFORD, GEORGE. Jamaican economist and member of the Pan-Caribbean black power group of the early 1970's. See also BLACK POWER.

BEGUINE. A creole dance originating in Martinique's Carnival.

BEKE. Martinique slang for a white man. The island, which has adapted the strict French sense of social classes, places whites at the top and blacks at the bottom, although most of the population is black. On the other hand, as Naipaul notes, race on Martinique is an inescapable issue, but in their Frenchness all Martinicans are equal.

BEM ARIADA. "Well-sandpapered," a Bahian term for a light mulatto.

BEMBA. A Spanish-American term for Negroid-appearing lips.

BENGUELAS. Africans shipped as slaves by Portuguese traders from Angola.

BENS DO EVENTO. "Contingency goods" sold at auction, regulated by Brazilian officials in the 1850's for the first time. "Bens" included cattle, beasts, and slaves.

BERBICE SLAVE REBELLION. An uprising in Dutch Guiana in 1762, which, because of the strong Calvinism of the slaveowners, was viewed as a war between Christians and heathens. As a result, when the rebellion collapsed, the surviving slaves were executed by the most extreme forms of tortures imaginable. The leader of the slaves, named Atta, was slowly roasted while his fellow slaves were tortured before his eyes.

BERING STRAITS. Lying between Alaska and Russian Asia, this was the presumed route through which the first Amerindians migrated to the New World, possibly between 25,000 and 20,000 B.C.

BEST, LLOYD. Trinidadian black power leader. See BLACK POWER.

"BETTER CLASS." A phrase used in Jamaica as a euphemism for the white elite.

BETTY. A young East Indian girl, in the British Caribbean, probably derived from the Hindustani beti, or daughter.

BIAFRAS see CASTAS DE RIOS DE GUINEA

BICHO. Mexican slang (c. 1930's) for blue-eyed whites.

BIDONVILLES. Haitian shantytowns inhabited by poor blacks, often constructed on the ruins of abandoned housing. See also FAVELAS.

BIG SIX. The economic "establishment" of Barbados through the 1940's, all white and whose trading monopoly on the island restricted opportunities for the "coloured" middle-class merchants in Bridgetown.

BIMS   see   UNPOLLUTED BIMS

BIMSHIRE.   Satirical West Indies name for Barbados, seen as a black version of English provincialism and stuffiness.   See also   BAJANS.

BIOHO, DOMINGO.   Same as KING BENKOS (q.v.).

BIZANGO.   An Afro-Haitian werewolf which eats children, analogous to the Kimbungo of Afro-Brazilians.   See also   BANTU-YORUBA TRANSFER.

B'JACK.   A Bahamian term for a poor, dark-skinned, clever boy.

BLACK BROTHERHOODS.   Colonial Brazilian religious organizations, called Irmandades, founded in 1639 and after by blacks and mulattos under Church sponsorship. The brotherhoods often collected funds to free slaves through purchases of cartas de alforria (letters of freedom).   Other slaves were granted their liberty by their masters in gratitude for long service (especially where the slave was aged, crippled or sick).

BLACK BUNDLES.   Slang term for black slaves imported to Barbados to develop its sugar plantations in the seventeenth century.

BLACK CARIBS.   A half-breed group of West Indians which originated in the seventeenth century when slaves were imported to the smaller islands of the Caribbean.   The greatest concentration today of Black Caribs are in Belize, or British Honduras, where they were resettled when St. Vincent became a British colony.   See also MOSCOS.

BLACK CONQUISTADORS.   The term denoting Hispanicized ladinos--Spanish-speaking blacks--who accompanied their masters as servants or soldiers to the New World. Many slaves, moreover, earned their freedom through participation in the battles of the conquest.

BLACK CULTURES RESEARCH INSTITUTE OF RIO DE JANEIRO.   A volunteer organization organized in the late 1970's to provide research and technical services, educational programs, visual aids, and other assistance to black communities and groups in the city seeking to cele-

brate or study Afro-Brazilian Culture. One of a number of groups funded by the Inter-American Foundation,
its future was imperiled when the latter agency was expelled from Brazil in 1977 by the Foreign Ministry.

BLACK ISLAM. Like Fanti-Ashanti culture, a religious
body imported to the New World that has survived culturally but not as an organized body of belief. Black
Muslims flourished in Rio de Janeiro and in the region
around Bahia, where they were called Musulmis, or
Malis (inhabitants of Mali). They worshipped Allah or
Olorum-ulua, a syncretistic blending of Allah with the
Yoruba chief deity, Olorum. They met not in mosques
but in the residences of their priests, or alufas, who
were assisted in cult ritual by ladanos (a term derived
from the Arabic imam). The religious side of the cult
gradually died out in Brazil, although cultural survivals
were left in the form of mandingas, or magical rituals.

BLACK ISRAELITES. A name Rastafarians have given to
themselves since they believe they are living in the
Babylonian captivity of Jamaican life.

BLACK JAMAICA. A book by W. P. Livingstone, published
in 1899, showing the acceptance by the colonial elite of
the Social Darwinist argument of unequal evolution of
races.

BLACK POWER. The contemporary black power movement
in the "Commonwealth Caribbean" (Trinidad, Jamaica,
Guyana, and Barbados) began formally in Guyana in
1960, although it was preceded a generation before by
the Jamaican black nationalist Marcus Garvey and by
the pan-Caribbeanist C. L. R. James, both of whom
were exiled for attempting to organize politically. The
Guyana circle formed the New World Group, whose
ideas were disseminated in a publication, New World
Fortnightly. Associates on other islands soon organized
a pan-Caribbean black power journal, the New World
Quarterly, with contributions from Lloyd Best in Trinidad, George Beckford in Jamaica, and Clive Thomas
in Guyana: all political economists seeking radical
changes in Caribbean dependent productivity. After
1968, intellectual leadership was exercised by Walter
Rodney, the historian who had been exiled from Jamaica,
and who now preached political power for blacks in the
Caribbean "commensurate with their own numbers."

Several political groups--Tapia and Moko in Trinidad, Ratoon and Ascria in Guyana, Forum in St. Lucia, and Abeng in Jamaica appeared, following Rodney's anti-imperialist and pro-black nationalist line.

BLACK REVOLT. An insurrection led by the newly outlawed Cuban Independent Party of Color in 1912 in Oriente province, the only region in Cuba with a majority of blacks in its population. The revolt was put down by Cuban forces, although the United States landed four Marine companies at Guantánamo and sent warships to Havana. Nearly half of the black troops were killed, about 3,000.

BLACK RIO. A movement of Afro-Brazilian cultural identity originating in the less-affluent "surburban" zones of the city of Rio de Janeiro in 1976-77. Black Rio challenged the traditional view of the Afro-Brazilian as a docile, assimilated Brazilian. Given the total absence of opportunities for black self-awareness in the past for Brazil, this modest start was perceived as a definite threat by the elite, leading to attacks on the Black Rio concept via the media, as an imported form of militancy promising violence. In spite of this resistance, branch groups have formed in other Brazilian cities: Black São Paulo, Black Salvador, Black Pôrto Alegre, even Black Florianópolis.

BLACK-SHOTS. A name for blacks serving in the Jamaican militia in the first part of the nineteenth century.

"BLACK STAIN." The theme proclaimed by such Brazilian intellectuals as João Pandia Calogeras and others, that the answer to the country's racial dilemma was to "whiten" the population. Within a century (of white immigration), Arthur Heyl Neiva wrote, "the nation will be white."

"BLACK TOMMIES." Negro troops used by British colonial officials to keep order in Jamaica and other islands.

BLACK WHITELASH. The condescending term coined by foreign journalists for the "loss" of Antigua and other Caribbean islands to black nationalists in the 1960's.

BLANCO. Literally, "white," but the term used in some Latin American countries for the light-skinned mestizo elite.

BLANCOS. Whites, the name used for Europeans (peninsulares) in the New World. See also HOMBRES DE LA OTRA BANDA.

BLANCO Y NATO. Colombian phrase for a white with a Negroid nose.

BLOOMSBURY CULT. According to Gordon K. Lewis, the belief among intellectuals before the mid-1930's that Caribbean non-whites were "simple and healthy" savages. The appearance of W. M. MacMillan's Warning from the West Indies in 1935, an exposé of West Indian social disorganization and economic dependency, helped counter this thesis.

BLYDEN, EDWARD W. (1832-1912). The first black from the Virgin Islands to be recognized for his scholarly work. Educated in Liberia, he eventually settled there and became Secretary of State.

BOA FORTUNA. A slave ship, ironically named "Good Fortune," which arrived at Belém de Pará in 1788 carrying slaves infected by smallpox. Although the ship was quarantined--200 slaves died on board--two slaves were sold secretly, spreading the disease to the city.

BOÇAL. A newly-arrived slave in Brazil, so-named because he or she could speak no Portuguese.

BODE. 1) A billy-goat, in Brazil. 2) Slang term for a mulatto.

BODEGAS. Taverns frequented by Cuban urban slaves, usually in the company of their carabelas (shipmates from Africa), or members of their "tribe" or "nation."

BOGAS ("Canoe men") see LIBRES DE COLOR

BOIAS FRIAS. "Cold meals," a slang term for the marginal day laborers who reside in the urban centers of the coffee and cattle-raising regions of the interior of the state of São Paulo, and who are trucked by landowners to fazendas on a day-by-day basis. João Goulart's Rural Worker Statute, promulgated in 1963, designed to extend legal protection to the working class of the rural areas, actually drove them off the land, as entrepreneurs

preferred to avoid complying with the law, hiring laborers instead on an itinerant basis. Most of the boias
frias are either caboclos or blacks.

BOIS-BOIS. The name for the King of Carnival in the
French Antilles (Rei Momo in Brazil), who is symbolic-
ally burned by revellers on the islands.

BOLIVAR, SIMON (1783-1830). The hero of Venezuelan Independence, a wealthy creole who devoted his life to the
overthrow of the Spanish Empire in South America. On
race, Bolívar's record is ambivalent: although he recruited and allied himself with the llaneros and fielded
troops who were largely zambos and blacks, he personally feared persons of color. In 1826, he wrote to General Santander that Latin Americans "are the abomin-
able offspring of those raging beasts that came to America to waste her blood and to breed with their victims
before sacrificing them. Later the fruits of these unions conmingled with slaves uprooted from Africa. With
such physical mixtures and such elements of morale,
can we possibly place laws above heroes and principles
above men?"

BOLIVIA-AFRICA CONNECTION. The flight of whites from
Rhodesia and South Africa in the late 1970's resulted in
many seeking a haven in the ostensibly unlikely nation
of Bolivia. These colonos have purchased land and employed cheap, peasant labor, and are recreating, in a
small way, their African life-style. A similar wave of
immigration to Bolivia, Argentina, Chile, and Brazil occurred at the end of the Second World War when former
Nazis and other European fascists fled their crumbling
regimes.

BOLIVIAN MINISTRY OF PEASANT AFFAIRS. One of the
first acts of the revolutionary government which came
to power in April 1952 under Víctor Paz Estenssoro's
MNR was to create a ministry to deal with Bolivia's
indigenous population. Its reformist spirit is illustrated
by the fact that the word indio, with its pejorative connotations, was expunged from government use, replaced
with the more neutral term campesino, which means
"peasant."

BOLIVIAN NATIONAL INDIAN CONGRESS. An officially-
sanctioned national meeting in May 1945 to discuss the

problems of Bolivia's rural Indian population. Little
real change resulted from the Congress's decrees calling for schools for peasants, reduced feudal obligation,
and help for the poor although some labor requirements
(pongueaje) may have been lightened, specifically in the
region of the yungas.

BOMA see NATIONS

BOMBA. The only surviving African dance practiced by
the largely Negro population of coastal Ecuador, and
then only at Christmastime, to the accompaniment of
songs in Spanish.

BOMBO. A Ki-Kongo word for a dead body which, in modern Jamaican usage, is considered offensive and may
result in a fine in court if used.

BOMFIM, MANOEL. One of the first Brazilians to refute
publicly the implications of the European-based racist
versions of Social Darwinism which swept the Latin
American elite at the conclusion of the nineteenth century. A physician from the poor northeastern state of
Sergipe, Bomfim cited contemporary anthropologists
to attack such racists as Le Bon, Gobineau, and the
Portuguese Oliveira Martins. Other writers, including
the influential Brazilian critic Sîlvio Romero, counter-
attacked, calling Bomfim's arguments advocating racial
equality "illusionary" and worse.

BOMILCAR, ALVARO. A journalist and social critic who
was one of the first Brazilians--in 1911--to write about
racial prejudice; his book, O preconceito de raça no
Brasil, was withheld from publication for five years by
the author to find a more "receptive audience." In
1920 he founded a nationalist group, Açao Social Nacio-
nalista, which, among other demands, called for racial
equality.

BONGO. The so-called "Convince Cult," a syncretistic
Afro-Protestant religion acknowledging Christ but wor-
shipping the spirits of the dead. Local fraternities (bongo) in Jamaica served for a time as centers of resistance to white domination, but in recent years have declined in influence, supplanted by the more activist Ras
Tafari movement.

BONGO MAN. An African.

BORDEAUX, GENERAL   see   MOSES GOTTLIEB

BORIQUEN.   Columbus's original name for the Island of
Puerto Rico, which he sighted in 1493.   The place was
inhabited by Taino tribesmen, four whom, women, were
seized by his sailors when they canoed out to his ship
to make contact.

BOYER, JEAN PIERRE.   A mulatto landowner who consolidated the independent sections of republican Haiti in
1818 and who annexed the Spanish colony of Santo Domingo after its citizens revolted.   See also   PETION,
ALEXANDRE.

BOZALES.   African slaves newly imported to Cuba in the
nineteenth century, most destined for rural sugar plantations away from the growing cities.   Rural slaves
were mainly bozales while urban slaves were criollos,
Afro-Cubans born on the island.

BRAN, BROM PEOPLES.   Africans from the coast of Senegal and Gambia, corresponding to the Spanish category
of gelofes.

BRANCO CABOCLADO.   A "caboclocized white," a Brazilian
term for a Caucasian of racially doubtful parentage, or
simply a light-skinned mulatto.

BRANCO DA BAHIA.   A term usually employed outside Bahia, used to mock the Bahian custom of calling mulattoes "whites," since most Bahian elite families were
believed to have been liberally mixed with black ancestry.
The term branco por procuração ("white by proxy"),
with an even more pejorative connotation, is used behind peoples' backs.

BREADFOOT NIGGERS.   Jamaican slang term for "small
islanders," the inhabitants of St. Kitts, Montserrat,
Antigua and so on.

BREADFRUIT.   A tropical fruit used as cheap slave food, first
taken by Captain Bligh from the Guianas to St. Vincent
in 1793 and sold for a thousand pounds.   See also   STAR-
APPLE.

BRIDE.   A Jamaican maroon term used either for the bride
or groom in a wedding ceremony.

BRITISH CARIBBEAN RACE RELATIONS. At the top of the social scale as on the bottom, society remained rigorously segregated until the post-World War I period, when the rise of spectator sports and the example of personally successful non-whites in commerce and, to a lesser extent, in politics, contributed to relaxation of racial separateness. In some places, education was offered as a palliative to non-white frustrations, and by the 1920's these educational opportunities began to produce a parallel elite to the entrenched white establishment.

BROSSA. A band of brigands, the offensive arm of villages descended from the runaway slave (maroon) "republics" in Mexican Oaxaca, employed as a form of resistance against outside encroachment.

BRUJOS see ZAHORIS

BUCCAN. A Carib word for the wooden rack or frame on which meat--including human flesh--was smoked or dried prior to eating. The word "buccaneer" is derived from buccan.

BUCCRAS. White masters (Guyana spelling). See also BUKRAS.

BUCHI. A Panamanian term for a wild or uncivilized man. It is derived from the English bushman.

BUCKLE, HENRY THOMAS (1821-1862). An English historian whose History of Civilization in England dismissed Brazil (which he had never visited) as a tropical orphan, cut off from the possibility of genuine progress by its exotic and luxuriant untamed nature. Buckle's view provided the antecedent to later, more overtly racist, interpretations of Brazilian life condemning that nation as decadent and "mongrelized."

BUCKS. A contemptuous term for Amerindians used by coastland Guyanese whose world (Naipaul reminds us) is more Caribbean than South American.

BUDDOE see MOSES GOTTLIEB

BUDIM. The supposed body odor of the African, as perceived by upper-class Brazilians. Owing to this stereotype, mulattoes during the eighteenth and nineteenth centuries became noted for their extravagant use of perfume, ostensibly to counter this "odor." See also CATINGA.

BUENA CASTA. "Of good family." See also SOCIEDAD DE CASTAS.

BUENO DO PARDO, BARTOLOMEU. A Portuguese noble and military officer who crushed a "quasi-kingdom of fugitive negroes" in the interior of Minas Gerais in 1757 and who allegedly returned to Lisbon with 3,900 pairs of ears as "proof" of his success.

BUKRA. A pejorative term used by rural workers in the Virgin Islands to refer to whites in general and planters in particular.

BUMBA. A hideout of fugitive slaves near Santiago, Cuba, in the seventeenth century. The settlement was granted treaty autonomy by the Spanish authorities but the agreement was broken and Bumba ultimately destroyed.

BUMBA-MEU-BOI. A folkloric enactment of the death and resurrection of an ox, performed in papier-mâché costumes by rural Brazilians, usually caboclos.

BUNGE, CARLOS OCTAVIO. A turn-of-the-century Argentine writer and son of a German immigrant who developed a theory about mongrelization of the Spanish American "race," calling the mestizo "impure, anti-Christian," and deadly. Virulently racist by today's standards, Bunge drew on pseudo-scientific ideas current during his day in Europe and the Western Hemisphere.

BUNGO TALK. The term for old fashioned expressions and turns of phrase spoken by Jamaican blacks, usually "Guinea birds," or slaves born in Africa.

BUREAU OF INDIAN AFFAIRS. A Mexican cabinet-level agency established in 1936 by President Lázaro Cárdenas. The Bureau sponsored an international conference on Indian affairs in 1940 and led to the creation, in 1941, of agencies in Mexico (and other Latin American republics) to promote education, sanitation, and the preservation of traditional indigenous culture.

BULTER, URIAH. A self-educated, Marxist labor leader in

Trinidad responsible for a general strike in 1937 and
labor agitation against exploitation of the poor throughout the Caribbean. He was ultimately arrested by the
British as an agitator.

BURHAM, FORBES. Prince Minister of Guyana after 1964
and leader of the country's blacks. His protagonist was
Cheddi Jagan, who is supported by the East Indians.
Burham's party, the People's National Congress, rep-
resents about one third of the population, the Afro-
Guyanese.

-C-

CABERRE INDIANA. A tribe indigenous to modern-day
Venezuela, known in pre-Columbian times for their manufacture of curare, which they made from swamp roots.

CABILDO. An informal club or social organization for
slaves and ex-slaves in Cuba, headed by a capataz de
cabildo, or leader.

CABOCLIZAÇÃO see VADIAGEM

CABOCLO. Term (literally, "copper hued") applied to a
Brazilian Amerindian or mestizo. In the Amazon region
and the Northeast, the term is often used indiscriminately to describe the rural poor, not unlike the word
"hillbilly" in English.

CABOCLO CANDOMBLE. A predominately African version
of the forbidden Brazilian cult of catimbo, found in the
region between Pernambuco and Bahia. See also CAT-
IMBO.

CABOCLO DE BEIRA. A river-bank caboclo.

CABRA. A Brazilian term for a person of mixed ancestry,
usually African, European, and Amerindian. See also
CABOCLO.

CABROCHA. A dark-skinned mestizo woman.

CACHOTS BRÛLANTS. Punishment cells in French island
prisons, usually windowless, with temperatures exceed-
ing 100 degrees, where subjects, usually blacks, were

chained flat on boards; they quickly wasted away or became demented.

CACIQUE. A Carib word for a chiefdom, ruling over a determinate number of villages or kinship groups. In 1500 Puerto Rico had eighteen chiefdoms in an estimated population of 45,000, Hispaniola had six in a much larger population of 500,000.

CACOS. Haitian black mercenary peasants, who hired themselves to political aspirants and who unleashed a wave of looting and terror to prepare the way for the taking of power. A 1915 caco uprising during the United States intervention was suppressed by the American marines after a period of guerrilla warfare. The power of the cacos diminished thereafter.

CAFE-AU-LAIT SOCIETY. A humorous reference to the Martinican elite, which is light-skinned mulatto in hue, and highly Frenchified.

CAFE COM LEITE. Meaning "coffee with milk," this Brazilian term refers to a morena, or coffee-hued mulatto woman. The term is usually linked with a connotation of sexual desirability, and is used by males in describing idealized mulata sexual partners.

CAFUSOS. Persons in Brazil of mixed African and Amerindian blood, so named after the penetration of the interior west from São Vicente (São Paulo) by Portuguese adventurers and their African slaves.

CAIDO. A Brazilian term for a dark-skinned person who powders his face and body in an attempt to pass for white or give the appearance of belonging to a lighter-skinned racial category.

CAKCHIQUEL. One of the principal nationality groups of pre-Columbian Guatemala.

CALABAR NEGROES. A group, or "nation," of blacks settled in Cuba.

CALDAS BARBOSA, DOMINGOS (1738-1801). A mulatto Brazilian poet who consciously attempted to demonstrate his cultural assimilation and his distance from Afro-Brazilian roots.

CALEDONIA BALL. One of the prestigious social events
in turn-of-the-century Jamaica restricted to whites.
The same system prevailed in the other British island
colonies; society in Barbados, for example, was dominated by five "gentleman's clubs," all lilywhite.

CALIXTUS III, POPE see NICHOLAS V, POPE

CALPULEQUE. Village leader in Aztec Mexico. See also CALPULLI.

CALPULLI, CALPULLEC (pl.). Aztec kinship groups,
roughly equivalent to the Spanish barrios or lineages.
Land was held by calpullec in common, with the group
as a whole deciding who would be permitted to cultivate
what amount.

CALUNGA, CULT OF. A Bantu religious cult whose survival in heavily industrialized Buenos Aires has been
documented by Bernardo Kordon.

CAMARGO, ADALBERTO. One of the few Afro-Brazilians
elected to the federal legislature. A paulista, Camargo
has been a member of the Foreign Relations Committee
and has argued for better relations between Brazil and
Black Africa. A businessman, he is the founder and
president of the Afro-Brazilian Chamber of Commerce.

CAMBAPE see CAPOEIRA DE ANGOLA

CAMBUJO. Literally, "donkey," a colonial Mexican synonym for mulato pardo. See also RACIAL NOMEN-
CLATURE, DISTINCTIONS; COYOTE.

CAMELO. A Brazilian street vendor or hawker in the
North, usually a caboclo. Portuguese immigrants often
have become street vendors as well.

CAMPANHA DE DEFESA DO FOLCLORE. An official Bra-
zilian campaign, in the mid-1970's, to recognize the
African roots of Brazilian culture, but, as Abdias do
Nascimento shows, in patronizing terms.

CAMPESINO. A word used to denote peasants, usually of
Amerindian origin, instead of the more racist word
"indio." The revolutionary Bolivian M.N.R. of the
early 1950's, for example, substituted "campesino" for
"indio" in all official communications.

CAMPO, DIEGO DE. Turncoat cimmarón leader during the so-called "War of the Negroes" in Santo Domingo in the 1540's. See also WAR OF THE NEGROES.

CANAAN. The English title of the novel Canaã, by the Brazilian Graça Aranha in 1902. The plot concerns the life of two German immigrants to the agricultural state of Espírito Santo, one of whom expresses the whitening ideal of the Brazilian elite, the other who dwelled on racial pessimism. Skidmore contends that Graça Aranha's own ambivalence--expressed through his protagonist--accurately reflected the debate over race within the elite itself at the turn of the century.

CÂNDIDO, JOÃO. A black seaman in the Brazilian navy who led the 1910 Naval Rebellion against mistreatment of enlisted men by the all-white officer corps. Seizing a number of dreadnaughts in Rio de Janeiro harbor, he ordered all intoxicants thrown overboard, then pointed his ships' guns at the city and demanded that his men's grievances be redressed. The mutiny was ended by a presidential amnesty, leading several high-ranking naval officers to resign in humiliation. Few lasting reforms, however, ensued.

CANDOMBLES. Cultural societies organized around African and Afro-Christian deities, especially prevalent on the Brazilian coast north from Bahia. Candomblés often took the name of tribes or places in Africa: Nago (Yoruba), Ewe, Quetu (a town in Dahomey), Oyo (a town in Nigeria), Ijesha (a district in Nigeria), Angola. See also NATIONS.

CANNIBAL. This was originally a Carib word that has been absorbed into the English language, as have "buccaneer," "canoe," "hurricane," and "tobacco."

CANUDOS see CONSELHEIRO, ANTÔNIO.

CAPATAZ. Another name for the black or mulatto capanga bodyguard who enforced discipline on Brazilian plantations among colono families by intimidation or the use of force. Maeyama considers the role of the capataz to parallel the colonial and slave-era capitão-do-mato.

CAPILDEO, RUDRANTH. Leader of the East Indian minority political party, the Democrats, of Trinidad in the late 1960's and early 1970's.

CAPITACION. A tax paid by landowners for the right to own slaves (Puerto Rico).

CAPITÃES-DO-MATA. Professional slave hunters in colonial Brazil, generally free blacks or mulattoes. The capitães were paid on the basis of bounties, and were known for their cruelty.

CAPITAL DOS PRETOS. Slang name for Bahia meaning "capital of the blacks." The region around Salvador is the most obviously Afro-Brazilian in character in Brazil.

CAPITÃO-DO-MATO. "Captain-of-the-forest," a term for a man, often a mulatto or free black, who was used to hunt escaped slaves in rural Brazil through the nineteenth century.

CAPOEIRA DE ANGOLA. A martial art practiced by blacks in Bahia, Brazil, once popular among young toughs and, in recent times, stylized into a ritualistic art form shorn of aggression. In Rio de Janeiro it is known as cambapé and in Recife as a form of Carnival Frêvo. See also LAGGIA.

CARABELAS. A Cuban slave term for persons--shipmates-- imported from Africa on the same vessel. See also BODEGAS, CABILDO.

CARACAS INDIANS. A warlike tribe inhabiting present-day Venezuela. They cultivated crops, domesticated wildlife, and engaged in hunting and fishing. Their military ranks were indicated by tattoos on their bodies.

CARAMURU. The Tupi name given to Diogo Alvares Correia, the shipwrecked Portuguese sailor, native to Vianna do Minho, who found himself in 1510 among the Tupinamba Indians on the coast of Brazil at a place now called Mariquita. Caramurú escaped being eaten and was taken under the protection of Paragassú, the daughter of the chief of the tribe. His full name, Caramurú-Assú, means "sea-dragon"; he was also called "man-of-fire."

CARGEROS ("Carriers") see LIBRES DE COLOR

CARGOS. Menial offices assigned to Indian youths in the

closed-corporate peasant communities of the highlands from Mexico to Bolivia. These "burdens" may range from carrying water to standing guard to cleaning a public building. As the youth gains experience, he is assigned to more responsible duties, such as planning the details of religious festivals, or helping divide communal produce. The carguero often must borrow money to pay for the costs of his job--to buy liquor for the fiestas, for example. The system, which reinforces communal ties and resists outside influences, is called the "fiesta complex" by anthropologists.

CARIB RESERVATION see SNAKECOE

CARIBS see ARUAKS

CARIMBA. A brand mark, burned into the flesh of the newly arrived slave upon landing and passing the required physical examination. The mark was the indication of legal importation; some slaves were given another brand, the private mark of the slave trader or monopolistic company.

CARNAVAL, TRINIDAD. The original Spanish pre-Lenten celebrations were changed under French influence in the 1780's. By the 1830's Mardi Gras had become a national fete, given to masked revelry, parties, dancing, and celebration. Blacks and Amerindians were originally forbidden from participating, and free blacks could only join under certain legal restrictions. With Emancipation in 1833, the celebrations embraced the entire population. The lower classes began to "picong," or ridicule, the higher strata of the colony; in more recent years, the government has come under satirical attack as well. By the 1890's, Carnaval began to acquire a middle-class aura, with merchants stimulating Carnaval activities for commercial reasons. By the 1920's it had arrived at its modern form: part touristic, part commercial, and part uninhibited spontaneity. With a rise in black consciousness in the 1960's, authorities in Port-au-Prince took steps to tone down politicization, banning a visit of Stokely Carmichael in 1969, for example. A Calypso artist, the Mighty Chalkdust, parodied the ban and won third prize in the annual calypso competition.

CARONA, LA. A dilapidated tenement in Havana known for

its high percentage of black families, and a target of efforts to erase the segregated housing practices in urban Cuba by the Committees for the Defense of the Revolution (CDRs).

CARPATA. The nom de guerre of the slave Bastiaan, who led the slave revolt of 1795 on Curaçao, and who was captured and executed.

CARRERA. A notorious island prison off the coast of Trinidad, populated mostly by blacks.

CARRIACOU. A small island with almost a purely Negro population, one of the few cases of such racial homogeneity in the Caribbean.

CARRIO DE LA BANDERA, ALONSO see CONCOLORCOVO

CARTAS DE ALFORRIA see BLACK BROTHERHOODS

CASA DE ESCRAVOS. The Portuguese agency overseeing the slave trade, established in 1486 by King João II (1481-1505).

CASA DEL ESTUDIANTE INDIGENA. A Mexican experimental residence established in the 1920's for Indian students recruited from rural villages for their educational promise, and subsidized by the government. To some extent this parallels Booker T. Washington's Tuskegee Institute, and, as Mörner notes, reminds one of efforts to train an Indian elite in the sixteenth century.

CASINO ESPAÑOL see NEGREROS

CASTA. A derogatory term for persons of mixed blood, whether slave or free.

CASTAS DE ANGOLA. Tribal members from the region in and around Portuguese Angola shipped as slaves to the New World. The "castas" included Benguelas, Congos, and Manicongos.

CASTAS DE MEZCLA. "Degrees of color admixture," carefully classified by Spanish colonial authorities according to what Sánchez Albornoz calls the "classifying tendency of the orderly, rationalizing mentality of the [eighteenth] century." Every mixture possible, starting from the three "pure" racial types, received a name.

CASTAS DE MOZAMBIQUE. Tribal members shipped from
Mozambique across the Pacific Ocean to Acapulco, Mexico, an unprofitable route which led to the curtailment
of the trade.

CASTAS DE RIOS DE GUINEA. "People from the Guinea
region," meaning blacks who were further subcategor-
ized by the Spaniards as gelofes, biafras, and mandin-
gos.

CASTAS DE SAN TOME. Africans shipped as slaves from
the port of San Tomé, in the Bight of Biafra, the major slave entrepôt for Dutch and English slavers after
the 1570's when their activities were forced southward
by Portuguese pressure.

CATIMBO. A pipe used to smoke tobacco in Northeast
Brazil, and the name given to an indigenous cult which
has been banned for its use of hallucinogens, including
hashish and marijuana. The priest, or catimbozeiro,
receives the spirits in behalf of the faithful, and thus
exercises great power. The cult shows few Afro-Brazilian influences, and has remained relatively unaltered
since the earliest days of colonization.

CATINGA. A Portuguese term for the supposed odor characteristic of the African. See also BUDIM.

CATIVOS. "Captives," a Brazilian word for slaves.

CAYES DE JACEMAL. A cluster of maroon sanctuaries in
Guadeloupe repeatedly attacked by French forces (nine
times between 1702 and 1781) but never yielding. Eventually, the settlements achieved de facto autonomy.

CEDULAS (of 1551 and 1558). Decrees governing treatment
of non-whites giving aid to a fugitive slave, or cimarrón.
Punishments included death or the same penalty inflicted
on the captured runaway--often mutilation, flogging, and
the fastening of iron weights to parts of the body for
periods of months or years.

CEDULAS DE GRACIAS AL SACAR. Certificates of racial
purity, available for purchase during the Spanish colonial period. Removing legal "caste" status, however,
was often not sufficient to overcome socioeconomic prejudice. A French traveller (Mörner relates) observed

around 1800 that the only benefit pardos received from such a royal document was the right of their women to wear a mantilla in Church. See also DISPENSAS DE COLOR.

CEMES. Amerindian saint figures, or santos.

CENTRO CIVICA PALMARES. An Afro-Brazilian cultural organization founded in São Paulo in 1927, becoming, according to Florestan Fernandes, the forerunner of the Frente Negra Brasileira.

CENTRO DE CULTURA AFRO-BRASILEIRA DE PERNAM-BUCO. A cultural organization which opened (and closed) in 1937 in Recife, aimed at raising Afro-Bra-zilian consciousness. See also FRENTE NEGRA PER-NAMBUCANA.

CENTRO DE PESQUISAS DAS CULTURAS NEGRAS. The cultural association research center in Rio de Janeiro presently dedicated to exposing, if discreetly, the ex-istence of racism in Brazilian society. It is linked in-formally to the Casa de Cultura Afro-Brasileira in São Paulo and the Grupo Palmares in Pôrto Alegre, Rio Grande do Sul.

CERCADO DE LIMA. A district of the city of Lima, Peru, established by royal authorities for Indian residents un-der the segregation decree of the Recopiliación of 1680. See also REDUCCIONES.

CHACHAS. A Catholic, white enclave inhabited mostly by French-speaking Virgin Islanders in St. Thomas. They are descended from colonists from Brittany who first settled on St. Bartholomew Island but who migrated to the Virgin Islands in the mid-nineteenth century. Find-ing themselves in the anomalous position of holding low-er-class economic status but "upper class" status in race and culture, they have kept to themselves in rela-tively closed communities afflicted by a high degree of consanguine degeneracy.

CHAKE INDIANS. A semi-nomadic tribe in the Maracaibo Lake Basin of Venezuela, part of the Motilone (cut-hair) nation, and organized into a relatively classless society whose life has changed little from colonial days.

CHAMISO see SOCIO-RACIAL CLASSIFICATIONS

CHANGO. A Yoruba candomblé indigenous to the region in
Brazil centered in the states of Pernambuco and Alagoas,
also known as batuque, an onomatopoeic term meaning
"drumbeat." On Cuba the cult is known as santería; in
Trinidad it is also called Changô. See also CANDOM-
BLES; BATUQUE.

CHARQUEADAS. Meat curing, or salting, plants in Rio
Grande do Sul, Uruguay, and Argentina. These used
slave labor until the brutal conditions so incapacitated
slave workers that wage laborers were substituted for
reasons of cost.

CHAVIN CULTURE. An ancient Sierra (Peru) culture which
developed in the upper Marañon Valley about 1400 B. C.,
extending beyond to Huánuco and Lima. Their religion
was based on a pan-Andean deity and concept of unity,
demonstrated by cultural ties with the peoples of the
Amazon basin. Dobyns and Doughty note that similarities in detail between Chavín art and contemporary Mesoamerican Olmec culture "provide evidence that these two
peoples may have shared many basic religious and artistic concepts." Both peoples worshipped sky, water, and
earth gods and developed powerful priesthoods for secular leadership. See also POST-CHAVIN CULTURES.

CHIBCHAN PEOPLES. A language-based division, located
in the Andean region, and responsible for the highly developed culture of prehistoric Colombia, including the
legend of "El Dorado."

CHICHA. Fermented maize, first brewed by the aboriginal
population of Peru after about 1800 B. C. See also
MAIZE CULTIVATION.

CHICHICASTENANGO DRUNKENNESS. An old social custom
in Guatemalan Indian communities, especially in Chichicastenango, where husbands and wives get publicly drunk
on alternate weekends. The sober partner, in turn,
cares for the incapacitated one.

CHIMBANGUELEROS. Venezuelan dances of African origin,
performed by persons wearing grass skirts to the chim-
banqueli drum.

CHIMU. An Amerindian civilization which expanded throughout present-day northern Peru in the fourteenth century

A.D., with its capital at Chan-Chan. The Incas conquered the Chimu empire in the mid-fifteenth century.

CHINEE. Slang term for Chinese in the Caribbean, many of whom were established as merchants by the 1930's and after.

CHINESE IN SURINAM. With abolition approaching and the curtailment of the slave trade by the early 1850's, Dutch authorities began to import Chinese contract laborers from Java. Between 1853 and 1872 a total of 2,500 Chinese came; after 1872, when the Chinese government began to restrict emigration under contract, they were replaced by Hindus from Calcutta and elsewhere in South India.

CHINOS. Name ("Chinese") by which African slaves from Mozambique were dubbed in Mexico, possibly for the fact that they were shipped across the Pacific Ocean to such Western ports as Acapulco. See also ZOBOS.

CHIQUE-CHIQUE, MANE. A fictional character invented by a Cearense politician in 1914 to refute author Monteiro Lobato's assertion that the Brazilian peasant was lazy, ignorant, and a national burden. Mané Chique-Chique, in contrast, was a model northeasterner, efficient, self-reliant, the "anonymous pillar of the nation." See also TATU, JECA.

CHIRINOS, JOSE LEONARDO. A zambo rebel against the Caracas Company and landowning class of Venezuela in the 1790's who followed the banner of Andresote's insurrection with a rising of his own in the town of Coro, the location of Venezuela's first slave rebellion in 1532. Chirinos and others had heard rumors that Carlos IV had freed the slaves but that slaveowners and local officials had suppressed the decree; his uprising was based on the unrealistic premise that support would come from partisans of the French Revolution. His movement rallied blacks, mulattoes, zambos, and Indians, and was crushed by Spanish soldiers aided by loyal Indians. Chirinos was captured and tortured to death in 1796.

CHOLO. A term with ethnic and social connotations. Cholos, in Bolivia, are Indians "on the make"; they usually speak both Spanish and their indigenous language; cholo women are known for their traditional clothing of unusually high quality. Cholos are considered somewhat akin to gypsies, stereotyped as commerce-minded, aggressive, and domineering. Before 1800 the term simply was used as a synonym for mestizo.

CHRISTOPHE, HENRI. The last of Haiti's revolutionary generals, and the ruler of the northern portion of the republic after the assassination of Jean-Jacques Dessalines in 1804. An ex-slave born on St. Christopher, he had settled in Haiti and volunteered to fight with Lafayette in the American Revolution, one of a force of 800 Haitians. In 1811 he crowned himself King Henri I, and established a rule of more-or-less benevolent despotism. Faced with growing rebellion, he killed himself in 1820.

CHUETAS. Spanish-language slang for descendants of converted Majorcan Jews, called chuetas either from the word "chuya" (pork, or pork-eater), "chuco," a call-sound to a dog, or "jueto," Catalán for "little Jew."

CIBONEY. One of the three principal Amerindian groups in the relatively sparsely populated Caribbean at the end of the fifteenth century. They were also known as the Guanahuatebey. The other groups were the Taino Arawak and the Carib. The Ciboney were probably the oldest culture group in the islands, and were among the peoples first encountered by Columbus when he reached Hispaniola. They were probably poor, relatively unclothed, and with no pottery, domestic utensils, or weapons.

CIMARRON. A "wild black," an escaped African slave. Cimarrones were the founders of the fugitive colonies, called palenques, quilombos, etc., which were sometimes crushed by colonial authorities and sometimes managed to preserve their autonomy.

CIMI (Conselho Indigenista Missionário). A Roman Catholic organization in Brazil with jurisdiction over Church-Indian relations, and considered subversive by the government in the mid-1970's. Under CIMI's auspices, Indian leaders held 13 national assemblies between 1974 and 1977.

CIRCULAR 29 OF MAY 31, 1891. Three years after the abolition of Brazilian slavery, the Finance Minister of the Federal Republic, Rui Barbosa, ordered the de-

struction of all historical documents and files related to
the slave trade and to slavery in order to "erase the
memory" of that shameful institution. As a result, historical research was set back several decades, until
scholars, in the 1960's, began to probe local archives
and other records not destroyed by the 1891 order.

CIRCULOS SOCIALES. Self-help and voluntary associations
in Cuba, nationalized after the Cuban Revolution in order to end de facto racial discrimination by social agencies.

CLARIM DE ALVORADO. The leading Afro-Brazilian newspaper of the Frente Negra, published in São Paulo. The
title means "Clarion of the Dawn."

CLASS AND RACE. Since racial categories are highly sub-
jective, Latin Americans frequently adjust meanings of
terms to specific cultural or class contexts. Morenos
of high economic status, then, may be considered by
peers to be "practically identical with whites" (Pierson),
while a lower-class preto uses the term "moreno" for
persons of lower-class status who are "almost identical
with pardos." See also TIRA-TEIMA.

CLASS CRITERIA see "MONEY WHITENS"

CLUB ATENAS. A social club in Havana for blacks in the
1940's, rivalling white clubs in sophistication but ob-
serving, in the process, the unwritten code of racial
segregation which prevailed on the island.

COARTACION. A process, first employed in Cuba and then
taken up in other Spanish colonies, whereby slaves could
purchase their freedom in installments. In 1788 the
Council of the Indies rejected the notion that slave
mothers who paid for their emancipation would also se-
cure the freedom of their children.

COCAMBA-COCAMILLA. One of a small number of surviving tribes inhabiting the Peruvian Amazon. They are
estimated to total about 100,000, although contact with
the outside is shrinking each group. Other tribes in
the region include the Aguaruna, Amuesha, Campa, and
Shipibo-Conibo.

COCHO. Literally meaning "dirty," this is a colonial Mexican term for a mulato pardo. See also COYOTE.

COCO POINT. An exclusive Antiguan resort for wealthy American tourists, attacked in the press in recent years for excluding non-whites and Jews from its patronage. It is owned by William Cody Kelly, a self-described descendent of Buffalo Bill.

CODE NOIR. The Black Code, a decree issued by Louis XIV of France in 1685 banning all non-Catholics from the West Indies, commanding that slaves be baptized as Catholics, and granting some rights to slaves including the right of marriage and to obtain manumission through purchase.

CODIGO NEGRO CAROLINO. A set of decree laws promulgated in the name of Carlos III by the audiencia of Santo Domingo in 1785. The laws banned the use of torture and mutilation of slaves as punishment, required that slaves be given the use of a garden plot (conuco) for their own use, and that slaves were to be properly clothed, fed, and instructed in religion. But all such liberalities were to depend on the slave's good behavior and comportment toward whites.

CODIGO NEGRO ESPAÑOL. A law code promulgated by Carlos IV of Spain in 1789, borrowing, in spirit, provisions of the 1785 Santo Domingo Statute and the French Code Noire of 1685. It limited the right of owners to mutilate, flog, and otherwise mistreat slaves; required that slaves be adequately housed and clothed, and that the office of protector of slaves be created in every urban center. It did not prohibit breaking up slave families, and it did not speak to the ways in which slaves could obtain their freedom.

COFRADIA. The group in an Indian community responsible for organizing the fiesta of a particular saint. Expenses must be borne by the members of the group although the fiesta is celebrated by the entire village.

COLONO. 1) A tenant farmer or Indian serf, in the Andean region. Regional terms for colonos in Bolivia include pegujalero (in valleys) and sayañero (on the Altiplano). 2) In the Caribbean, the term refers to independent farmers, mostly white, who grow sugar cane on contract for industrialized refineries. Some colonos own their land; others lease it. The colonos' role parallels that of the Brazilian senhor de engenho, although the latter, through the end of the nineteenth century, probably enjoyed higher social status.

COLOURED. The British West Indian term for mulatto.

COME-AROUND. A beggar or petty thief, in Jamaica. The word may have come from the Spanish camarón, meaning parasite.

COMPADRAZGO. The institution of naming godparents, usually from a higher socio-economic class, to newborn children. Many godparents were Spaniards or creoles, their act linking the families in an informal network of protection and patronage.

COMPAGNIE DE SENEGAL. The company which purchased the monopoly for the slave trade from Africa to the French West Indies from the French West India Company in 1672, and which, after the defeat of the Dutch in 1678, acquired control of the major Dutch slave trading posts in West Africa as well.

COMUNIDADE OBA-BIYI. A "terreiro," or autonomous candomblé community in the city of Salvador, Bahia, which in the late 1970's moved to expand its traditional activities by establishing children's groups, study facilities for Afro-Brazilian issues, and a base for relationships with organizations outside the community. The group is primarily dedicated to the preservation of the Afro-Brazilian tradition within Brazilian life.

CONCOLORCOVO (ALONSO CARRIO DE LA BANDERA). An Argentine mestizo author of the late eighteenth century, author of El Lazarillo: A Guide for Inexperienced Travellers Between Buenos Aires and Lima (1773).

CONFRADIA DE LOS NEGRITOS. "Brotherhood of the Little Negroes." A lay brotherhood of free blacks in Spain in the fifteenth century. To raise funds, some would sell a fellow member into slavery, then purchase his freedom at a later date. Fraternal bonds, Rout shows, were very strong.

CONFRADIA DE SAN COSME Y SAN DAMIAN. A Spanish New World brotherhood, established in Santo Domingo in the early 1600's, which accepted both freedmen and slaves but excluded some Africans if their place of origin was considered undesirable.

CONGA see NATIONS

CONGO see CANDOMBLES; NATIONS

CONGO, KINGDOM OF THE. One of the major sources of
slaves for the Latin American trade in the sixteenth
century. The "Congo" was the region roughly bounded
by the river Zaire (Congo) on the North, the river Dande
in the South, the sea on the West, and the river Kwango
on the east.

CONGREGACIONES. Another term for mission villages for
Amerindians in Spanish South America, known as well
as REDUCCIONES.

CONJUNTO FOLKLORICO NACIONAL. Cuba's National Folklore Dance Troupe, given a prominent role after the
1959 Revolution, but, at least to some critics, considered by Cubans to represent an exotic form of theater,
ridiculing the Afro-Cuban heritage rather than instilling
respect for it.

CONQUISTADOR. A fifteenth or sixteenth century Spaniard
who participated in the campaign to subdue the aboriginal
population of the New World and establish the hegemony
of the Spanish Crown and Catholic Church.

CONSANGUINE DEGENERACY see CHA-CHAS

CONSEJO DE LAS INDIAS. The Spanish Council of the Indies. Established in 1524, it determined overseas policy and served as a court of judicial appeal.

CONSELHEIRO, ANTONIO (1828-1897). A backlands mystic
from Quixeramobim, Ceará, whose messianic vocation
created the holy city of Canudos, Bahia, and led his
caboclo faithful in dogged resistance to the hated military arm of the federal government. Conselheiro called
himself a reincarnation of St. Sebastião and Jesus Christ,
and vowed divine intervention to redress social injustice
and domination by white society of the coast. The Canudos rebellion was finally crushed by massive armed
force in 1897. See also BAPTIST FREE CHURCH (JA-
MAICA).

CONSPIRACY OF THE TAILORS. A would-be revolt for independence in Salvador, Bahia, in 1798, led by four free

blacks, Luis Gonzaga das Virgens, Lucas Dantas de Amorim Torres, João de Deus Nascimento, and Manoel Faustino Santos Lira. The conspirators were arrested, hanged, and had their bodies torn into four pieces and exhibited publicly.

CONUCOS. Small plots of land in the Dutch Leeward Islands which slaves were allowed to cultivate for their own use.

CONVENCÃO NACIONAL DO NEGRO. A national meeting of Brazilian blacks, held in São Paulo in 1945 with Abdias do Nascimento as President.

CONVINCE CULT see BONGO

COPACABANA SODALITY see INCA, ALONSO VIRACOCIIA

COOBA. A casual woman servant, in Jamaica. In more recent days the term has come to be used to describe a womanish man.

COOLIES. The pejorative term used to describe East Indians imported into Trinidad as indentured laborers up to 1917.

COOLIE-TOWN. Name given by whites to the East Indian ghetto of Port of Spain, Trinidad, in the early twentieth century.

CORAVECAS. Amerindians of the Bororoan language group in southern Santa Cruz in Bolivia.

COR DE CINZA. Literally, "ashen." A term used to describe medium-hued Brazilian mulattoes or caboclos.

CORO INSURRECTION OF 1532. The first known slave revolt in modern-day Venezuela, in the hamlet of Coro, the site of the uprising of José Leonardo Chirinos two-and-a-half centuries later, in the 1790's.

CORRECTOS, LOS. Redfield, in his Tepozlán study, describes the class distinction between the correctos, Amerindians who wore shoes and followed city customs, and los tontos, rustics who lived further from the urban center and who followed "primitive" native customs in medicine, religious practice, and dress. When the Mexican Revolution came to Tepozlán in 1911 the "tontos" rose against whites and "correctos" alike, and many of the latter fled to Mexico City for safety.

CORVEE. Co-operative family labor in Haiti, where poor peasants or younger sons from more affluent rural families rent out their services. Since patrons must feed their workers, the corvée has largely disappeared from the rural countryside owing to the low wage scale as compared to the high cost of feeding a work gang.

COSMIC RACE. The title of a book-length essay by Mexican philosopher José Vasconcelos, referring to the Latin Americans, whom he called "the treasury of all the previous races, the final race, the cosmic race." The book, published in 1925, emphasized Vasconcelos' praise for the Latin American spirit as culturally superior. See also MESTIZAJE.

COSTA CHICA. The coastal highlands of Mexico facing the Pacific Ocean, a common location for palenques, rural habitations of escaped slaves during the seventeenth and eighteenth centuries.

COUTINHO, AZEVEDO. An eighteenth-century Brazilian bishop noted for his hostility to French reformist thought and as a defender of African slavery, which he called a "licit trade" whose legitimacy had never been doubted among the nations since antiquity.

COVARES. A now-extinct Amerindian group related to the Coravecas, native to eastern Santa Cruz in Bolivia.

COYA. An Inca queen. At one point, Gonzalo Pizarro, brother of the conquistador, was urged by supporters to marry an Inco coya and proclaim himself Emperor.

COYOTE. A Peruvian term for zambo. Rout cites this term and others to show the thinly disguised contempt the Spaniards held for such peoples.

CREATIVE SYNCRETISM. Michael Craton, in his study of West Indian slave families, challenges the traditional view emphasizing the ways that slavery destroyed family structure. Rather, he emphasizes the ways in which the slaves' own form of family and their capacity to act covertly triumphed over adversity. This "creativity"

included accepting cousin-mating and premarital inter-
course, adjustments by slaves to deal practically with
the new environment of the plantation system and with
shifting demographic conditions.

CREOLE. The spoken language of the Haitian peasantry
which is a blend of French and West African languages.
Approximately 10 percent of the population is bi-lingual,
the rest speak Creole only. The first Creole newspaper
appeared in 1943.

CREOLESE. The Guyanese term for the local patois dialect.

CRIAS. Slave children born and reared in the Big House of
Brazilian plantations, often the illegitimate children of
the master. See also IRMÃOS DE CREAÇÃO.

CRIOLLO MORENO. A black born in the New World, of
bozal parentage.

CRIOLLOS. Creoles, members of the Hispanic elite born
in the New World, and, in consequence, not eligible for
the highest positions in the colonial hierarchy, reserved
for peninsulares, or persons born on the Iberian peninsula. As time passed, creoles comprised an ever larger
proportion of the social and economic elite, and increas-
ingly chafed at their second-level status. Most criollos
were white, although mestizos in some countries were
able to rise to the top of the creole group.

CRIOULO. A Brazilian term for a medium-skinned mulatto.

CROW, JOHN. Jamaican term for a black man.

CRUZ E SOUZA, JOÃO DE (1861-1897). An Afro-Brazilian
poet whose writing has been called an "unconscious" example of racial memory, although on the surface his
poetry was highly acculturated.

CUADRILLAS. Gangs of slaves working together in the
mines or on public works. The 1778 census showed
that 60 percent of all slaves in Panama were so engaged, mostly in gold mining.

CUARTERON. A quadroon, someone of one-fourth European
parentage.

CUBANGO see BANTU RELIGIOUS INFLUENCE

CUBAN MIGRATION TO THE UNITED STATES. Cubans who have come to the United States after the fall of Batista have been disproportionately white in comparison to the racial proportions of the Cuban population. This "whiteness" increased, in fact, as the 1960's progressed. See also RACE POLICIES OF THE REVOLUTIONARY CUBAN GOVERNMENT.

CUBAN SLAVE TRADE. Since the impetus for the importation of slaves came relatively late the Cuba--in the 1830's and after--most traditional sources of slave supply had closed. Some planters bought their slaves from other islands, and even from Brazil in extreme cases. By 1860 the price of a slave had risen to over 1,000 dollars; most slaves by that time were obtained through private pirate expeditions to the African coast.

CUCUMBI. A secret ceremony within the ritualistic system of Afro-Brazilian candomblé.

CUFFIE. A Jamaican term, of Ghanaian origin, for a man born on a Friday. The Twi word is Cofi.

CUIJLA. A Mexican maroon colony on the West coast, near present-day Guerrero. See also MANDINGO.

CUMBES. A Venezuelan term for fugitive slave communities, elsewhere known as palenques. See also MAMBISES.

CUNGA see NATIONS

CURACA. A Peruvian Quechua village chieftain. See also JILICATA

CURAVES see ECORABES

CURIBOCA. A cross between a black and an Amerindian, in Brazil. Also called cafuso.

-D-

DAGGA. A rebellious black soldier in Trinidad who, in 1834, according to lore, attempted to walk east until he got back to Africa.

DAHOMEY-Z-EPAULES. A whirling Haitian dance performed with the top part of the body upright and shoulders rotating in time to drum rhythms.

DARK SAMBO. A person, in the British Caribbean, "between black and brown."

DAVALOS, GIL RAMIREZ. Governor of the audiencia of Quito in the mid-sixteenth century who sent troops to attack zambo tribesmen in the maroon enclave known as El Portente. The campaign failed when the zambos reverted to guerrilla resistance, and preserved their autonomy.

"DEDO NA COZINHA." "Finger in the kitchen," a slang Bahian term for someone with presumed Negro ancestry.

DE LAS CASAS, BARTOLOME. A sixteenth-century Spanish colonial bishop, champion of the spiritual rights of the Amerindian population of the Americas, and a staunch advocate of the importation of African slaves to New World lowlands in order to replace the less-hardy native population, which was becoming decimated by the brutal conditions of forced labor.

DELGRES, LOUIS (1772-1802). The mulatto commander of Fort St. Charles in Guadelupe in 1801 and a leader of the liberal faction against the suspension of the French Revolution's ban of slavery. Defeated in 1802, he and his troops committed mass suicide.

"DE LUIE NEGER VAN CORONIE." "The lazy blacks of Coronie," a phrase describing the stereotyped view of the Coronie district of Surinam as placid, lazy, remote. One reason for the stereotype is the fact that the unrefined oil produced in Coronie is more expensive than refined oil imported from Holland. It is inhabited by former slaves who took the land after it was abandoned by their masters after abolition in 1863.

DENIS, PIERRE. A French visitor to Brazil in the first decade of the twentieth century who endorsed the "whitening" thesis of Lacerda and others, and who characterized Brazilian blacks as indolent and morally inferior, ravaged by alcoholism and lack of hygiene.

DESCENT RULE. A system whereby persons are judged

socially in terms of their racial or ethnic descent (as in the United States) rather than by their racial image (as in Latin America) as persons independent of their ancestry. Harris found that the descent rule was absent for rural Northeastern Brazil, where siblings who were phenotypically different were assigned to contrasting racial categories in conformity with actual phenotypical contrasts which they manifested. But he also found that ambiguity was built into the system, and that definitions of racial types vary widely from community to community and from person to person.

DESSALINES, GENERAL JEAN-JACQUES. Commanding general of the black Haitian forces which defeated the French in 1803 and who, on January 1, 1804, declared Haitian independence, the first such instance in Latin America. Dessalines, a former slave, established dictatorial rule, killed most of the remaining whites in the new republic, and used his troops to enforce an agricultural system which has been called the basis of the modern impoverished peasantry of Haiti. He was assassinated in 1806.

DIAS, HENRIQUE. An Afro-Brazilian and a hero of the Portuguese struggle against the Protestant Dutch in the early sixteenth century. He was rewarded by being accepted into the Portuguese royal Order of Christ.

DIASPORA, DOUBLE. Roger Bastide speaks of the dispersion of Africans themselves, through the importation of slaves to the New World and elsewhere from Africa, and that of African cultural traits, which transcend ethnic groupings.

DIET, AFRICAN INFLUENCE ON. Among the foodstuffs brought to the New World, or utilized there, by Africans were palm oil, chilies, okra, and the guinea fowl. Afro-Latin dishes include angu (a corn porridge), caruru (a shrimp and pepper gumbo), xinxím (palm oil, shrimp, and chicken), and efó (a puree of shrimp, greens, and palm oil).

DIEZMOS. Tithes of 10 percent of income, collected in support of the Catholic Church, called dizmos in Brazil. Indians were exempted from tithes and sales taxes (alcabalas) but had to pay tribute and supply obligatory, unpaid labor.

DINERO BLANQUEA, EL ("Money whitens") see DISPEN-
SAS DE COLOR

DIRECTORY OF INDIANS. A system to regulate Indian
labor established for Pará-Maranhão by the reformist
Pombal administration in 1757, and which followed the
legal emancipation of Indian slaves in 1755. The administration was entirely secular, excluding priests and
missionaries, and served to deliver Indians to frontiersmen, soldiers, and landowners. In this sense, the directory simply transferred the Indians from one form
of bondage to another. The system was never introduced in Brazil as a whole, since it was opposed by
local authorities.

DISPENSAS DE COLOR. Licenses attesting to racial "purity" and sold by the Spanish Crown in the eighteenth
century to upwardly mobile non-whites.

DISSOCIATION, PRINCIPLE OF. A form of social behavior
in which members of a marginal society can avoid the
tensions caused by cultural clashes and conflicting demands by adhering to a syncretistic religious group or
other ethnic or cultural fraternity.

DISTURBANCES OF 1937-38. A lower-class protest movement which swept the Caribbean islands of Jamaica
(where sugar workers demanded restoration of wages
lowered by landowners), Trinidad (where oil workers
attacked the punitive system of labor control employed
by managers), and elsewhere. Conservative officials
sought simply to suppress the disturbances, while lib-
erals viewed the peasantry as simple folk and offered
naive prescriptions for economic improvement.

DIXON, ALEXANDER. The first black man to win a seat
in the Jamaican legislative Council, at the turn of the
century. This was made possible, in part, by the creation of a competitive civil service in 1885.

DJARIK. A long sarong, worn by Javanese women in rural
Surinam.

DORACES. A Panamanian Amerindian group, from the
province of Chiriquí.

DOUTOR. "Doctor," usually referring to a doctor of laws.

In rural Brazilian towns until the mid-twentieth century, the term was often used by caboclos and blacks to address any white whose clothing or demeanor suggested authority or superior status. In contrast, Brazilian whites often address non-whites, especially blacks, as "rapaz" ("boy").

DREADLOCKS. The wild-looking coagulated ringlets popularized as a hair style by the Jamaican Rastafarians in the mid-1970's, and popular throughout the Caribbean.

DROP-PAN. A gambling game introduced to Latin America, especially to the Caribbean, by Chinese laborers imported to the region. One buys a ticket (tai shiin) from a vendor, who drops it into a pan and pulls out a winner, like a raffle.

DUKE, THE. Trinidadian calypso artists. See also MIGHTY STALIN.

DUKUN. A Javanese witch doctor, in Surinam.

DUPPY. A Jamaican term for disembodied spirits which linger after a person's death in the community and which are greatly feared.

DZULOB. A Mayan word for "aliens," or "foreigners." See also MAZEHUALOB.

-E-

"E A MULATA QUE E MULHER!" A Brazilian saying-- "The mulata is the woman!"--illustrating the stereotypical view of the woman of mixed race in Brazil as the idealized sex object. One variation on this theme went, "Brazil is a hell for blacks, a purgatory for whites, and a paradise for mulatas." Another version, more explicit, claimed that, "white women are for marrying, black women for service, and mulatas for fornication."

EAST INDIAN ASSOCIATION. A white-dominated political party in pre-1950 British Guiana which yielded to the bi-racial People's Progressive Party along with the black-only League of Coloured Peoples.

EAST INDIAN IMMIGRATION TO THE NEW WORLD. Be-

tween 1838 and 1917, nearly 500,000 East Indians came
to the region of the West Indies, primarily British Guiana (about half of the total), Trinidad, and Dutch Guiana.   About 13 percent were Brahmins or high castes,
another 8 percent artisans, and about a third low castes
and outcasts.   A fifth were Muslims and less than one
percent Christians.   After 1917 immigration slowed to
nearly a halt owing to ethnic and racial tensions in the
places where the East Indians had settled.   See also
COOLIE.

ECORABES.   Extinct Amerindian group related to the Coravecas, native to southern Santa Cruz in Bolivia.

EDWARDS, PRINCE EDWARD C.   A Rastafarian leader in
the 1950's, and the convener of an all-Jamaican conven-
tion of followers in 1958.   It lasted twenty-one days,
with nightly celebrations around bonfires of automobile
tires and other "eccentricities" (see Norris) that earned
the Rastafarians the bad reputation which subsequently
has developed among upper-class Jamaicans.   This ap-
prehension exploded two years later, when the Rastafarians were accused of fomenting armed revolution.
See also HENRY R.B., REVEREND CLAUDIUS.

EFIK   see   NAÑIGOS

EFOR.   An African tribe, related to the Efik people, transported to Cuba and to Brazil as slaves, and participants in a secret religious society centered around the
supreme god Abasi.   See also NAÑIGOS, ABASI.

EMANCIPADO.   Africans in mid-passage seized by British
antislavery patrols and freed on Cuba.   There, although
supposedly free, most were enslaved by Cuban planters.

EN BUENA GUERRA.   The official justification offered by
Spanish officials for allowing African slaves to be purchased from Portuguese traders in the fifteenth century:
that is, that the slaves had been taken prisoners in
war.

ENCINA, FRANCISCO ANTONIO.   Chilean historian and
chronicler of the victorious War of the Pacific (1879-
1883), which he, like other members of the Chilean
upper classes, attributed in part to Chile's "superior"
race mixture, a combination of the Basques and Goths

from Europe and the "tenacious" Araucanos native to Chile.

ENCOMIENDA. A legal institution of the Spanish colonial system under which Amerindian populations were distributed among Spaniards, who, in exchange for affording them protection and religious education were given the right to exact tribute in the form of labor. Frequently, the encomenderos asked for women to be used as concubines, although formal trading in female slaves for purposes of prostitution was forbidden by the New Laws of the Indies.

ENGAGES. Whites brought to the French Caribbean colonies along with slaves. The engagés were indentured workers, and could obtain release from their contracts after a specified period of time or the accumulation of a certain amount of cash.

ENGANCHE LABOR. A form of plantation labor in Northern Peru in the nineteenth and early twentieth centuries, reinforced by debt peonage. The serranos recruited to the coastal plantations which used this harsh form of labor eventually formed a working class movement.

ENMORE RIOTS. An insurrection of sugar workers outside Georgetown, British Guiana, in 1947, which was attributed in part to the fact that the men drivers (whites and East Indians) who were put in charge of women's work gangs often raped their charges with impunity. This followed an old practice in the region of assigning women and children to creole gangs, which were given light work during seasons when men were needed for heavier tasks. Multiple rapes of the black women and children were common until at least the early 1940's.

ERMINE WHITES. "Blancs d'hermine," whites of the highest economic class in Guadelupe. Most are high civil servants, planters, or businessmen.

ESCOGEDOR. A tobacco sorter, the best position in the tobacco industry for a skilled worker, and, in Cuba up to the 1930's, one from which blacks were excluded.

ESCURO. "Dark," a Brazilian term for a caboclo or mulatto.

ESMERALDAS. A rural jurisdiction of the audiencia of

Quito, populated during the early eighteenth century by groups of predatory zambo bandits. A similar group, also of zambos, terrorized the Mosquito Coast of Nicaragua; still another in the zone beyond Cartagena in Nueva Granada in the late eighteenth century.

ESPINOSO, MANUEL. A Venezuelan slave who was accused by another slave, under torture, of having masterminded the slave uprising planned for June 24, 1749. Along with other presumed leaders he was executed in the following year.

ESTANCIAS. Cattle ranches. From Mexico to Argentina, slaves utilized as laborers generally were given the greatest degree of relative freedom and trust than slaves in any other endeavors.

ESTATE STRATIFICATION. A form of social stratification under which status is determined by law, custom, and frequently by hereditary relationships between groups based on obligations for labor or servitude.

ESTIRPE. A Spanish word for lineage, stock, or race. Estirpe real means someone of royal lineage.

ESZE. A term of Curaçao and the islands of the French Antilles for persons who are reputed to be able to turn themselves invisible.

ETHNIC GROUP. One characterized by cultural or religious traits, not to be confused with "race," which strictly speaking is a biological term dependent upon genetic distribution.

EURINDIA. A concept popularized briefly by the Argentine writer Ricardo Rojas in the early 1920's, seeking to identify a New World aesthetic combining values of European and American origin.

EXPOSTOS. Abandoned infants of rival Brazilian agricultural workers during the colonial period, usually of caboclo parents. Many children were left to be found by plantation owners or churchmen, who raised them and later used them as laborers.

EWE see CANDOMBLES; NATIONS

EX-SLAVES. Brazilian references to ex-slaves were very

specific. Livres were free slaves, whereas libertos
were "freed" slaves, also referred to as forros ("those
with savings"), or "the manumitted." If ex-slaves'
backgrounds were unspecified, they could be simply
called "ex-escravos."

-F-

FAENA. A work group of Indians or peasants put to re-
pairing roads, walls, and other hacienda property, usually on Sunday mornings after all of the week's work
had been completed.

FANTI-ASHANTI CULTURE. Originating on Africa's Gold
Coast, the religious belief system has left a mark not
only in the Guianas but in enclaves among Afro-Americans in the United States and in the British-colonized
islands of the Antilles. Religious influences, however,
have waned, although cultural influences have survived.

FAVELAS. Shacks of wood and tin located in the slums of
major Brazilian cities in the Center-South, usually con-
centrated in settlements of several hundred or thousand
as shantytowns. In Brazil, most favelados are non-
white, although poor whites occasionally become favela
inhabitants as well, fueling the notion among some affluent Brazilians that discrimination in their society is
economic rather than racial. Favelas correspond to
mucambos in the Brazilian Northeast, colônias prole-
tários (Mexico), barriadas brujas (Peru), contregiles
(Uruguay), and bidonvilles (Haiti).

FEBRUARY REVOLUTION. A popular movement supporting
the principles of black militancy which erupted in Trinidad in February 1970 and which lasted in the form of
strikes and demonstrations for two months. The mobil-
ization was led by the National Joint Action Committee
(NJAC), which in turn evolved out of the black power
movement's two local organizations, Moko and Tapia.
NJAC, led by Geddes Granger, a recent graduate of
the University of the West Indies, called for economic
independence and the removal of the white power structure thought to dominate the Caribbean. Demonstrations
of between eight and twenty thousand Trinidadians, mostly blacks, characterized the movement, which was ended
when Prime Minister Eric Williams declared a state of
emergency and imposed martial law. As a result, half

of Trinidad's army rebelled. See also LA SALLE, LT.
REX; BLACK POWER.

FEDERAL WAR OF 1859-1863. A Venezuelan civil war
    rooted in racial hatred of the white elite. After a
    bloody series of battles, the issue cooled down, and
    brought about some degree of socioeconomic levelling.
    The war is treated in Rômulo Gallegos' novel, Poor
    Negro.

FEITOR. An overseer on Brazilian plantations utilizing
    slaves. After abolition in 1889, the feitor remained on
    the plantation, becoming a foreman or administrator of
    the new work force, made up of freed blacks and im-
    migrant (Italian and Japanese) colonos.

FEN CULTURE. Predominant among the slaves brought
    from Dahomey to the French Antilles and Guiana and
    to Louisiana, where many slaves first came to Haiti
    and were later sold to the mainland.

FESTAF. An international African cultural festival, held
    in Lagos, Nigeria in January 1977. Of the six Brazil
    representatives sent by the Foreign Ministry, five were
    white, provoking a storm of complaints from African
    representatives and moving the Brazilian government to
    dismiss the festival as illegitimate. In turn, a regional
    FESTAF planned for July-August 1978 to be held in
    Salvador and Rio de Janeiro was boycotted by the Bra-
    zilian government although 200 Afro-Americans attended
    during the four weeks. The Journal Nacional, a nightly
    television program, and the Voz do Brasil, a nation-
    wide radio program, warned Brazilians not to partici-
    pate in spite of the fact that Brazil played the host for
    the four-week event.

"FIESTA COMPLEX" see CARGOS

FIGA. Afro-Brazilian fertility symbol, in the form of a
    clenched black fist with the thumb extended between
    the forefinger and middle finger. Often worn as an
    amulet.

FILHOS DE CRIAÇAO. "Natural children" or "protégés,"
    illegitimate children of white fathers and black or mu-
    latto mothers in Brazil during slavery (and after). They
    were tolerated and sometimes given financial support,
    but within the boundaries of inferior racial status.

FOLKLORIZED. "Foclorizado," a Brazilian term meaning
to be exploited through the patronizing of an elite which
pays lip-service to one's talents and contributions to
Brazilian life, but which does little to acknowledge special problems or needs. The phrase is used with specific reference to Afro-Brazilians. By denying that racial discrimination exists in Brazil, the elite worsens
the dilemma by trivializing the Afro-Brazilian's role
and denying the validity or legitimacy of any protest.

FON GROUP. A cultural group, Dahomean in origin, predominant in Haiti and North/Northeast Brazil, especially in the
region around Maranhão originally settled by the French.

FORD MOTOR COMPANY AMAZON SCHEME. A proposal,
made in 1929, by Henry Ford to transport blacks from
the United States to work on Ford-owned and rubber
plantations on the Tapajós River. The plan was with-
drawn after it raised bitter objections in Manaos, the
chief city of the Brazilian Amazon region. Newspaper
editorials attacked the would-be immigrants as "the
worst unassimilable element of North America" and
"dangerous, persecuted, unhappy people."

FORROS. Manumitted slaves. See also EX-SLAVES.

FORTY THIEVES. The establishment lawyers and bankers
who control the economy of Bermuda's Front Street,
and therefore dominate decision-making on the island.
Their name derives from the fact that many Bermudan
fortunes came from piracy and smuggling in past centuries. In 1959, the Forty Thieves was led by Sir Henry
Tucker of the Bank of Bermuda, integration was achieved
within a decade, and Tucker appointed Premier of Bermuda. See also FRONT STREET.

FOUET. A term used by slaves for overseers who made
the slaves dance, sing, and talk for potential custom-
ers--by using whips.

FRASCOMANIA. A term coined by Albert O. Hirschman to
describe the Mexican "penchant for failure," a tendency
to see everything in the gloomy light of doubt and to
view the Mexican character as weak, backwards, and
racially flawed.

FREE PAPER. A legal document carrying with it emancipation status, in the British Caribbean.

FREE WOMB LAW. A national law passed by the Brazilian
    parliament in 1871, granting freedom to children born
    of slave mothers within a short number of years (with
    compensation paid to owners) or at the age of 21 (with-
    out compensation). Conservatives supported the meas-
    ure, since it promised to extend the life of slavery's
    legality for the foreseeable future. See also SEXAGE-
    NARIAN LAW.

FRENCH ANTILLES VOODOO. A cult, probably imported
    from Africa by the same tribes who brought Voodoo to
    Haiti, which, on Guadelupe and other French islands,
    emphasized the worship of reptiles and other animals,
    and plotted against whites. Vestiges of the cult are
    still found among inhabitants of the island of Martinique.

FRENTE CIVICO CONTRA LA DISCRIMINACION RACIAL.
    A Cuban antidiscrimination association founded by the
    Batista dictatorship in the 1950's, in part to counter
    Communist activity in this area. The Frente was con-
    trolled by the Batista trade union confederation (CTC).

FRENTE NEGRA BRASILEIRA. The "Black Brazil Front,"
    a political movement originated in São Paulo in the early
    1930's, and fairly successful among lower middle-class
    urban Afro-Brazilians. By 1936 the movement had
    spread to other cities and had elaborated a timid but
    courageous platform demanding better treatment for
    blacks. With Vargas's prohibition on political parties
    after the promulgation of the Estado Nôvo in 1937 the
    Front was closed.

"FRENTE NEGRA GIRLS." Young black women who joined
    the São Paulo based Black League and who were, in
    turn, blacklisted by would-be employers who feared
    hostility and other forms of militancy.

FRENTE NEGRA PERNAMBUCANA. A brief-lived (1935)
    group of militant blacks in the Northeastern Brazilian
    state of Pernambuco, linked to the Frente Negra Bra-
    sileira as well as to the left-wing Aliança Nacional Li-
    bertadora.

FRONT STREET. The name of the principal street in Ham-
    ilton, Bermuda but also a code word--like Wall Street--
    for rich, smug control by a largely white economic and
    social elite. See also FORTY THIEVES.

FUNAI see MORRER, SE PRECISO FOR

FUNDO.   The Chilean equivalent of a <u>hacienda,</u> or large
agricultural property or estate.

-G-

GAFEIRA.   Afro-Brazilian slang for a <u>samba</u> parlor, a
bar where lower class blacks congregate to dance,
drink, and socialize.

GALLEGO.   A nickname given in Argentina and Chile to
Spanish peasant immigrants, who stereotypically are
considered to be undernourished, with raven-black hair,
and stingy.   Gallegos are supposed to exploit and dominate their children and to favor honest work over education.

GALVEZ, ZOILA.   The "Marian Anderson" of Cuba in the
late 1930's, and one of the first mulatto women in the
country to gain the same public status as whites.

GAMA, LUIZ.   One of the few mulattoes active in the Brazilian abolitionist campaign of the 1880's.   A lawyer
from São Paulo, Gama approached abolitionism from a
moralistic and theologically-based position.

GAMIO, MANUEL.   A Mexican intellectual and <u>indigenist,</u>
one of the early champions of the interests of the Indian <u>peon</u> and a defender of the concept that Latin American nations should modernize in the economic and tech-
nological sphere but base its future evolution on what
Victor Alba calls Indian-derived spiritual values.   See
also CASA DEL ESTUDIANTE INDIGENA.

GAÑANES.   Indians from mission or hacienda villages who
exchanged their labor in exchange for wages determined
by contract.   Since all Indians had to pay tribute under
the Spanish colonial system, many may have been driven
to seek wage labor in order to meet their financial obligations.   In any case, the rise of this system helped
diminish the influence of the repartimiento in areas
where labor was scarce.   Landowners helped create
further incentives for wage labor by depriving Indian
villages of their lands.

GANDUL. A vagrant, or lazybones. The word is used to describe Indians who sit in public places.

GANGA-ZUMBA see BANTU RELIGIOUS INFLUENCE

GANGS. Groups of slaves on Jamaican plantations organized together according to age and work potential. Gangs of children, attended by a female slave, were called "small gangs."

GARVEY, MARCUS (1885-1940). A Jamaican-born black nationalist, who, on a visit to England and France in 1912 began to plan for a movement--the first in the Western Hemisphere--to organize blacks and improve their economic status. Meeting little success in Jamaica, he emigrated to the United States during the First World War, where he established the Universal Negro Improvement Association, which grew from its base in New York City into a nationwide movement. He organized a shipping company to transport blacks to Liberia, where they could live out from under the shadow of whites. The line failed, and he was jailed for a time. He was deported in 1927 and returned to Jamaica, where he founded the People's Political Party. Still unsuccessful, he was arrested, and finally left for England. He died on board the ship which was to bring him back to Jamaica in 1940.

GAUCHOS. The wind-burned cowboys of the Argentine, Uruguayan, and Brazilian pampa, often rustlers, highwaymen, and Indian hunters. Of mixed racial origin (like the Brazilian caboclos), their legendary roughness and barbaric habits dismayed criollo intellectuals, who saw the European side of the Argentine and Uruguayan sociocultural heritage to be threatened by the leather-clad nomads.

GAZA STRIP. Slang term for Wrightson Road, Port-of-Spain, Trinidad, which is a bar and red light district formerly catering to United States navy personnel stationed at the nearby navy base.

GAZO. A near-albino white, with pale blue eyes. The term is used in Brazil to distinguish gazos from generic "whites," who may or may not, in the opinion of the speaker, have some non-white ancestry.

GEBEL-EL-TARIK (TARIQ IBN-ZIYAD). The Moorish

general who crossed from North Africa into Spain and
by 716 A.D. had consolidated Islamic rule in Iberia.
Many of his troops were probably black Muslims from
sub-Saharan Africa, supplanting the descendants of other
Africans who came to Iberia in earlier centuries as
soldiers or slaves.

GENS DE COULEUR. The French term for mulattoes in
the Antilles. Many were descendants of the illegitimate
children of planters and their female slaves. Although
granted free status after the promulgation of the Code
Noir in 1685, they were still restricted from carrying
arms and from engaging in most occupations. Many
strongly supported the French Revolution, which ultimately led to the restoration of their full legal rights.

GENTE DECENTE. A term used in nineteenth-century Mexico for someone of white skin, literally meaning "de-
cent folk." See also PELADO.

GENTE DE COLOR. "Colored people," the generic term
used after 1860 in Cuba to describe non-whites, who
previously were divided into pardos (mulattoes) and
morenos (blacks). Knight suggests that this act, taken
by itself, might have been a significant index of deter-
iorating social and racial relations.

GENTE-DE-COR. "Colored people," a term used increas-
ingly in post-1960 Brazil to lump together all non-white
groups, much as "blacks" in the United States refers to
non-whites of all hues.

GE-ROUGE. One of a number of Haitian "divinities," a
religious cult form caught up in the movement towards
syncretism and profoundly influenced by the dominant
Dahomean religion.

GHIRINO, JOSE L. A free zambo who headed a slave insurrection at Coro, in the Viceroyalty of Nueva Granada, in 1795. He was captured, hanged, and quartered.

GIBARO. The product of a union between a zobo (part-In-
dian and part-African) and a mulatto woman. See also
ZOBO.

GILBERT, NATHANIEL. An Antiguan convert to Methodism
in 1757, the first black brought into the Methodist faith,

and the father, as it were, of the creed as it evolved
to a position of dominance.

GOBINEAU, J. ARTHUR DE (1816-1882). A French racial
determinist of the middle nineteenth century, who, like
Henry Thomas Buckle, wrote about Brazil in disparaging
terms, and who considered Brazil's heritage of racial
miscegenation to be an insurmountable weakness. A
diplomat, Gobineau was assigned to Brazil after his
pessimistic Essai sur l'inégalité des races humaines
was published in 1853. He called the Brazilian population "totally mulatto, vitiated in its blood and spirit,
and fearfully ugly." Skidmore links his vehemence to
his bitterness at having been assigned to what he considered a backwater and dead end for his personal career.

GOELDI, EMILIO. A Swiss immigrant to Brazil and a
physical anthropologist, who founded a research center
in the northern city of Belém in 1885 to study Amerindian culture. Neither Goeldi nor any of the other
pioneer anthropologists in Brazil, including Hermann
von Ihering (the founder of the Museu Paulista in São
Paulo), devoted any attention to Afro-Brazilian history
or culture.

GOMEZ, JUAN GUALBERTO (1854-1933). A Cuban mulatto,
journalist, and abolitionist. He was a close friend of
José Martí and other revolutionaries, and was repeatedly jailed for sedition. He spoke out publicly against
the Platt Amendment and helped shape evolving Cuban
nationalism.

G.O.N.G. A pro-independence political movement on Guadelupe established in 1963, influenced by the Cuban revolution, and profoundly nationalist. The G.O.N.G. advocates adoption of creole as Guadelupe's official language and cancellation of French economic privileges
and monopolies on the island.

GONZALEZ, LELIA DE ALMEIDA. One of the first Afro-
Brazilian women to hold an academic position at a Brazilian university (the Federal University of Rio de Janeiro) and a founder of the militant Unified Black Movement Against Racial Discrimination (1979).

GORGOTOQUIS. Amerindian peoples of "Amazon" culture

type who became extinct by the mid-sixteenth century. The group was native to the central Santa Cruz region of modern-day Bolivia.

GOTTLIEB, MOSES. The organizer of a major slave revolt on St. Croix in 1848. He was known also as Buddoe, or General Bordeaux. The insurrection led to the proclamation of abolition by the colonial governor but Gottlieb himself was exiled to Trinidad, where he lived the rest of his life. See also LABORERS' REVOLT OF ST. CROIX.

GRANDS BLANCS. The French equivalent of peninsulares, whites born in the metropolis and residing in the New World. Their children often became petits blancs, or poor whites, a parallel but somewhat different term for criollos, or creoles. Ironically, while the grands blancs behaved like local nobility, their representatives to the French General Assembly after 1789 voted with the Third Estate.

GRANGER, GEDDES. Trinidadian black power leader of the N.J.A.C., and a key member of the group of intellectuals responsible for the two-month-long February Revolution in 1970. See also FEBRUARY REVOLUTION.

GRAN KAPITANG. A district leader in a Dutch Guiana maroon settlement of Bush Negroes in the eighteenth century. Maroon villages were organized roughly along military lines. The tribal chieftain was known as the gran man.

GRÃO ESCOLA DE SAMBA QUILOMBO. The Quilombo Samba School, drawing more than a thousand members from four poor bairros of Rio de Janeiro. In the late 1970's the group openly endorsed a policy of emphasizing the Afro-Brazilian heritage in its Carnaval pageantry.

GREASER. A vulgar slang expression in the United States for a Mexican or other Latin American.

GREMIO RECREATIVO E CULTURAL. An organization promoting cultural awareness among blacks organized in the early 1920's in São Paulo.

GREMIO RECREATIVO KOSMOS. A São Paulo-based cultural organization among Afro-Brazilians which, unlike other (less-active) groups of the 1918-24 period, carried out an educational program, published a literary newspaper, and sponsored a drama group.

GRIFO. A Puerto Rican term for a person of Caucasian phenotype but with some identifying Negroid features, such as frizzy hair.

GRINGO. A foreigner, in Latin America, usually referring to a white. The derivation is unclear, although it may come from the word "griego," or Greek.

GROS NEG. A Haitian term for a member of the affluent rural peasantry, a tiny group of no more than 5 percent of the larger rural black population.

GRUPO DE TRABALHO DE PROFESSIONALS LIBERAIS E UNIVERSITARIOS NEGROS (GTPLUN). A group of 200 black Brazilian professionals, organized in 1974, and devoted to improving social services and training facilities for the poor-mostly non-white--in and around the city of São Paulo.

GRUPO OLORUN BABA MIN. A group of black artists, established in Rio de Janeiro in 1974, seeking to express their Afro-Brazilian heritage in theaters, neighborhoods, and other public locations. Funded by the Inter-American Foundation, the group's efforts were curtailed when the military government forced the Foundation out of Brazil in 1977 for interference in internal Brazilian affairs.

GUACUCO. A Panamanian word for Negro or Negroid.

GUADELUPE RIOT OF 1976. A violent strike provoked by economic and racial grievances which led to five deaths and more than sixty injuries.

GUAJIRO see POOR CARIBBEAN WHITES

GUANAHUATEBEY see CIBONEY

GUANCHES. A name for Canary Islanders, some of whom, by the last quarter of the sixteenth century, still served as bondsmen in Spain.

GUANDA see NATIONS

GUARANI. A major Amerindian language native to southern Brazil, Paraguay, Uruguay, and northern Argentina. Its speakers moved into eastern Bolivia in the fifteenth century. After the conquest, guarani speakers were gathered under the protective wing of Spanish Jesuits, who organized them into semi-autonomous "republics." Guarani is more closely related in culture to the "Amazon" or tropical forest type. It is the major indigenous language today in Paraguay, and the third largest group in Bolivia, after Quechua and Aymará.

GUARAÑOCA. An Amerindian people in southern Santa Cruz, Bolivia, belonging to the Zamucoan language group and "marginal" cultural type.

GUARAYU. Amerindians of "Amazonian" cultural background now residing on a reservation established by the Bolivian government in northern Santa Cruz. The tribe briefly abandoned Christianity in the early nineteenth century after the intervention of a messianic leader, Luis, who led his followers in a movement devoted to a return to ancient practices.

GUAYQUERI INDIANS. Inhabitants of Margarita Island, off the Venezuela coast, and one of the few population groups of the Americas to have been studied biologically. Their genetic distribution, in fact, shows them to be a mestizo group 46 percent Caucasoid, 13 percent Negroid, and 41 percent Amerindian.

GUIMARÃES. A town in northern Portugal where slave auctions are known to have been held as early as 1258. Slaves were imported from the Barbary coast or purchased from Muslim traders in North Africa, but on the whole the cost of acquiring them was too high to result in the institution becoming firmly rooted either in Portugal or in the kingdoms that later became the modern nation of Spain.

GUINEAU BIRDS. A term used in the English Caribbean for slaves born in Africa.

-H-

HAIR TEXTURE. In Latin America, especially in Brazil, hair texture holds equal or greater importance in de-

termining everyday classifications of race. In Bahia,
Pierson notes, one often hears the expression "Ele é
um pouco escuro, mas o cabello é bom." ("He is a
bit dark but his hair is good," that is, straight.)

HAITIAN-AMERICAN DEVELOPMENT COMPANY. The
major foreign investor in Haiti during the 1930's and
1940's, employing thousands of black workers and holding nearly 11,000 acres, mostly cultivated in sugarcane.

HART, JIM. A United States citizen living in Guyana, the
military leader of the Rupununi revolt Rebellion on January 1, 1970. The Rupununi is a ranching area in the
remote South settled by white immigrants who have tak-
en advantage of border disputes between Guyana and
Venezuela to stir up the local Amerindian population
and seek annexation with Venezuela. Ninety-three rebels
fled across the border after the revolt.

HEEGAARD, ANNE (1790-1859). A free mulatto and mistress to the Governor of the Virgin Islands, von Scholter, who freed the slaves in 1848 in part as a result
of her personal urging. With abolition she allegedly
cancelled a large debt owed to her by von Scholter.

HEMBRAS. Female slaves. Usually less able to perform
manual labor, they sold for from 10 to 25 percent less
than male slaves, or varones.

"HENDE DI TERA FRIU." "People from the cold land,"
an old Papiamento name for Dutchmen in the Netherlands Antilles.

HENRY R.B., REVEREND CLAUDIUS HENRY. "R.B."
stands for "Repairer of the Breach." A Jamaican who
had lived in the United States, then returned home in
1960 and promised Rastafarian followers that he would
lead them back to Africa. Fifteen thousand "tickets"
were sold for a shilling each, and hundreds of families
sold their possessions in preparation for the voyage.
When Henry R.B. was arrested, police found some
arms, and a letter addressed to Fidel Castro asking
for aid in "liberating" Jamaica. He was sentenced to
ten years imprisonment, and his son organized a band
of Castro-like guerrillas, who were captured after a
few deaths. All of this sharply increased fears and
racial tensions on the island and throughout the Carib-

bean, and led to links between Rastafarian groups and black power intellectuals at the University of the West Indies.

"HIGHLAND INDIANS." A generic term applied by English-speakers to Aymará and Quechua peoples in the Bolivian and Peruvian altiplano.

HISTORY WILL ABSOLVE ME. Fidel Castro's autobiographical statement explaining the basis of the Cuban Revolution. On the matter of race, Castro is silent, suggesting, as Hugh Thomas points out, that Cuba for revolutionary purposes was to be considered a racially homogeneous nation. Later, for circumstantial reasons, the color issue surfaced, when black rebel soldiers, for example, were turned away from the Havana Hilton and other places in the capital while whites were admitted. Castro's first pronouncements on race and racial discrimination came in a speech on March 22, 1959.

HOG HUNTER. An early synonym for maroon--when that term simply designated men who hunted wild hogs in the islands of the Caribbean. Later, the term "hog hunter" also came to refer to runaway slaves.

HOMBRES DE LA OTRA BANDA. "Men of the other band, or tribe," a phrase used in the New World to describe peninsulares, Europeans who came to settle and who were considered sickly, susceptible to disease, and pallid. In contrast, the creoles saw themselves as robust and well-adapted.

HOUGAN. A voodoo initiation priest. See also PAPA-LOA.

HOUNSI. Voodoo priestesses. See also MAMAN-LOA.

"HOUSE-KEEPER." The mulatto mistress of a white man, in Jamaica and Barbados.

HUANYAM. An Amerindian tribe of "Amazon" culture and Chapacuran language in central Beni, Bolivia.

HUARIS. Pre-modern Andean peoples who spread their influence through territorial conquest and who, after 600 A.D., had captured most of Peru as far north as the Chicama Valley and Cajamarca. See also TIAHUANA-COS.

HUICHOLES. An Amerindian people native to Tepic and Jalisco, Mexico, who as late as the mid-1920's refused to come into contact with Mexican society and who survived, isolated, in rural pockets out of touch with the marker economy of the reach of the government. See also LACANDONES.

HUMPHREYS, THOMAS. A Tortola Quaker whose money helped establish the Institute for Colored Youth in Philadelphia.

HUNGENIKON. Choir-master in Voodoo society. The man or woman (also called reine chanterelle) who "launches" (envoie) the songs and stops them. She helps the priest and takes his place when he is possessed or when for one reason or another he cannot conduct the whole ceremony.

HUNSI. Man or woman who has passed through voodoo initiation and who helps the hungan or mambo.

-I-

ICAZA, JORGE. An Ecuadorean novelist whose works, especially The Huasipungo, extoll the virtues of Amerindian life to the point (according to Mörner) of inverted racism. Representative of indigenismo, the novelist wrote in reaction to the pessimism of the Social Darwinists and positivists on the same subject. See also INDIGENISMO.

IJESHA see CANDOMBLES

ILLAPA. The Inca weather-god, associated by converts with the Catholic St. James.

ILLESCAS, ALONSO DE. A ladino, and leader of escaped black slaves in northwestern Ecuador in the mid-1650's. He eventually dominated a palenque Empire that included the provinces of Esmeraldas, Imbabura, and Pinchicha, and successfully resisted all effort of the Spanish authorities to retain control.

INCA, ALONSO VIRACCOCHA. The indigenous governor of the Aransayas and a convert to Catholicism who established a sodality at Copacabana, on the shore of Lake

Titicaca (present-day Bolivia) in the early 1580's to encourage further Indian conversions. The shrine has become the center of a regional pilgrimage which has lasted over the centuries.

INCAS. The major imperial power of pre-Conquest South
America. At the height of the Inca Empire in 1520,
the entire territory from modern-day Ecuador to northwestern Argentina was subdued, bringing linguistic uni-
formity (Quechua) and strict administrative control to
the region. Headed by a hereditary emperor and a
large, bureaucratically-organized hierarchy, the Incas
achieved a sophisticated degree of social control, advanced agricultural technology (although they did not
use the wheel), and cultural-religious expression. Inca
roads, often stone-paved, ran for an estimated 15,195
kilometers from Cuzco. Peasants, especially subjugated
peoples, lived harsh lives but had all of their needs
cared for, and received incentives for productivity. The
Inca civilization fell to Francisco Pizarro in 1532, at
a time of internal divisiveness. The degree to which
the Spaniards imposed their "conquest culture" on the
Inca Empire illustrates what, according to Dobyns and
Doughty, was the result of the fact that Spanish colonial
and Inca colonial cultures were so alike. The Spanish
elite simply substituted itself for the Inca elite, and
the lives of the population were not dramatically altered.

INCONFIDENCIA OF BAHIA. An abortive revolt in 1798 in
the Brazilian city of Salvador, directed by mulattoes of
working-class and artisan origin, and put down with brutality by the Portuguese Crown.

"INDIAN DOGS." Mestizo-criollo vulgarism addressed to
Amerindian peasants, first used in the eighteenth century.

INDIAN SLAVERY. The first large-scale attempts to achieve
a controlled labor force in the New World involved en-
slaving the Amerindian population, but the Spanish soon
found out that the indigenous population of Meso-America
was not suited for the type of intense labor demanded.
In the English colonies of North America and in Brazil,
the population density and ecological environment acted
as well to encourage officials to consider alternative
sources of labor. The Spanish and Portuguese chose
African slavery, although, as Knight observes, once the

decline in the Indian population was checked and the
mesticization of the native population evolved, it became possible to reduce reliance on the slave trade,
which had always been expensive and turn once again
to local labor forces.

INDIERO. A Spanish Indian-hunter in the early days of the
Spanish occupation of the Caribbean. Most of the slaves
from Curaçao, Aruba, and Bonaire were taken to Hispaniola.

INDIGENA. A more socially-acceptable term for Indian,
used in the nineteenth century especially to designate
Amerindians who had become partially or wholly acculturated into the Europeanized side of national life. See
also SOCIAL CONCEPT OF RACE.

INDIGENISMO. A movement which flowered in the 1930's
in reaction to the racist pessimism of the Bunge-In-
genieros-Nina Rodrígues school. Indigenistas held up
the simple Amerindian as morally and culturally superior to the decadent representatives of European "civilization." Some indigenistas were less extreme--includ-
ing Ciro Alegria, Diego Rivera, and Miguel Angel As-
turias--portraying the Amerindian's simple dignity without exaggerating his inherent strengths.

INDIO. A term used to relegate Amerindians to lowest social group. It also serves as simple epithet or vulgarity.
See also CAMPESINO.

INDIOBRUTO. A pejorative Spanish term imputing a brutish
character to Amerindian laborers in Peru and Bolivia.

INDIOS DE CORDA. Already-enslaved Amerindians, permitted by Portuguese authorities in Brazil to be kept
in slavery and thus the center of a loophole which permitted slavehunting expeditions by bandeirantes and others. Jesuits attempted to protect the peoples under
their jurisdiction--a form of bondage in itself--but were
driven out of Brazil after 1755 when the Portuguese
government declared all Amerindians to be free, a
legal fiction which led to further depradations.

INDIOS MITAYOS. Indians performing mita labor. See
also MITA.

INDIOS NABORIOS. Nicaraguan Amerindians technically free during colonial days but subject to various forms of labor servitude.

INDIOS PICOTAS. Indian workers in colonial Peru distributed to hacendados (landowners) by caciques and corregidores, despite legal prohibitions of the practice.

INDIOS PONGOS. A Peruvian term for domestic servant. Colonial officials forbade the use of Amerindians as domestic servants, but the existence of the term, and the reality of rural life, meant that the law was unable to be enforced.

INDOCUMENTADOS. Migrant workers without documentation, of Colombian origin, who have crossed the Venezuelan border illegally in search of work. In 1979, up to 400 of the migrants--mostly Amerindian in origin, were alleged to have been massacred in the frontier states of Zulia, Táchira, and Mérida, near the Colombian-Venezuelan line.

INGENIEROS, JOSE. Argentine writer in the early decades of this century whose anti-Negro passion consumed his creative energies and led him to call blacks products of a lower race. Like his compatriot Carlos Bunge, Ingenieros based his outlook on racist Social Darwinism, seeking in the theme of racial inferiority an excuse for Argentina's chronic political instability.

INGLES. "Englishman," a Spanish word used in interior Venezuela to denote Antillean black immigrants--English-speaking--who came as immigrants, especially during the reign of the mestizo Juan Vicente Gómez (1908-1935).

INJERTOS. Children of mixed Chinese-mestizo origin in Peru. Stewart notes that coolies imported to the west coast of South America were invariably male, and that cultural barriers and factors of isolation forced the coolie men into homosexuality as an outlet. Miscegenation with Peruvian women came later, and produced the injertos.

INQUILINOS. Permanent rural workers attached to farms in Chile and elsewhere. They are allowed to reside on the fundo (estate), unlike day laborers, or jornaleros.

Part of his wages are paid in kind and some use of the land is provided.

INSTITUTO RIO BRANCO. Brazil's elite foreign service training academy, organized on the French model, and noted for its historical conservatism and its de facto exclusion of blacks. In 1978 its first black was admitted--Monica Meneses--but the symbolic nature of her appointment was muted when she complained publicly that she was a mulata, not a black. Some African students have attended as guests, but a program funded by the Inter-American Foundation of Washington, D.C. to help prepare Afro-Brazilians for the entrance examination was cancelled when the Brazilian government protested in 1978 and expelled the Foundation from the country on the grounds that it was provoking racial unrest.

INSTRUCTION OF 1789. A decree within the Spanish colonial empire regulating treatment of slaves, based to some degree on the French Code Noir of 1685. Priests and government inspectors were empowered to report abuses against slaves (although little enforcement could have been possible), and the asiento, or slave monopoly, was replaced by free slave trade, to assure a better supply (Mörner). Landowners opposed the Instruction as meddlesome.

INTERRACIAL MARRIAGES. Throughout the post-Conquest period, marriages between persons of different racial groups in Latin America have for the most part occurred between persons not far from one another in terms of the social standing of their groups. Of the 186 marriages celebrated in the Oaxaca chapel in 1756, for example, at least half united persons of the same ethnic group and most of the rest were between ethnic "neighbors" (Mörner). In Brazil, the female member of the couple is usually darker, indicative of the fact that women of color have attained a degree of social (and sexual) desirability to the point where marriage has become an accepted form of upward mobility for them. Except for rare cases (usually celebrities like the soccer hero Pelé) marriages in Brazil between black men and lighter-skinned women are rare, and are frowned upon by society. See also COMPADRAZGO.

IRMÃOS DE CREAÇÃO. "Brothers/sisters of the family,"

a term used in colonial Brazil for slaves reared within
the big house, often "natural" children of the master,
and somewhat comparable, as Pierson notes, to poor
relations in the households of medieval Europe although
they remained slaves unless manumitted.

ITAGUAI. An agricultural colony southwest of the city of
Rio de Janeiro, established in the 1930's, and settled
by both Japanese and Brazilian farmers. The Japanese
prospered: they were aided by their own government
representatives in Brazil, were given certain benefits
by the federal government, and managed to develop an
efficient organizational framework and close business
and social relationships. Some have criticized the Brazilian government for not aiding its own people in the
same way.

ITZCOATL. Ruler of the Aztec Empire between 1428 and
1440, and the leader responsible for the conquests which
brought the Empire wealth and power. Itzcoatl rewarded the principal Aztec chieftains with lands and titles
after his victory, and ordered all histories burned, to
be rewritten during his reign.

IXIAMA; ISIAMA; YDIAMA. An Amerindian group of Tac-
anan language and "Amazon" cultural type in northern La
Paz and western Pando, Bolivia.

IZCALO REVOLT (1932). An uprising among El Salvadorian
Indians which led to widespread slaughter and dispersion
of most of the survivors in the region.

-J-

JAGAN, CHEDDI. A Marxist, and leader of Guyana's East
Indian population. See also BURHAM, FORBES.

JAGUNÇO. A ruffian or outlaw in the Brazilian backlands,
usually a caboclo.

JAMAICAN DIALECT. Another word for "patois," the mixture of English, Spanish, Twi (the language of the Akan
peoples of Ghana), and other African languages, spoken
in Jamaica, especially by the common people.

JAMAICAN EBONY. A bundle of ebony rods lashed together
and used as a whip to flog slaves.

JAPANESE IMMIGRATION TO BRAZIL. Before 1908, Japanese emigration to the New World went primarily to the West Coast of the United States, to Hawaii, to Canada, and to Peru. But restrictions imposed by Washington led Japanese settlement societies to look elsewhere, and the first group of emigrants to arrive in Brazil came in 1908--781 settlers. Most were settled on isolated agricultural colonies in the south, and therefore avoided conflict with Brazilian society, either cultural or social. In the 1930's, nationalists began to seek immigration restrictions, especially of non-Caucasians. Acts of imperialism in Asia by Japan led some Brazilian intellectuals--including Miguel Couto, Xavier de Oliveira, Félix Pacheco, and Arthur Neiva--to campaign against further immigration. Led by Couto, the "Japanophobes" charged that Japanese settlers posed threats to Brazilian national security, and the results of the campaign led to Article 121 of the 1934 Constitution, which imposed immigration quotas. The Brazilian government, however, did not completely enforce the restriction, and Japanese settlers continued to arrive, especially to colonies in São Paulo state. Angered, the anti-immigrationists revived their campaign, and effective restriction was achieved in 1938 and was broadened under the Brasilidade campaign of the Estado Novo. In all, the Japanese in Brazil were treated well by the Vargas government, in contrast to the wartime experience of other Japanese in Spanish American countries and in the United States.

JAPONES. Portuguese word for Japanese. See also NIHON-JIN.

JEWISH GAUCHOS. More than 10,000 refugees from the Russian pale settled in Santa Fé, Argentina, to take up farming and cattle ranching. Their story is told by A. Gerchunoff in a volume translated as The Jewish Gauchos of the Pampas (1955).

JEWISH MAROONS. Gilberto Freyre claims that the Djukas maroon settlements of Dutch Guiana were inhabited by former slaves who had been converted to Judaism and who continued to practice their faith as rural fugitives. Some of the blacks, in fact, were sent into the forest deliberately by their Portuguese Jewish masters when Dutch tax collectors levied an unusually high head tax on slaves. See also MAROONS.

JEWS IN THE FRENCH ANTILLES   see   PIETER

JEWS IN THE NETHERLANDS INDIES.   Settlement began in
1651, when 50 Sephardic Jewish colonists were allowed
to immigrate to Curaçao by the Dutch West India Company.   When the Dutch government took over direct control of the islands in 1815 good relations continued, and
Jews became relatively integrated into colonial society.
Some East European Jews settled in Curaçao after 1926,
and additional refugees from Nazism came to the islands in the 1930's.

JIBARO   see   XIVARO

JIGGA.   A dance leader, in Jamaica, probably from the
term "to jig."

JIGGER-FOOT.   Epithet used against West Indians in Bermuda, where the newcomers are considered uppity and
likely to precipitate social unrest.

JILACATA; HILACATA.   An Aymará chieftain, the highest-
ranking official of an ayllu, or community.   The title
was revived after 1953 to accompany Bolivian land reform.   In Quechua, the equivalent term in CURACA.

JOBABA UPRISINGS.   Two major slave insurrections swept
the copper mines at Jobabo, Cuba, in 1533 and again
in 1713.   The eighteenth-century revolts were never
firmly put down until 1798, when the slaves in the region were declared freed.

JOCHINA.   A Botocudo Indian who was captured by a Portuguese
military expedition during the early nineteenth century
and eventually taken to Europe.   In England, he became
the focal point of an early campaign to publicize the
plight of the aboriginal populations of the New World.
Jochina's story, as well as details about the life of his
tribe, was published in an ephemeral pamphlet published
in four small editions in London, Birmingham, Exeter,
and Edinburgh in 1822, and was only uncovered by historians in the late 1970's.

JODEN SAVANNA.   The "Jewish Savanna," a territory along
the Surinam River settled in the seventeenth century by
Portuguese Jews who had fled to Brazil, then to Cayenne,
and then--after it fell to the French--to Dutch Guiana.

JORNALEROS.   Peasant day-laborers.   See also INQUILINOS.

JUEZ REPARTIDOR.   An administrative functionary in colonial Nueva España and Peru who distributed Amerindian
laborers to landowners under the system of encomienda,
and later under the repartimiento, under which Indian
peasants were assigned to mine and agricultural labor
on a rotating basis throughout the year.

JURUPARI.   An aboriginal divinity in Amazonian Brazil
whom Catholic missionaries identified with the devil.

-K-

KANAIMA.   Professional Guyanese Indian-killers, hired by
prospectors and landowners to commit murder.   In their
fear, Amerindians have cast the very-human kanaima
into the form of a myth: he represents death itself,
and all deaths are attributed to the kanaima.

KAPO.   Leader of the black Protestant Pocomania cult in
Jamaica in the 1960's, a proponent of class integration
and race unity.   See also POCOMANIA.

KARDECISM.   A spiritualistic cult popular in Brazil, named
after the French medium Allain Kardec, the pseudonym
of Hippolyte Rivail (1804-1869).   Afro-Brazilians joined
the movement because it allowed them to maintain their
beliefs in reincarnation, a central theme of Bantu religion, yet be identified, at the same time, with a religious institution acceptable to Europeans.

KESHWA; KISHUA   see   QUECHUA

KIELSTRA DESAS.   Javanese villages, transplanted to Surinam under the authority of J. C. Kielstra, governor
from 1933 to 1943, with the presumption that family
groups would prove more stable settlers than individual
contract laborers.   Five such desas were inaugurated
before World War II cut off immigration.

KILL HOG.   To slaughter a hog and make a feast of celebration, a term used by Jamaican maroons during the
eighteenth century in their fugitive settlements.

KIMBUNGO.   A werewolf in Afro-Brazilian folklore, given

to devouring children and swallowing them through a
hole in its back. See also BIZANGO.

KING BENKOS. Cimarrón leader in the early seventeenth
century in Nueva Granada. See also SAN BASILIO.

KING'S NEGROES. A term in Jamaica for maroons who,
having won de facto freedom by successfully resisting
recapture and winning peace treaties with colonial officials in 1739 and 1795, themselves turned to bounty-
hunting of newly escaped slaves and to owning slaves of
their own.

KINGSTON RIOTS OF 1965. An uprising of urban blacks
against the conspicuous Chinese shopkeepers of the
slums. They are considered to have been more socioeconomic than racial in their motivation.

KJOTSUNI; KOTSUÑ see URU

KLEURLINGEN. The Dutch term for mulattoes, the dominant group in the middle class of the islands of the
Netherlands Antilles.

KROMANTIS. The African cultural grouping predominant in
Jamaica, of Gold Coast origin.

KRU EMIGRATION TO THE WEST INDIES. The Krus, a
West African tribal group, were unusually successful at
avoiding enslavement due to their seafaring skills and
to their strategic geographic location on the Kru coast.
They were considered good agricultural laborers, and
were encouraged to settle voluntarily in the British Caribbean by planters, especially in the 1830's, when the supply of slaves began to dwindle. Between 1,000 and
1,200 Krus are believed to have migrated to British
Guiana, Trinidad, and Jamaica. Gradually, however,
their places began to be taken by East Indian laborers.

KRUMIROS. Scabs, used to break strikes in early twentieth-
century Brazil. Frequently they were caboclo migrants
from rural areas, or Portuguese immigrants.

KUBI. A Jamaican name given to a man born on a Tues-
day. See also CUFFIE.

KUMINA. A possession cult native to Jamaica, in which

the spirit of an ancestor, during the stage known as myal--is believed to take over the dancer's body.

KWAYANA, EUSI. Guyanese black power advocate and head of the Afro-Guyanese Ascria group.

-L-

LABORERS' REVOLT OF ST. CROIX. A violent insurrection of blacks in St. Croix, V.I., in 1878 protesting the continued existence of contract servitude, which kept the island's blacks in near servitude despite the decree of abolition in 1848. The mob attacked Frederiksted and sacked the establishments owned by white merchants; plantations were also burned before reinforcements arrived from St. Thomas. The revolt led to a reform of the labor laws which had precipitated the unrest.

LABORIOS see NABORIOS

LACANDONES. An Amerindian people in rural Usumacinta, Mexico, who by the 1920's had still refused to end their isolation from the "civilized" world of the national state. See also HUICHOLES.

LADANOS. Sacristans of the nineteenth-century Brazilian Black Muslim cult. See also BLACK ISLAM.

LADINO BAN OF 1503. Queen Isabella warned that ladino slaves were fleeing once they arrived in Hispaniola (and offering a dangerous lesson in rebelliousness to the local indigenous population, prohibited the further landing of ladinos in the Spanish New World). The decision was reversed after her death by King Ferdinand, who was aware that native Caribbean tribes were becoming decimated by disease and the effect of forced labor. By 1514, the number of ladinos on the island had surpassed the total number of whites.

LADINOS. 1) Indians in Central America and elsewhere who have adopted Spanish forms of dress and behavior. Ladino-ized Indians usually live in their own communities; in towns they live in separate barrios (districts, or neighborhoods) away from other Indians. 2) Spanish-speaking African slaves, at first recruited from the

slave population which had been transported to Spain
(and Portugal).

LAGGIA. A combat dance, practiced by descendants of
slaves in the French Antilles, and related to the Brazilian capoeira.

LAKU. The Haitian extended family around which Voodoo
practices are based. See also VOODOO.

"LAND OF THE SIX RACES." A popular name for Guyana,
whose heterogeneous population includes Africans, East
Indians, Portuguese, Chinese, Europeans, and Amerindians.

LA PIEL MAS BLANCA. "Whiter skin," an attribute of
many immigrants to South America from Northern Italy,
giving them higher status than the darker-skinned Southern Italians, even among settlements of Italian colonos.

LA-PLACE. Title in a Voodoo society for the master of
ceremonies. Armed with a sword or machete he leads
processions, presents arms, pays homage to the loa
and helps the officiant.

LAPOUGE, GEORGES VACHER. A late nineteenth-century
French disciple of Count Gobineau who condemned mixed
races for their casual genetic inheritance, holding that
race conflict results in the weak driving out the strong.
Lapouge, who was widely read in Brazil and elsewhere,
illustrated his thesis with the example of the Antilles,
where whites have "almost disappeared," and Haiti, seen
as a center of African barbarism. In Mexico, Lapouge
saw the Indians as having taken over.

LA SALLE, LT. REX. Leader of a black power faction
within the army of Trinidad which revolted in April
1970, against general conditions and against the government of Sir Eric Williams. The mutiny spread, but
was put down with the arrival of requested aid from
Venezuela and the United States. A truce was nego-
tiated, with the army relaxing its stand against black
power symbols within the enlisted ranks. Six United
States warships sailed from Puerto Rico at the government's call, backing the cease-fire; LaSalle and twenty-
six others were tried for treason and sedition.

LAST SUPPER, THE. A film (1978) by Cuban Tomás

Guitièrrez Alea, the producer of "Memories of Under-development." The plot concerns the inability of Cuban landowners to adapt to the industrial revolution in the late eighteenth century, and powerfully portrays the will of plantation slaves to mock their masters--and the punishments suffered for their audacity.

LAVEAU, "QUEEN" MARIE. The most famous leader of New Orleans Voodoo, in the late eighteenth century, known for her ability to manufacture magic potions which became in demand not only among her followers but among members of the white elite.

LEAGUE OF COLOURED PEOPLES. A pre-1950 black-only political party in British Guiana which yielded to the bi-racial People's Progressive Party in 1950. See also EAST INDIAN ASSOCIATION.

LEGAL VS. SOCIAL STATUS. Law in colonial Spanish America recognized different social categories than social status. The "legal" hierarchy started with "Spaniards" and descended through Mestizos, Indians, free blacks, mulattoes, zambos, and finally to the slaves. "Social status" categories started with peninsulares, then descended to criollos, the mestizos, mulattoes, zambos, and free blacks, slaves (domestic, then agricultural), and then Indian peasants.

LEI AUREA. The "Golden Law," Brazil's decree abolishing slavery on May 13, 1888.

LE JEUNE CASE. A celebrated incident in 1788 in Saint Domingue, 14 slaves in the northern province of Plaisance approached a colonial court with the charge that Le Jeune, a planter, had brutally tortured two women slaves by roasting them in order to extract confessions. A commission appointed to investigate found the women still alive but in a horrendous state, and Le Jeune disappeared. Nonetheless the case was dismissed after a negative verdict. An appeal led to a second acquittal in spite of all of the evidence.

LE MANIEL. A major colony of fugitive slaves in French Saint-Domingue in the eighteenth century which achieved a measure of recognition from colonial political authorities.

LENCAS. Aboriginal Indians living in Honduras, descended from the Mayas.

LEPEROS. "Lepers," a slang term for semi-employed Mexicans, usually of Indian stock, who inhabited the outskirts of Mexico City during the colonial period and into the nineteenth century and frequently resorted to stealing, begging, or crime in order to support their families.

LES AMIS DES NOIRS. An eighteenth-century French humanist society founded to combat slavery in the territories. They influenced the French Revolutionary Government of 1790 to decree abolition in the French Caribbean, although slavery was reintroduced in Guadelupe and Martinique by Napoleon until final abolition came in 1848.

LEVA-PANCADA. A "whipping boy," a slave child who, according to Freyre, was substituted to receive punishment earned by the master's child. See also MULEQUE COMPANHEIRO DE BRINQUEDO.

LIBERTO. A descendant of slaves whose freedom was granted a "free womb" law passed during the nineteenth century in various countries, including Argentina, Brazil, Uruguay, Peru, and Paraguay. Most such laws legally bound the youth to his mother's master until his legal majority, and in practice many were kept in servitude beyond that point, either through coercion or contractual arrangements which skirted the "free womb" legislation.

LIBRES DE COLOR. Free blacks. Although emancipated, they were subject to many of the same restrictions held against slaves. In Colombia, libres could not even use walking sticks, a symbol of prestige, and were kept from even such unskilled positions as bogas (canoe men) or cargeros (carriers), which were reserved for Indians.

LICENCIADOS. Slaves shipped through the fiscal arrangement of the licencia, a royal authorization allowing an individual or company to trade in slaves to a specified port or region. As many as a half a million licenciados may have arrived in the New World prior to 1810.

LIMA SLAVE REVOLT OF 1578. Launched by the urban

slaves of the city during the invasion of the English ship captain, Sir Francis Drake, in 1578.

LIMPEZA DE SANGUE. The Portuguese equivalent of the Spanish certificate attesting to the legal condition of "pure" or "clean" blood.

LIMPIEZA DE SANGRE. A Spanish colonial document affirming the holder's "purity of blood," or certified whiteness. These were able to be bought by persons needing such documentation for social reasons.

LINGUA GERAL. The term used for the Afro-Brazilian língua franca used by blacks (and some whites, mainly the paulista bandeirantes who penetrated the interior in search of gold and Indian captives), based to some degree on Nagô, but a constantly-changing blend of Tupí-Guaraní and other languages as well. In Bahia, the língua geral was more exclusively Nagô.

LISTON. A measuring stick, divided into "palmos," used to measure the height of slaves brought from slave ships to such Spanish American ports as Portobello and Buenos Aires.

LIVRES. Ex-slaves, in Brazil. See also EX-SLAVES, WORDS FOR.

LLANEROS. Venezuelan mestizo cowboys, similar in origin to the Argentine and Uruguayan gauchos, who in 1817, joined with Bolívar against the Spanish and raised the spectre, among white criollos and peninsulares, of racial war. They were led in battle by their chieftain, José Antonio Paez.

LLULU. The Hualcán name (Quechua) for a child, literally meaning "unripe."

LOA. Supernatural being in Voodoo. This word is usually translated as "god," or "divinity." In fact, a loa is more a genie, demon or spirit.

LOANGAS. An African "nation" of Uruguay, transformed into a Carnival troupe. Bastide calls this "the last avatar of Africa" in the Rio de la Plata. See also NATIONS.

LOBATO, MONTEIRO see TATU, JECA

LOBO.   Literally, "wolf," a colonial Mexican synonym for a mulato pardo.   See also COYOTE.

LOGS.   Slang term used to describe Negro slaves in Barbados and other Caribbean islands in the seventeenth century.   See also BLACK BUNDLES.

LONELY LONDONERS, THE   see   WEST INDIAN DIASPORA

LORO.   "Parrot," a Mexican term used during the colonial period for a mulato pardo.

L'OUVERTURE, TOUSSAINT   see TOUSSAINT L'OUVERTURE

LOWLAND INDIAN SLAVERY.   Harris asserts that labor systems based on enslavement of lowland Amerindian groups failed because the captured peoples were not accustomed to harsh agricultural labor; many died from conditions brought about by exhaustion; others from disease; still others by suicide.   By the end of the seventeenth century, nearly the entire Amerindian population of the Caribbean and the large portion of the aboriginal population of Brazil had been wiped out.   Their places were taken by imported African slaves.

LUBOLOS.   A dancing procession of African origin, held during Carnaval in Montevideo.

LUCKHOO, J. A.   The first Indo-Guianese to be made a King's Counsel, in the nineteenth century, and the head of the leading East Indian family dynasty in Guyana.

LUCUMI.   A term used in Mexico, Colombia, and Cuba for slaves of Yoruba origin.   Elsewhere, the term used was nago.

LUNEROS.   Mestizo and Indian peasants in Mexican villages who are paid wages for one day of work per week, often Monday (thus the name comes from the word lunes).

LUPACA KINGDOM.   A functionally autonomous enclave established in 1567 by Spanish officials in Chucito Province on the present-day Peruvian shore of Lake Titicaca, to preserve the separateness of the Aymará-speaking inhabitants.

LUSITANIAN RACISM.   A philosophical school represented

by the writing of Afrânio Peixoto (especially his early
novel A Esfinge, published in 1911) and others during
the late 19th and early 20th centuries. The view rejected Anglo-Saxon hegemony as the necessary compo-
nent for racial stamina and health; rather, it endorsed
Brazil's Portuguese heritage as more tolerant and flex-
ible, since the Portuguese mixed freely with Indians and
blacks. Nonetheless. Peixoto and his colleagues wel-
comed the "whitening" of the Brazilian population and
labelled the non-whites of Latin America as sub-races.

-M-

MACEHUAL. Aztec word for a rascal or lawbreaker.

MACHIGUA. A name applied to Indians in the Panamanian
region of San Blás. The word means "child" in the
Cuna language.

MACRO-CHIBCHA. A language family of peoples native to
Central America (Nicaragua through Panama) and South
America.

MACUMBA. A fetish-worship cult popular among Afro-
Brazilians, and rooted in Bantu religious practice. See
also BANTU RELIGIOUS INFLUENCE.

MÃE-DE-SANTO. A candomblé princess. See also PAI-
DE-SANTO.

MAIZE CULTIVATION. The original Andean Amerindians
lived on the coast, and engaged primarily in hunting,
gathering, and fishing. Around 1800 B.C., however,
pottery making and maize (corn) cultivation transformed
the native population. The addition of maize to their
diets allowed adaptation to a more stable sedentary life,
and the fermentation of maize into chicha, or maize
beer, influenced religious practices, since maize was
identified with fertility. Peasants who drink chicha today still pour a few drops on the ground in homage to
the ancient Earth Mother.

MAKARA. An Efik word for the ruling elite, or class. It
may be the root of the West Indian term bakra, a member of the white planter class.

MAL D'ESTOMAC. "Belly ache." One of a number of

maladies considered "Negro diseases" in Trinidad and other Caribbean islands during the colonial period. Stomach troubles were often caused by dirt-eating, which poor blacks often practiced out of despair.

MALICIA INDIGENA. "Native cunning," a phrase used to impute sexual prowess to Amerindian or non-white persons, especially males.

MALUNGOS see IRMÃOS DE CREAÇÃO

MAMAN-LOA. Haitian voodoo priestesses, considered hounsi, or brides of the gods.

MAMBI. A Caribbean term for a poor white.

MAMBISES. A Cuban term for communities of fugitive slaves, generally known as palenques throughout the rest of Spanish America and quilômbos in Brazil.

MAME. A pre-Columbian tribe of peoples in present-day Guatemala.

MAMELUCOS. A Brazilian term for the early mestizos who lived more according to Amerindian customs than in European style, and who in turn were regarded as uncivilized. Some of the early bandeirantes fit this category. See also BANDEIRANTES.

MANCEBIA. Concubinage, an accepted form of cohabitation in Brazil and other places throughout Latin America, where divorce has been illegal and sexual freedom (for males) always socially tolerated.

MANCHA DE PLATANO. "Stain of the plantain," a pejorative phrase applied to Puerto Rican peasants by urban dwellers.

MANCHAS. "Spots," or marks, a term used by customs officials to classify skin disorders of any kind found on arriving slaves. Some represented disease, but unless the sores were running the slaves were usually admitted.

MANDAMIENTO. A form of exploitation of Indian peasants in Guatemala and elsewhere, a version of the older repartimiento system of forced labor.

MANDINGA. A successful maroon settlement in the Vera-

cruz-Oaxaca region of present-day Mexico, established
after a slave revolt in 1735. After eight years, the
Spanish authorities sued for peace, as it were, and
agreed to recognize the settlement's autonomy. The
maroons were occasionally recruited by the Spanish to
serve as a police force and to intimidate Indian peons
in the region.

MANDINGAS. Rituals associated with the Black Muslim religious cults of Rio de Janeiro and Bahia during the
nineteenth century which were heavily dominated by interest in magic. As a word denoting sorcery, "mandinga" survives in many Latin American countries
where Muslim slaves had been imported, including Argentina, Uruguay, and Cuba.

MANDINGO see NATIONS

MANEIS. A derogatory name taken from the common name
Manoel. It was used by Italian anarcho-syndicalist labor organizers in Brazil, for Portuguese workers, who
were considered insensitive to labor issues and willing
to serve as strike breakers.

MANICONGOS. Blacks from Angola shipped to the New
World, mostly the Indies, by Portuguese traders.

MANIFESTO OF BLACK BRAZILIAN WOMEN. Announced
to a small audience in Rio de Janeiro on July 2, 1975,
declaring opposition against the degrading and disre-
spectful treatment of non-white women by Brazilian society.

MANOA. The legendary capital of El Dorado, for which
Sir Walter Raleigh and others searched down the coast
from the Orinoco in Venezuela to the Amazon.

MANTOUBA. A jungle mountain town on Guadelupe inhabited
by descendants of East Indian laborers who came to
Guadelupe and Martinique after the abolition of slavery
in 1848.

MANUMISO. Word for liberto (freed one) in Venezuela,
Colombia, and Ecuador.

MANUMISSION. The act of setting a bondsman free through
legal means, usually through payment to the owner.

Slaves in Spanish and Portuguese America could obtain
their freedom to an extent more readily than their slave
counterparts in North America, but freedom itself did
not always mean that the slave could leave and pursue
his own life. Often, slaves granted free status had to
remain in service to the master, or to his wife in case
of the owner's death, for an indefinite period. The
most common reason during the colonial period for manumission to be granted was for extraordinary service,
usually in battle. The 1785 Código Negro Carolino offered freedom to slaves who denounced slave conspiracies, saved a white person's life, or worked faithfully
for thirty years. See also SEMILIBERATION.

MANUMISSION, OPPORTUNITIES FOR. Rout summarizes
three factors governing the prospects for manumission
for Spanish America as a whole (the situation in Brazil
was similar): 1. Urban slaves stood a better chance
than rural slaves; 2. Ladinos and criollos morenos were
more likely to earn manumission than bozales, or first-
generation slaves; 3. Mulattoes, especially the offspring
of Spanish fathers, were more likely to win freedom
than blacks.

MANUMISSION IN COLONIAL SPANISH AMERICA. Generally, women, children, and mulattoes were represented
disproportionately among slaves emancipated by their
masters. Johnson, for example, attributes the phenomenon to relative levels of acculturation in the dominant society, slave replacement costs, and the ability
of individual slaves to accumulate savings. The traditional explanation stresses owner paternity of slave children and "a reward system associated with concubinage."

MARABOU. A mulatto in the proportion of 88 to 40, defined according to the 128 divisions of racial origin used
in colonial Saint Domingue.

MARAN, RENE (1887-1960). A Martinique-born novelist
whose Batoula received the Prix Goncourt in 1921. The
novel describes the hardships of slavery on the island.

MARECHAUSSEE. A roving band of fugitive slave hunters
who exercised police functions and fought the maroons
in colonial Saint Domingue. Most of its members were
mulattoes, who were required to serve for at least three
years and thereafter join the local militia under white
commanding officers.

MARLY. An early West Indian novel (1828) portraying a Jamaican "coloured" (mulatto) youth who studies in the University of Edinburgh, only to come home to racial discrimination. The author is unknown.

MAROONS. Communities of runaway slaves. The term is used generically, throughout the hemisphere. It is derived from the Spanish word cimarrón, which originally signified formerly domesticated farm animals, such as the pigs, which had reverted to the wild state. Scholars identify different types of maroon societies depending on the status of their members. By the nineteenth century, most marronage was practiced by creoles, Negroes born in the New World. Many maroon societies attempted to recreate new Africas, although their societies, as long as they survived, generally exhibited more New World traits than Old.

MARRANOS. "New Christians," converted Jews who despite their professions of loyalty to the Spanish Church and Crown were forbidden to emigrate to the New World by royal policy. See also MORISCOS.

MARRONS see MAROONS

MARTIN, FRANCISCO. A member of an early expedition to Venezuela who was captured by Amerindians and who lived for years among them until he was kidnapped by Spaniards and brought back to "civilization." He ran away to rejoin his tribe but was kidnapped again and deported to Nueva Granada, away from his wife and children and adopted customs.

MARTINS, OLIVEIRA. A Portuguese historian whose works, at the beginning of the twentieth century, incorporated the views of Aryan supremacy and European-based racism that were accepted by many members of the Latin American elite. His writings were attacked by the Brazilian writer and physician, Manoel Bonfim, who accused Martins of using racist arguments as an excuse to maintain the status quo and to impede social progress.

MASAMORREROS. Independent mining prospectors in the Spanish colonies. Free blacks, or libres, were usually prohibited from becoming masamorreros, although some exceptions are known.

MASU GADU. A god of Dahomean origin sacred to the Bush

Negroes of Dutch and French Guiana, especially in the maroon villages in the forest interior.

MATIGNON. According to Gastmann, the name of the most important family of poor whites in Jabrun, Guadelupe, said to be descendents of eighteenth-century colonial-era aristocrats.

MATRICULAS. Brazilian civil registries, a major source for social historians interested in slavery.

MAWLA. A military-religious official in the Islamic legions used against the Christians in Iberia. Many were sub-Sahara Africans, freed after long service to the Moors and elevated to positions of medium-level authority in the ranks.

MAYEQUES. Indian peasants who worked as slaves or serfs for Aztec overlords, usually for a limited period of time before being allowed to return to the status of freedmen.

MAYOMBE SYNCRETISM. Merger of Cuban Bantu religious magic sects with Catholicism. The principal Mayombé deities include Salabanda (St. Peter), Insancio (St. Barbara), and Ashola Aguengue or Mother of Waters (Our Lady of Charity).

MAZEHUALOB. Mayan word for "natives," in contrast to "dzulob" or aliens. Thus the Mayans maintained the same kind of dualist perceptions as the Spaniards.

MELHORANDO A RAÇA. "Improving the race, or breed" see WHITENING.

MENELIQUE. Italo-Brazilian word for a black, probably derived from the term moleque.

MENENDEZ, JESUS. A Cuban labor leader assassinated in 1947, one of the first Afro-Cubans to achieve prominence in Cuban society before the 1960's.

MENNONITE SETTLEMENTS IN PARAGUAY see NUEVA GERMANIA

"MEN OF HUMBLE COLOR" see REGIMENT OF BROWNIES AND DARKIES

MESTIÇO. A Portuguese term used to refer to any person of mixed racial origin, including African, European, and Amerindian. The Spanish mestizo is primarily a term connoting a mixture of European and Amerindian parentage.

MESTIZAJE. A nineteenth-century intellectual movement, fomented by Mexican philosopher José Vasconcelos and others, based on the premise that the mixed-blooded population of Latin America comprised a "cosmic race," a superior blend of genetic and cultural factors. Its proponents advocated mestizaje as a strong integrating force to overcome national differences and achieve political hegemony.

MESTIZOS, EARLY. The first generation of mestizos in the Spanish and Portuguese colonies took part in the last stages of the Conquest. Juan de Garay and fellow mestizos from Asunción established the settlement at Santa Fé and later at Buenos Aires. The Chilean mestizos helped subjugate the Araucanian Indians; in Brazil, the offspring of Portuguese sailors (called mamelucos, referring to their primitive style of life) remained loyal to the Portuguese cause. Some few mestizos became loyal to their maternal group, and were considered deserters and traitors by their compatriots.

METIS. Half-breeds, a term used until the turn of the twentieth century for Brazilian mulattoes.

MEU NEGRO, MEU NEGO, MEU NEGRINHO. An old-fashioned (vintage 1930's) Brazilian term of endearment ("my little Negro") used not only by whites to blacks and blacks to other blacks, but, as Pierson shows, by whites to other whites. Beggars, he added, also used the term in appealing to whites for alms, or to mulattoes "if [they] appeared well to do." Clerks also used the term in addressing customers. The feminine form of the term is "minha negra...."

MEXICAN NATIONAL INDIAN INSTITUTE. A government-funded entity established in the mid-1940's, devoted to preserving national Indian culture, language, and folklore. It is located in San Cristóbal Las Casas in Chiapas.

MIGHTY CHALKDUST see CARNAVAL, TRINIDAD

MIGHTY STALIN. A leading Trinidadian Calypso singer

whose songs, in the late 1960's, began to take on a
political and racial consciousness. His "Martin Luther
King" won second prize at the 1969 Carnaval; first prize
went to the Duke's "Black Is Beautiful."

MILAN, GABRIEL. A early governor of the Danish Virgin
Islands (1684-86) and one of several Jews who served
Denmark in the colonial office. After 1814, when Den-
mark became the first modern nation to pass laws pro-
tecting the rights of Jews, many came to settle in St.
Thomas, the capital of the Virgin Islands.

MILPAS. Garden plots worked by repartimiento laborers
to provide their own food. See also REPARTIMIENTO.

MINA. A light-skinned slave woman from the Bahia region
taken as companion or concubine by Portuguese masters
and prized for their sexuality.

MINAS. Slaves shipped from the Gulf of Guinea, considered
to be the best place of origin for human captives in Africa. In actuality, the term was inaccurately applied,
since slaves who embarked from the Gulf came from
varied tribal groups, including Ashantis, Ewes, Yorubas.

MINE LABOR. In Latin America, Indian slaves were generally used in mining, while African slaves were reserved for plantation work. Brazil provided an excep-
tion, as did some of the gold and silver districts in
Nueva Granada. Black slaves were considered too expensive to use in the high-risk silver mining areas of
Potosí (Upper Peru). Two of every 3 Indian slaves there
died, and the mitayos (miners) were chained together to
prevent escape.

MINTY ALLEY. A novel by the historian and writer C. L. R.
James, which emphasized the ethnic separatism within
polyglot Trinidadian society in the early twentieth century and later.

MISCEGENATION. Marriage or cohabitation between persons of different races. In the Americas, the term is
usually applied to mixed relationships where one partner
is Caucasian. An aura of sensuality and forbidden ero-
ticism often attends discussion of the practice. W. E. B.
Du Bois called antebellum miscegenation "stark, ugly,
painful, beautiful," and Gilberto Freyre employed the
concept to provide the basis for his hypothesis that

Brazilian race relations were more humane because of the tolerance of the Portuguese colonist and his purported appreciation of the erotic attraction of the African slave and Native Brazilian women, who he blames for "seducing" the European.

MISCIBILIDADE. "Miscibility," a term used to describe the Portuguese propensity (according to Gilberto Freyre) for miscegenation in their conquered territories.

MISTURA DANADA. A "damned mixture," a term used in Brazil to refer to offspring of either racially or ethnically mixed unions. It is only faintly pejorative.

MITA. A system of forced labor during the later years of the colonial period. See also REPARTIMIENTO.

MITAMAES. People forcibly removed and relocated by the Incas, in order to lessen the potential causes of rebellion.

MOCAMBO, MUCAMBO. A waterside shack or hovel made of bamboo or wood, in the Brazilian Northeast. The word comes from the African slave word for a jungle hideout for runaway maroons. See also QUILOMBO.

MOCHICA. A coastal civilization native to present-day Peru in the first millennium A.D., known for its use of irrigation in agriculture and its pottery.

MOKE see VULGARISMS

MOKO. 1) A Jamaican word of Ibo origin designating an area in which Ibo people settled after or during slavery. It is derived from the Ibo term Mgboko, for a market in Iboland. 2) A Trinidadian black power association formed in the late 1960's. See also BLACK POWER.

MOLEQUE. A Brazilian term for a black urchin, or "streetwise" young black boy, portrayed as typically engaged in stealing, begging, or making trouble. See also MULEQUES.

MONÇÕES. Bands of Portuguese and mulato adventurers who penetrated the rivers of interior Brazil to raid Indian villages or otherwise loot or find precious minerals. The name comes from the Portuguese word for "monsoon."

"MONEY WHITENS." A phrase referring to the fact that
in Latin America persons of color can enjoy status usually afforded to whites (or, to affluent persons) if they
can demonstrate their "economic fitness" through upward economic mobility. This calculus of identity in-
volves adding up a person's education, manners, dress,
wealth, and coloration, in what Harris calls a system
of merits and demerits in which class criteria modify
racial identity.

MORANT BAY. The Jamaican site of a major uprising of
blacks in 1835, following in the island's tradition of
slave rebellions in the seventeenth, eighteenth, and nineteenth centuries.

MOREJON, NANCY. The most prominent of the post-revolutionary generation of Cuban poets. The daughter of
a Havana worker, she studied French literature and was
influenced by the symbolistes before, as Peter Winn
notes, her awakening black consciousness was drawn to
the Antilles poetry of Aimé Cesaire and Edward Braith-
waite.

MORENO. A polite "code word" in Brazil for blacks. See
also PARDO.

MORISCOS. Muslims from Iberia converted to Catholicism
before and after the Reconquest, but themselves expelled
in 1509, as had been the "New Christians," or marranos: the converted Jews.

MORRER, SE PRECISO FOR, MATAR, NUNCA. "Die if
necessary; kill, never." The motto of Cândido Rondôn's
Indian Protective Service, established in 1910 by the
Brazilian government after continued hostility against
settlers on the agricultural frontier moved the army to
consider means to pacify the Amerindian tribes. Over
the years, however, the Protective Service evolved into
a bureacratic agency not only unable to protect its charges but, through its representatives, given to exploit and
even murder Amerindians. Allegations documenting this
mistreatment came to light in the middle 1960's and led
to the closing of the Protective Service and the creation
of a new agency, the National Indian Foundation, FUNAI.

MORUA, MARTIN. A Cuban black and a member of the national Congress under the United States occupation, when
discrimination against non-whites intensified. As pres-

ident of the Senate, Morúa, in 1912, introduced a successful bill that outlawed any political party based on
ethnic exclusivity. The law had the effect of proscrib-
ing the Independent Party of Color, which had been organized in 1908, moving its leaders to rebel, in Oriente
province and in Las Villas, regions populated by more
than 50 percent blacks. See also BLACK REVOLT.

MOSCOS. "Mosquitoes," the name given to the inhabitants
of the Mosquitia marshes (Mosquito coast) region of
eastern Central America. Most are considered to be
the descendants of Negro-Indian unions, in comparison
with the more Negroid Black Caribs of Belize (British
Honduras). See also BLACK CARIBS.

MOTECUHZOMA. The Aztec name for their chieftain, captured and finally murdered by Cortes in 1521.

MOURA ENCANTADORA. "Moorish enchantress," a sexual
stereotype cited by Gilberto Freyre as an explanation
for the willingness of the Portuguese invader to mix
sexually with indigenous women. Given the greater degree of acculturation between Spanish and Moor before
the Reconquest, Freyre's theory is called into question,
since the Spanish conquistadores were far less active as
agents of miscegenation and concubinage with native wom-
en.

MOZOS. A Nicaraguan term for migrant harvesters.

MUCAMBOS. Shantytowns composed of wooden or bamboo
huts, usually perched on flood-prone river banks in the
coastal Brazilian Northeast. See also FAVELAS.

MULATA. Brazilian term for a woman mulatto. See also
E A MULATA QUE E MULHER.

MULATO BLANCO. A person with a known Negroid parent
but with Caucasian features. The term was used widely
in Costa Rica, especially in the eighteenth century on
baptism records.

MULATO CHINO. A term used in Cuba and elsewhere in
Spanish America for a mulatto with Oriental features or
skin-color.

MULATO CLARO. A Latin American term for a light-
skinned mulatto.

MULATO LAVADO.   A light, or "washed" mulatto.

MULATTOES.   Persons of mixed Caucasian and Negroid ancestry.   In the United States they did not constitute a
separate caste in the South except among economically-
independent blacks in some cities.   Mulattoes were
treated much in the same way as blacks of darker pigmentation, although some slaveholding families preferred
to select young mulattoes for domestic service.   Those
mulattoes who received special treatment from whites,
Genovese observes, were usually recognized as kin,
and the treatment was not universally favorable.   The
mulatto, especially the mulatto slave, received the same
treatment as his blacker brethern.   In Latin America
mulattoes tended to enjoy an intermediate status between
descendants of European and pure Negroes, and some
have written of a "mulatto escape hatch," whereby persons of color could attain upward social mobility by accepting the value system of prevailing white society, especially if their skins were relatively light-hued and
their features more Caucasian than Negroid.   The word
is probably derived from the word mulo, connoting the
hybrid offspring of a horse and mule.

MULECON.   A male slave between the ages of seven and
twelve.   Female slaves of the same ages were called
muleconas.

MULEQUE COMPANHEIRO DE BRINQUEDO.   Literally, a
"little black playmate," in nineteenth-century Brazil, a
slave child provided for a master's child to be his constant companion until at least adolescence.

MULEQUES.   Nineteenth-century Cuban trader slang for
slaves between the age of twelve and sixteen.   See also
MOLEQUE.

MULHERES DE COR.   "Colored women," a term used in
nineteenth-century Brazil to describe non-whites with
whom white men intermarried.

MULTIRACIAL ILLEGITIMACY.   One of the ironies of the
Latin American "pigmentocracy" was that, given that
lighter skin was undeniably more socially desirable,
women of color often preferred concubinage with Cau-
casians than with men of their own phenotype.   Mörner
notes that eighteenth-century travellers remarked that
the absence of public prostitution was due to the will-

ingness of mulatto women to engage in sexual union with
white men--whether or not this was true, the fact remains that such liaisons produced a substantial number
of illegitimate births of racially mixed parentage, and
that this in turn fed existing prejudices against them, a
vicious circle.

MUNJOLO see NATIONS

MUSTIFINO. Probably derived from the word "mustee," a
creole variant of the Spanish "mestizo," and "fino" (for
"fine"). Used to designate a mulatto in colonial Jamaica.

MUSULMIS. The Black Muslims of Brazil. See BLACK
ISLAM.

MUTIRÃO. A form of communal labor in rural Brazil performed by peasants and the rural poor--mostly caboc-
los--in a regional economy in which the bulk of the population has little or no access to cash.

MUTUAL-AID SOCIETIES. In pre-Castro Cuba, Brazil, and
other countries in the hemisphere with large indigent
black populations, folk religions and cults have func-
tioned as communal aid societies, especially where there
is little tradition for the State to provide social services
to the poor. Thus Cuban santerías and Brazilian candomblés have developed auxiliary roles, often unper-
ceived by outsiders.

-N-

NABORIOS (or LABORIOS). Indians in eighteenth-century
Mexico exempt from formal repartimiento labor requirements but subject to drafts for low wages by mineown-
ers.

NABUCO, JOAQUIM (1849-1910). The leader of the Brazilian abolitionist movement, the son of a planter and
a slaveowner, and an eloquent spokesman for ending
slavery on moral grounds.

NAGO. 1) Fon name for the Yoruba. 2) The principal candomblé imported to the New World from Africa. See
also NATIONS.

NAMBICUARAS. A Brazilian Amazonian tribe which became notorious for an ambush in 1907 of an expedition
led by Col. Cândido Rondon, the future head of the Indian Protective Service. Rondon was shot by an arrow,
but its tip was deflected when it hit his leather belt.
By the 1970's, the Nambicuaras had dwindled in number from an estimated 20,000 in 1900 to under 500.
The tribe was resettled on a reservation when its territory was opened to outsiders by a new highway. See
also WASUSUS.

NAÑIGOS. Members of a secret society among the Calabar
Negroes in Cuba, based culturally on the Efik or Efor
nation, who practiced African cult rites. A parallel
white society of the same name sprung up later, founded by a French-Cuban mestizo, blending nañigo cult
practices with Christian-utopian formulations. See also
NATIONS.

"NÃO E TÃO PERSISTENTE." The commonly-held insinua-
tion, in Brazil, that white men sexually lack black
men's prowess, giving rise to stereotypes about black
sexuality detrimental both to whites and blacks.

"NÃO SEJA GENTINHA." "Don't be like common people,"
a phrase widely used among affluent Brazilians in the
1930's and after. Other similar usages were "não ligue
a povo miudo" ("don't attach yourself to vulgar people,")
and "não se incommode com a gente baixa" ("don't get
involved with the riff-raff").

NATIONAL JOINT ACTION COMMITTEE (NJAC). Trinidadian black power and anti-imperialist movement. See
also FEBRUARY REVOLUTION.

NATIONS. Loosely-defined groupings of blacks according
to point of origin in Africa. Historians speak of four
"nations" in the Rio de la Plata region, Conga, Mandingo, Ardra, and Congo, the more important further
subdivided into "provinces." In Montevideo, the Congo
"nation" was divided into six "provinces": Cunga, Guanda, Angola, Munjolo, Basundi, and Boma. Brazilians
organized their non-white troops into separate battalions
organized by "nations," and religious fraternities for
blacks were similarly divided. After abolition the concept vanished and non-whites were grouped according to
whiteness and physical characteristics (e.g. prêtos,

pardos). The "nations" continued to flourish, however, as centers of traditional culture, as the civilizations became detached from the ethnic group which imported them and took, as Roger Bastide notes, "a life of their own." These "nations," in the form of candomblés in Brazil, attracted not only blacks but mulattoes, caboclos, and even whites.

ÑATO. A Caribbean region term for Negroid-appearing nasal structure.

NATURALES. A name used for Indians by the arriving Spaniards.

NAYGUR. A vulgar slang term for Negro in the Virgin Islands.

NAZCAS. A pre-modern Andean people occupying the Nazca-paracas region of south coastal Peru. Their tapestry, metalwork, and pottery were particularly skillful; their ceramics utilized polychrome painting and molds to reproduce hundreds of vessels of the same type. Nazca kilns were capable of heating pottery to temperatures in excess of 1000° F.

NEEGRISH. A Jamaican term meaning "mean" or "despicable," used by blacks for other blacks in their disfavor.

NEGERENGELS. "Negro English," the dialect of blacks in Surinam. In the early 1960's, nationalists campaigned to replace Dutch as the official language with negerengels or talkie-talkie. Among more stolid citizens, children caught speaking negerengels have their mouths washed out with soap.

NEGO. Brazilian student slang, the equivalent of the North American expletive "nigger."

NEGREGADO. Pejorative Brazilian term, "Negro-like," meaning disgraceful, infaust, or given to manual labor.

NEGREROS. Cuban term for merchants in slaves. Their influence extended as far as Madrid, and by the 1850's, the entire Cuban bureaucracy was under their sway. Their institutional center was the Casino Español, the club of the wealthy and powerful.

NEGRIER. 1) A French slave ship. 2) The ship's captain.

NEGRITO. A pickaninny.

NEGRITUDE. Pride in black culture and the Afro-American heritage. The idea was born in the West Indies, seeking to help the black resist assimilation and find the roots of his ancestral culture.

NEGRO. One of the major races of mankind, characterized by slight body hair, small ears, wooly or frizzed head hair, brown to brown-black eyes, a low-bridged nose, and full lips. The term "Negro," in Latin America, often holds pejorative connotations, depending on the context in which it is used. Pierson found that in Bahia in the late 1930's the term was often used as an epithet, and almost always was used to convey the slave origin of the black person referred to. Today, the term is usually avoided in day-to-day conversation.

NEGRO AZUL. A "blue Negro," a Colombian term for a near-pure black.

NEGRO DAY. Old-time expression in Jamaica to designate Saturday, when slaves often were released from general tasks and allowed to work their own crops. See also NEGRO-GROUNDS.

NEGRO-GROUNDS. A portion of land on a Jamaican estate traditionally set aside for slaves to cultivate.

NEGROS, BODA DE. "A Negro wedding," a Chilean slang term for a boisterous party or gathering.

NEGROS ATEZADOS. "Blackened" blacks, considered safe by the Spanish Crown, and the only (literally, bozales) to be allowed to be shipped to the New World after 1595. Even Muslim-influenced gelofes were excluded after the 1530's, as were ladinos after the Santo Domingo slave uprising of 1522.

NEGROS CIMARRONES. Maroons, or escaped slaves, who often engaged in banditry as well as fortifying themselves in fugitive settlements in the wilderness. See also MAROONS.

NEGROS DE GANHO. Brazilian slaves permitted to travel free within city limits to earn money, part of which could be used to buy their freedom.

NEGROS DE GELOFES (JALOF). A Portuguese term for
slaves sold in Spain after 1462, most of whom came
from the region bounded by the Senegal River and Sierra
Leone. Later, the term mandingo was used as a synonym.

"NEGRO SUJO." "Dirty nigger," a vulgar expression whose
frequent use in Brazil calls into question Gilberto Freyre's view that collective representations of blacks in
Brazil as uncouth, ignorant, and uncivilized are only of
folkloric value. Even Pelé (Brazilian soccer star),
Pierre-Michael Fontaine notes, has been called a "negro
sujo."

"NEO-INCAS." Holdouts after the fall of Cuzco who resisted the Spanish Conquest for forty years until the
1670's, and who included Quechua and non-Quechua
speakers.

NEORRIQUEÑO. A Puerto Rican born in New York City or
residing there for a long period of time.

NEW JEWEL MOVEMENT. A group of college-educated,
middleclass Grenadan black militants who seized power
in March 1979 in an unprecedented coup d'état after
frustrations caused by the inability of the island's socioeconomic hierarchy to absorb them boiled over. The
group, soundly anticolonial, consolidated its hold on the
government by cultivating relations not only with the
general population but with the middle class. Other
Caribbean governments, taunted by the NJM's spokes-
men for being "afraid of their own people," were shak-
en in their complacency and have taken steps to follow
the NJM in style if not in substance.

NEW WORLD FORTNIGHTLY. The publication of the or-
iginal Caribbean black power movement, the New World
Group, founded in Guyana in 1960. See also BLACK
POWER.

NHONHO. Term used by Brazilian slaves for a small child;
from the Portuguese menino.

NICHE. A Cuban term roughly equivalent to the English
word "nigger."

NICHOLAS V, POPE. The author of a papal bull, in 1454,

which served as one of the two major religious justifi-
cations for the enslavement of sub-Saharan Africans;
the second was the bull issued by Calixtus III in 1456.
The documents gave not only legitimacy to the Portuguese effort to explore and dominate the African coast,
but also, as Rout notes, the air of a "crusade."

NIGER, PAUL (1917-1962). A Guadelupe-born poet and
writer and leading member of the anti-French indigeniste
movement.

NIGRICIA. Nineteenth-century name among slavers for
Nigeria.

NIHONJIN. The term used by Brazilian-born Japanese for
themselves, as distinguished from the Portuguese term
"japonês," which the nihonjin use for foreign-born Japanese. Nihonjin means "Japanese" in the Japanese language.

NINA RODRIGUES, RAIMUNDO. A Bahian-born mulatto
physician who held the chair of forensic medicine at
the Bahian medical school in the 1890's until his death
in 1906. He was a pioneer in Afro-Brazilian ethnology,
and the first scientific researcher of the African background of Brazilian to tackle the question of the legacy
of slavery and miscegenation. He was a doctrinaire
racist, influenced by Le Bon, Gobineau and others, and
believed that the genetic inferiority of the Afro-Brazilian
was an immutable scientific fact. He divided mixed
races into three groups: "superior types," degenerates,
and social unstable persons somewhere in-between.

NITAYNOS. The ruling class nobility of the Arawaks. See
also TAINO INDIANS.

NOVENARIO. A sadistic form of punishment for Cuban
slaves, in which a flogging sentence was stretched out
over nine consecutive days, often leading to death. Some
plantations constructed special stocks called tumbaderos
where flogging was administered.

NUBES. A cataract-like eye affliction common to slaves
during the colonial period. There is no known medical
reason for the disorder, or for the high incidence of
pterygium (uñas en los ojos), another form of vision
impairment centered in the cornea.

NUEVA GERMANIA. A German colony founded in Paraguay, in the forested area east of Asunción, by socialist visionaries in 1887. Friedrich Nietzsche's sister was the wife of the group's leader. An estimated 12,000 German-speaking immigrants came to Paraguay in the early twentieth century, many of them Mennonites from the United States, Canada, Germany, Switzerland, and the Netherlands.

NYA-BINGHI. An invented black power organization supposedly headed by Emperor Haile Selassie, dedicated to the worldwide extermination of the white race. The conspiracy was fabricated in 1935 on the occasion of the Italian invasion of Ethiopia by a fascist journalist, Frederico Philos, but Jamaican Rastafarians have picked up on his claims and turned them into sources of black pride, forming Niyabinghi groups with the password "death to the whites." See also RAS TAFARI MOVEMENT.

ÑYANGA see ẎANGA

-O-

OBATALA. The chief Yoruba deity worshipped in Brazil among the Nagôs, or Afro-Brazilian Yorubans. Obatala, the skygod, is considered to be androgynous; he is also known by the name Orishala. See also ALZAN.

OBEAHISM. Witchcraft, in Jamaica, from "obayi," the Twi language word for sorcery. It has been outlawed in the island since the Slave Law of 1760, which was modified in 1938 to fit modern conditions.

OBIA. White magic. See WISI.

OBRERO. A blue-collar laborer, usually enjoying higher status than semi-employed day laborers (jornaleros).

OCTARON, OCTARONA. Terms used in colonial Costa Rica for persons of mixed blood, presumably with minimal Negroid ancestry but enough to earn a "mixed blood" designation.

OGE, VINCENT. A French-educated mulatto who led a slave uprising in Saint-Domingue in 1790, and who was captured and tortured to death after it failed.

OGUN. War-god of the Nago sects, adopted by Amerindian
sects in the forest regions of Brazil under the name
"Ogun of the White Stone," "Ogun of the Seven Cross-
roads," and so on. The phenomenon illustrates the
strong influence towards syncretism in all areas of
ethnic and racial intermingling in the hemisphere. See
also ZARABANDA.

OLIVARRIAGA, JOSE DE. Spanish colonial official stationed
in Nueva Granada in the early eighteenth century. In
1720 he reported to the Crown that at least 20,000
cimarrones were organized in cumbes, or fugitive slave
colonies, throughout the region, especially in what today is southern and southwestern Venezuela.

OLIVEIRA LIMA, MANOEL DE (1867-1928). Brazilian statesman and historian who chose to live in the United States
and Europe, in part out of his disgust with Brazilian
backwardness. He frequently warned that without European immigration the "supremacy of the whites" in Brazil might be "drowned by the spreading of inferior races." Oliveira Lima's extensive private library was donat-
ed to the Catholic University of America after his death.

OLMECS. A Mesoamerican civilization in the Gulf Coast
lowlands between 1150 and 400 B.C. The Olmecs were
superb sculptors, leaving monolithic heads carved into
basalt and granite or immense proportions.

OLORUM-ULUA. The chief deity of the nineteenth-century
Brazilian Black Muslims. See BLACK ISLAM.

OMASUYO. A regional Amerindian dialect of Aymará in
west central La Paz, Bolivia, as well as the name of
the Aymará-speaking province of the Inca Empire along
the eastern shore of Lake Titicaca.

OMOLU. The Yoruba god of smallpox, associated in Latin
America with St. Sebastião, who is portrayed shot
through with arrows, and pocked with arrow wounds.

ORDENANZA PARA MINAS. A decree promulgated in Valdivia, Chile, in 1545 to regulate black labor in the
mines. Indian laborers were forbidden to work for
blacks and morisco slaves could not acquire mine ownership.

ORIGINARIOS see AGREGADO

ORISHALA see OBATALA

ORIXA. A West African divinity, half saint, half spirit.
When candomblé was outlawed by Brazilian authorities,
the orixás were syncretized with Catholic saints. Ogun,
for example, became identified with St. Anthony; Xangô,
the thunder god, merged identity with St. Jerome; Yan-
san, the goddess of winds, with St. Barbara.

OSHUNMARE. The Nigerian-Yorubean god of the rainbow,
worshipped in Brazil by believers of candomblé and
batuque.

OUR LORD OF MIRACLES. A Catholic holy figure whose
festival, in October, parallels the festival of the pre-
conquest Inca Pachacamác oracle. As such, the "Na-
zarene," or Our Lord of the Miracles, has come to
represent a special figure in the panoply of Roman
Catholic saints and personages revered by the Indian,
black, and mestizo population of the Andean region.

OYO see CANDOMBLES

-P-

PADRINAZGO. The godchild-godparent relationship, which
anthropologists demonstrate was transformed under the
Hispanic colonial system to a secondary role, with the
compadrazgo relationship between parent and godparent
assuming more importance owing to the need for protection among the peasantry and the desire for legitimacy and authority among the elite.

PADRON. An overlord, usually but not exclusively function-
ing within a system of slave labor. See also PATRÃO.

PAEZ, JOSE ANTONIO see LLANEROS

PAGELANCE. An Afro-Brazilian syncretistic cult found in
the region of the Amazon, the result of what Roger Bastide calls a conscious desire by participants to retain
both African and Amerindian influences.

PAI-DE-SANTO- "Saint-father." A candomblé priest. See
also BABALORIXA.

PALENQUE. A village of runaway slaves, or maroons. They were often defended by armed guards using poisoned arrows and booby-traps.

PALENQUEROS. An Andean term for almost pure blacks who live in isolation and who maintain African religious and social practices.

PALES MATOS, LUIS (1898-1959). A black Puerto Rican poet whose works portrayed the bitterness of life among the poor non-whites in the Caribbean.

PALMARES. A long-lived maroon community of 30,000 inhabitants in rural Brazil between 1630 and 1695 led by a near-legendary ex-slave, Zumbí, who was executed by royal troops after the destruction of the settlement. Brazilian maroons practiced European Catholicism, and even passed the religion on to Amerindian tribes they encountered. See also MAROON.

PALMATORIA. A rod used to beat the palms, knuckles, or soles of the feet of malcontent slaves.

PALMEO. The customs clearance inspection, performed on incoming slaves at the port or in the barracones, the slave barracks within the city limits.

PANAMA RIOT. Also known as the Watermelon Riot, an incident in Panama City, Colombia, in 1855 caused by a dispute between an American traveller and a black merchant, José Manuel Luna, over payment for a watermelon. Numerous deaths and arrests followed.

PANAMANIAN CIMARRONES. Outlaw slave fugitives waged constant bandit attacks on Spanish caravans of cargo across the isthmus in the late sixteenth century. They were so successful that in two cases the Crown offered their leaders a general pardon and decreed autonomy for their palenque settlements, in Santiago del Principe (1579) and Santa Cruz de la Real (1582). See also KING BALLANO.

PAPA-LOA. Priests of Haitian voodoo who lead the societies of initiates. They are also called hougans.

PAPIAMENTO. The basic language of the Dutch Leeward Islands, a mixture of African, Portuguese, and Dutch developed by slaves but spoken, in time, by whites on

the islands also. Officially adopted as the language of
the regional Catholic Church in the nineteenth century,
Papiamento (from the archaic Portuguese verb papear,
to talk) received a stamp of legitimacy.

PAQO. An Aymará shaman or witchdoctor known for his
"white magic" and healing abilities.

PARAGUASSU. The daughter of chief Itaparica of the Tupinamba peoples, who became the concubine of one of
the sailors who had been shipwrecked or deserted from
an early Portuguese expedition in the early sixteenth
century. Once donatario Thomé da Souza landed in the
Bay of Todos os Santos (Bahia), she was helpful to the
settlers. Paraguassú has been portrayed as a Pocohan-
tas-like figure in Brazilian history texts, and her hus-
band, Diogo Alvares Correia, has become a legendary
figure to whom (Pierson notes) living descendants proud-
ly trace their lineage. Paraguassú was taken by Alvares Correia to Portugal, where she was known as
Catarina, and was legally married. See also CARAMU-
RU.

PARDO. A generic term used to describe Brazilian mulattoes of all hues of skin pigmentation. Definitions differ
from region to region: in the Amazon, where few blacks
settled or were brought as slaves, pardos are often
Amerindian mestizos. In Bahia, with a predominately
Afro-Brazilian population, the term usually refers to
mulattoes. In the 1960's, pardo was frequently used
as a polite code word for "black" or "Negro." Afro-
Brazilians have complained that they are often called
"pardo" or "Moreno" in their presence but referred to
as "prêtos" behind their backs. See also MORENO,
PRETO, MULATTOES. Pardo is also used in Spanish
America to designate a person of mixed white and Negro or Indian and Negro parents.

PARDOS LOROS. "Light pardos," or brown-skinned persons, an eighteenth-century term used in Costa Rica.

PARRAINAGE. The process by which Negroes, "by definition a lower-class person" (Bastide), choose godfathers
and godmothers from white patrons in exchange for protection or aid. Since parrainage operates in accordance
with hierarchical principles color subordination is maintained and preserved.

PARTIDO INDEPENDIENTE DE COLOR. A Cuban political party of blacks, suppressed in 1912 after an "uprising" which Booth and others consider to have been trumped up.

PASAS. "Raisins," a term used in the Caribbean for Negroid hair.

PATIÑO, SIMON ITURI (1864-1947). A full-blooded Aymará Indian, unschooled, who became one of the wealthiest men in the world after amassing a fortune based on tin mining. Nonetheless, Patiño was ostracized from the leading social circles in La Paz because of his origins. He lived much of his life in Europe, marrying his daughters into European nobility and playing the role of a diplomat and philanthropist. The Patiño foundation is the only educational and scientific foundation in Bolivia.

PATOIS. The native creole language on the Virgin Islands, a mixture of English, Dutch, Danish, and African dialects.

PATRÃO. The Portuguese term for master or lord. Genovese notes that paternalism, whereever it exists, undermines solidarity among the oppressed by linking them as individuals to their oppressors. See also PADRON.

PATZCUARO. A Mexican village, the site of the First Inter-American Indian Congress in early 1940 under the Cárdenas administration's Bureau of Indian Affairs.

PAU DE FUMO. A piece of wood around which tobacco leaves are wrapped for transport. The term is also used in rural Brazil as a pejorative word for blacks, referring to the fact that the wood darkens with use.

PE. A voodoo or macumba altar, decorated with melted candles, flowers, crosses, bottles of rum, statues of saints, rosaries, and pots containing the souls of the dead.

PEAKA PEOW. A gambling game introduced by the Chinese into the British Caribbean. See also DROP-PAN.

PEÇA DA COSTA. "A piece of the (African) coast," a crude term for an African slave imported into Brazil. Also, "Peça da Africa."

PEGUJALERO. A valley-dwelling Bolivian colono. See also SAYAÑERO.

PELADO. A nineteenth-century Mexican term for someone with brown skin, synonymous for riff-raff. See also GENTE DECENTE.

PELIGRO NEGRO. The "black threat," a common theme used in Cuba and elsewhere in the nineteenth century to combat arguments supporting abolitionist movements.

PELO MALO. A Caribbean expression for Negro hair, literally, "bad hair."

PELOURINHO. The Afro-Brazilian "heart" of the city of Salvador, Bahia, made famous by Jorge Amado's novel about race and racial attitudes in Brazil, Tent of Miracles.

PENAL CODE OF 1890. A harsh series of Brazilian laws designed to check vagrancy and other forms of social deviance in the wake of the abolition of slavery in 1888. Black capoeira gangs became the target of police repression, and budgets for police, militia, and jails increased throughout the country, accompanying the general feelings of anxiety about urban crime.

PENINSULARES. New World residents born in Spain. Peninsulares comprised the highest echelon of colonial society, and held a near-monopoly of military, administrative, and clerical positions of influence. See also CRIOLLOS.

PEONAJE. "Peonage," an agricultural system whereby the peon, usually an Indian or mestizo, is tied to the land by paternalistic links or bound by debt. This contrasts with the somewhat more restricted forms of labor utilized during the colonial period and after, such as coloato.

PEON EFFECTIVO. A part-time wage-laborer. The term is used in the Bolivian Yungas, the subtropical valley of the eastern cordilliera.

PEONES ACASILLADOS. Itinerant mestizo and Indian peones, usually from Mayan villages in Mexico, who hired themselves out for day wages to the hacendados as the encomienda system began to break down at the end of the eighteenth century.

PEONES ALQUILADOS. Rural laborers in Mexico living in villages near the hacienda and usually landless, although subject to the tienda de raya's domination.

PEONES DE RAYA. Lower-class Mexican farm workers, mostly Indian or mestizo, who lived on haciendas and earned bare sustenance wages plus food for nine months work per year.

PEOPLE'S PROGRESSIVE PARTY. A Guyana political movement headed by Dr. Cheddi Jagan and supported by a constituency of East Indians, who number just over half the population.

PERUVIAN DECREES OF 1821 and 1822. Decrees issued by Simón Bolívar's liberating armies promising freedom for slaves who served against Spain, prohibiting slaves from being used as a medium for exchange, and providing education for their children. The 1823 Peruvian constitution gave freedom to all newly-born children of slaves, despite opposition from landowners.

PERUVIAN DECREE OF 1825. The formal basis for modern relations between Peru's native population and its European-rooted elite, decreed by Simón Bolívar. Indian communities were promised communal land, although in practice land became distributed to creoles and mestizos who won, through the courts, legal battles over disputed claims, sweeping aside Indian ownership.

PETION, ALEXANDRE. A Haitian mulatto who ruled southern Haiti after the death of Dessalines in 1804, until 1818. Educated in France, he distributed the lands of the former great French estates to his troops and generally created a free market economy lacking the military brutality characterizing Christophe's kingdom in the North. He was succeeded by another French-educated mulatto, Jean-Pierre Boyer, who managed to reunite north and south and to annex the eastern part of Hispaniola, the colony of Saint Dominque.

PETIT MARRONAGE. Temporary desertion by slaves to avoid labor, to defy a master, or to visit without permission friends or relatives on other plantations. It was punished with less severity than other violations, and became almost a part of the system, an escape valve for slaves in dealing with unpopular masters.

PETITS BLANCS. The French name for the indentured laborers who were brought to the French and Dutch Antilles from French Atlantic provinces by settlers in the seventeenth century and who, in time, migrated to the port cities where they became artisans or sailors. Their places on the land were taken by slaves.

PIAR, MANUEL (1777-1817). One of Bolívar's best generals who, after allying with the llaneros--mestizo cowboys of rural Nueva Granada--was executed for insubordination. Since Piar was a Curaçao-born, dark-skinned mulatto, historians have drawn the conclusion that Bolívar sought to make an example of the incident to forestall further rebelliousness. He wrote, in fact, that Piar had started to "provoke a war of colors."

PICAROON SOCIETY. The satirized socio-political environment of Trinidad where a social climber, stereotyped as a "gay troubador," an homme moyen sensual, was also expected to enter politics.

PICKLING. Rubbing salt into the wounds of a flogged slave, excused by the planters for its ability to stop infection.

PICKNY. Jamaican version of pickaninny, itself possibly derived from the Spanish pequeños niños.

PICQA-WARAÑQU KORAKA. A hereditary upper-level administrative official in the Inca Empire, superior in rank to Picqa-Pacaka Korakas and non-hereditary Picqa-Coñka-Kamayoqs.

PIETER. The principal city of the French Antilles island Pointe-à-Pitre, named after one of the first Jewish settlers of Guadelupe who arrived in 1654 after being expelled from Brazil by the Portuguese. Allowed to settle in Martinique and Guadelupe by the governor, Du Parquet, they introduced a more efficient method of sugar cane cultivation, the mainstay of the economy of the islands ever since. Jews were forced to leave after the Code Noir of 1685 but allowed to return after the proclamation of the First French Republic.

PIEZAS. "Pieces," the term used by Cuban slave traders to describe their merchandise.

PIGMENTOCRACY. A phrase coined by Lipschütz to describe the location of New World ethnic groups within a social structure dominated by a European elite.

PIJOTEROS. A phrase used to describe Italian immigrants by Argentine creoles, referring to the newcomers' supposed stinginess. Educated or not, all pijoteros are called gringos.

PIKIMACHAY CAVE. A site in Peru near modern Ayacucho where carbon dating techniques have estimated that hunters inhabited the cavern around 17,650 B.C., give or take some 3,000 years on either side. Given its altitude of nearly 3 miles above sea level, anthropologists believe that migrating peoples to the region must have arrived well before to be able to have acclimated there.

PIMENTA DE REINO. "Black pepper," an Amazonian term for tightly-rolled kinky hair.

PIMPÃO. A wise-guy, being street-wise, or rowdy. The term is used in Brazil to describe mulattoes.

"PINGAR UM ESCRAVO." To "drip" a slave--a common form of punishment in Brazil in which molten tallow was dripped onto the body of a man or woman lashed to the ground, often applied to the sexual organs.

PINKS. Black prostitutes, in Jamaica.

PIPIL NATION. An Amerindian people who dominated present-day El Salvador in the late fifteenth century. They were a Nahua-speaking Toltec people whose culture originated in present-day Mexico, and were organized into seven chiefdoms linked through a federation.

PIPILTZINTL see TLACOPIPILTZIN

PIQUETS. The name given to black Haitian mercenaries in the southern part of the island. See CACOS.

PIXAIM. A term used in the Brazilian Amazon for the kinky hair of a Negro.

POBRES. Literally, "poor people," in Portuguese. The term also is used to refer to blacks in rural and semi-urban Brazil.

POCHO. A somewhat pejorative term used by Mexicans for Chicanos, or for other Mexicans who have become "Americanized."

POCOM, POCOMAN. Pre-Columbia groupings of Indian peoples, native to present-day Guatemala.

POCOMANIA. A revivalist religious sect popular among black Jamaicans, akin to the Ras Tafari movement, but pre-dating it.

PO DE ARROZ. Rice powder, used by fans of Fluminense soccer club of Rio de Janeiro, the team of the affluent and white upper classes. Anthropologists point to the use of rice powder--which is thrown in the air--as the elite's flaunting of its wealth, "whiteness," and ability to throw around superfluous property. See also URUBU.

POEY, JUAN. A wealthy creole planter in early nineteenth-century Cuba who helped develop towns by attracting immigrants and leasing them small farms. Poey and other creoles encouraged agricultural innovation and helped lay the basis for the sugar cane plantations which came to dominate the island in the early decades of the century.

POMBEIROS, PUMBEIROS. Mulatto or black slave hunters who themselves dealt in Bantu and West African natives in the sixteenth and seventeenth century. Captives of the pombeiros were shipped from Luanda, the present-day capital of Angola.

PONGUEAJE. Compulsory personal service paid by Indian laborers to landowners in Bolivia until 1945 when it was abolished, at least on paper.

PONTOS RISCADOS. Religious patterned drawings used in Afro-Brazilian candomblé. See also ABASI.

POOR CARIBBEAN WHITES. A nineteenth-century term for small independent farmers, day laborers, midwives, policemen, artisans, and a host of others generally competing with jobbing slaves and free blacks. The poorest

of the lot were unemployed, but most were able to earn
a living, and were upwardly mobile in society. Working-class whites were called "walking bukra," "red
legs," "mambi," "guarjiro," and a host of other, usually pejorative, names.

PORK-KNOCKERS. Guyanese frontiersmen, usually black
but also East Indian, who comb the forests beyond the
Savannahs prospecting for minerals. They enjoy a reputation for roughness, and are feared by local Amerindian peoples.

PORTENTE, EL. A Pacific Coast region maroon enclave,
in present-day Ecuador, populated by zambo descendants
of blacks and Indians in the region. The blacks had
originally been imported by the Spanish to work as
slaves in the gold mines along the Cauca River in Colombia, and had escaped south. See also DAVALOS,
GIL RAMIREZ.

PORTUGUESE LANGUAGE, AFRICAN INFLUENCE ON.
The many words introduced by African slaves include
bangué (a sugar mill; a wheelbarrow), batucar (to beat
a musical instrument), cachaça (rum), camundongo
(mouse), careca (bald), fubá (cornmeal), ioio ("massa"),
mandinga (sorcery), moleque (urchin), quitanda (a mar-
ket-stall), samba (a dance,) tanga (a loincloth; a sparse
bikini); and xingar (to scold).

PORY PAPY, PIERRE-MARIE (1805-1874). A mulatto from
Martinique who studied law in France and returned to
become one of the first non-whites accepted into political life on the island. He was elected as a deputy
to the Second and Third Republican Assemblies in 1848
and 1871-74.

POST-CHAVIN CULTURES. Around 400 B.C., the pan-
Andean Chavín culture began to decline, leaving in its
wake disparate regional ethnic cultures including the
Nazca peoples on the south coast of modern Peru, Lima
on the central coast, Huaylos, Pucará, and Cajamarca
(the latter a modern name) on the altiplano. The most
impressive culturally was the Moche, or Mochica group,
around modern-day Trujillo. Their technology was relatively advanced, especially in textile production and weaving as
well as artistic realism. Their largest monument
was the "Temple of the Sun" in the Moche Valley. Moche

tribesmen sailed cargo rafts to guano islands and used
the product to fertilize their garden plots of maize and
other crops. In that they conducted large scale warfare for the acquisition of territory, they can be considered "civilized."

POTOGEES. West Indian term for the Portuguese, often
used when conveying the image of the Portuguese island
resident as crafty shopkeeper, who is quick, (as V. S.
Naipaul notes) "to talk of nigger this and coolie that."

POTOSI. The silver-mining region of Upper Peru, or Bolivia, the heart of Spain's South American economic
prosperity, and the site of forced labor where two of
every three Indian mitayos were worked to death. See
also MITA DE MINAS.

PRANCING NIGGER. A malicious study by Ronald Firbank
in 1921 of black West Indian life, centered in the small
towns of Jamaica.

PREGOS. "Nails," a Bahian term for very dark black
youths.

PRE-PLANTATION SLAVERY (CUBA). Before the 1750's,
when tobacco and cattle-raising were the chief agricultural activities in the island, labor requirements
were low. As a result, Cuba remained largely white;
slaves were few, and as often engaged in domestic service as in field work; and racial tensions were low.
White masters and their slaves often worked together
in the fields or on the cattle haciendas. By the late
1700's, however, Cuba's sugar revolution transformed
the island's economy and brought irreversible changes
to the labor system and to race relations.

PRESERVED RELIGIONS. A term frequently applied to surviving Afro-Latin American cults, as opposed to "living
religions," a category which included Haitian Voodoo.
Preserved religions are ones in which little innovations
occur, and where little guidance is offered for survival
in a modernizing world. Brazilian Orisha is considered
a form of "preserved Voodoo."

PRETO. "Black." The category in the Brazilian spectrum
of racial terminology carrying lowest status, usually
used to describe a person of African descent with black

pigmentation and pronouncedly Negroid features. See
also PARDO.

PRETO RETINTO. A very dark prêto.

PRETRES-SAVANES. So-called "hedge-priests," in Haiti,
who integrate a few fragmentary prayers into the structure of socially-accepted Voodoo.

PRIMERA, LA. A collective term designating the upper
echelon of Nicaraguan society, its socioeconomic elite.

PRINCIPALES. Senior Indian officials who unofficially gov-
ern self-enclosed highland Indian communities and who
are responsible for the assignment of cargos.

PROCURADOR SINDICO. "Protector of slaves," an official
whose jurisdiction was created by the Cödigo Negro Español of 1789 and who was charged with the responsibility of investigating violations of the code and arguing
the case for victimized slaves in civil court. If the
owner were to be found guilty of major infractions, the
procurador could demand that the slave be sold or, if
permanently injured, be supported by the owner.

PROGRESSIVE LABOR PARTY (BERMUDA). An all-black
party established in reaction at the slow pace of Bermudan integration, despite legal steps taken between
1959 and 1968 to achieve total desegregation on the island.

PROJETO DE EMANCIPAÇÃO. A Brazilian government
project, elaborated in the mid-1970's with the aim of
creating new reservations for Indian tribes, and shelved
after protests from pro-Indian groups in mid-1979. The
opponents charged that the plan would have stripped Indians of the meager protection heretofore provided for
them.

PROTOMEDICO. A royal health inspector, who examined
slave cargoes before disembarcation in New World ports.
In case of epidemic disease, entire shiploads were quar-
antined, usually not on board ship but within the city
walls. Blacks free from signs of illness were often
allowed to be disembarked immediately.

PROVINCES see NATIONS

PRUEBA, LA. A ship en route from Valparaiso, Chile, to
Callao, Peru, which was seized by slaves on board,
who killed 24 of the 36 white passengers and set on a
course for Africa. They were met by a United States
ship, Perseverance, and overtaken. The slaves were
executed and their heads displayed on stakes.

PUEBLO. "The people," from the original use of the term
for village.

PUEBLO ENFERMO. "The Sick People," the title of a
book-length essay published in 1909 by Bolivian Alcides Arguedas. Like his contemporaries Bunge and
Ingenieros in Argentina, Arguedas blamed the mestizo
and the mulatto for his continent's economic backwardness and its gloomy future prospects.

PUEBLOS DE INDIOS. Villages restricted to Amerindian
populations during the Spanish colonial period. They
were also known as Repúblicas de Indios.

PUERTO RICO, SLAVERY IN. Although island planters
faced a chronic shortage of labor well into the nineteenth century, slavery never played a dominant role.
The number of slaves increased rapidly after 1820 but
soon declined thereafter; when slavery was abolished in
1873 there were only 29,335 slaves on Puerto Rico.
On the other hand, the non-white population represented
nearly half of the island's total population.

PUKUMINA. The syncretistic religion of Jamaica, combining the African possession cult of Kumina with Christianity. The movement emerged out of the 1860 re-
vival which swept the island, according to Barrett, in the
generation following emancipation. See also POCOMANIA.

PUNISHMENTS, DIFFERENTIAL. In eighteenth-century
Santo Domingo and elsewhere, civil officials passed
laws ostensibly serving to drive a social wedge, in
Rout's term, between blacks and lighter-complexioned
persons. Freed blacks and mulattoes could not be
rented homes in town, for example, but the rule could
be suspended for tercerones and cuarterones. Freed
blacks or mulattoes showing disrespect toward a white
person could be given 25 lashes, in public, but tercerones and cuarterones received short jail terms (up
to four days) and a small fine for the same offense.

The Uruguayan cabildo followed a similar pattern, and restricted jobs requiring manual labor to morenos.

PURCELL, JOHN JOSEPH. A leading member of the Catholic Church hierarchy in British Guiana in the early 1900's, and a mulatto. Purcell was noted for his ardent arguments with Protestant theologians, as Lewis notes, "almost as if inviting the colonial white congregation to admire the Newmanite zeal of a coloured priest."

PUTAMAYO. A rubber-gathering region along the Putamayo River, a northern tributary of the Peruvian Amazon near the boundary between Peru and Colombia. In 1911, an English commission headed by Sir Roger Casement revealed the existence of unspeakable horrors against Indian and imported Barbadian rubber workers, blaming the dominant rubber company in the area, J. C. Arana Hermanos, for brutality and sadism. The Peruvian government promised to investigate, but little was done once the foreign observers withdrew. Casement retired from the British Foreign Office in 1912 as a hero, although his reputation became tarnished over the Irish-English dispute. News that he had been an active homosexual further served to discredit him, but it came after his contribution to the Amazonian workers had been made.

-Q-

QUASHEBA. 1) The colored mistress of a white man, in colonial Jamaica. 2) A woman born on Sunday.

QUAW. A black with grey eyes, or an albino Negro.

QUEBRA-QUEBRA. A rampage, committed by a mob of rural caboclos, or, in more recent times, by the urban poor, as when the stations and trains of the Central do Brasil were destroyed by angry passengers when service in and out of Rio de Janeiro was cut.

QUECHUA. South America's most numerous Amerindian language group, and the tongue of the Incas. About one million Bolivians speak Quechua today, as well as large numbers in Peru, Ecuador, and all of the remaining outposts of the Incan Empire, or the TAWAN-TISUYU.

QUETU see CANDOMBLES

QUILOMBO. 1) A Brazilian grass-roots movement among
    Afro-Brazilians, surfacing in the late 1970's, challeng-
    ing the traditional role of the Escolas de Samba, and
    seeking a more historically authentic view of the Afro-
    Brazilian heritage. See also BLACK RIO. 2) The news-
    paper of the Black Experimental Theater (Teatro Exper-
    imental do Negro) in 1950.

QUILOMBOS. The Brazilian version of the Spanish-American
    palenques, or cumbes, villages or settlements of es-
    caped slaves. Blacks lived unmolested for several dec-
    ades in what was called the "Negro Troy," the quilombo
    (or "Republic") of Palmares, which was finally assault-
    ed and destroyed in 1695. Carneiro suggests that local
    economic difficulties produced the conditions which made
    slave escapes possible: with economic distress, land-
    owners were not as well-organized to pursue runaways,
    and many may have actually encouraged the flight of
    slaves to avoid having to feed and clothe them during
    periods of great difficulty.

QUIMBAYA INDIANS. A tribe in present-day Colombia
    whose numbers are known to have declined from 15,000
    in 1539 to only 69 in 1628, a terrible illustration of the
    fate met by many groups within the Amerindian popula-
    tion during the sixteenth century.

QUIMBOISEURS. French Antilles name for sorcerers, prac-
    ticioners of Voodoo-related religious cults. Martinique
    folklore holds that all quimboiseurs are members of a
    secret society under a Voodoo king whose reign extends
    to the entire Lesser Antilles.

QUIPUS. String-knot mnemonic devices used by the Incas
    to keep records.

QUIRIGUA. A site in present-day Guatemala where pre-
    Columbian Amerindians carved massive stone stelae,
    testimony to their advanced state of artistic culture.

-R-

"RAÇA BRAVA." "Rough people," a term applied in the
    coffee region of São Paulo for immigrants from Cal-
    abria, reputed to be extremely pugnacious.

RACE. As generally used, the term refers to any human
group with definable common characteristics, although
the scientific definition is based on the frequency of re-
curring genes, and is neither cultural nor social. Genes
determining racial classification control eye color, skin
pigmentation, texture of hair, and anthropometric features as well as blood type. The hereditary composition, the genotype, is the primary consideration, since
physical appearance, or phenotype, may be influenced
by environmental conditions.

RACE POLICY OF THE REVOLUTIONARY CUBAN GOVERN-
MENT. The Castro regime officially outlawed legal
racial discrimination on March 22, 1959, opening all
clubs, beaches, and public and private institutions to
persons of all racial and ethnic backgrounds. Zeitlin
notes that blacks have strongly supported the revolutionary government although many have noted that inequality
of opportunity persists in Cuban society despite official
commitment to equality. Most agree that the Castro
government has come farther than any other Latin American regime in facing the race problem and attempting
to deal with it. Only 9 percent of the hundred members of the Central Committee of the Cuban Communist
Party in 1965 were black or mulatto, although these
groups represent about a third of the Cuban population.

RACIAL DISTRIBUTION. Roughly speaking, in the New
World the "Indian" is found in the highlands as well as
in low and unproductive tropical zones (according to
Mörner); whites reside mainly in the low temperate
zones; and blacks in low and productive tropical regions.

RACIAL ENDOGAMY. When it is pursued in Latin America,
and especially in the Caribbean, it tends to characterize
marginal small groups like the poor whites of Barbados
and Grenada or the consanguinely degenerate Cha-Chas
of St. Thomas.

RACIAL NOMENCLATURE, DISTINCTIONS. As time passed,
terms for racial categories began to acquire different
usages from viceroyalty to viceroyalty and from region
to region. Thus Peruvians in the early nineteenth century defined zambos as crosses between blacks and mulattoes, whereas in Venezuela and elsewhere the term
described persons of Indian-black mixture. Until 1560
or so, Afro-Indian crosses in Peru were called mulattoes.

RACIAL TERMINOLOGY. Words hold different connotations
from country to country in Latin America. The word
"Negro," because of its association with slavery, is
considered in bad taste in Guyana; the preferred word
is "African," which, Naipaul notes, will cause deep offense in Trinidad. In Surinam, euphemisms are used
in place of the term "Negro"; a notice in a newspaper
describing a missing black youth called him "a dark-
complexioned boy with curly hair." See also MORENO;
PRETO.

RACISM IN LATIN AMERICA. The struggle of newly independent Latin American nations to achieve national integration and establish socioeconomic stability brought
to the surface feelings about racial inferiority which
had been simmering for generations. Domingo F. Sarmiento and Juan Alberdi interjected the concept of "whitening" Argentina's population into nineteenth-century
presidential politics. In Peru, in 1889, Clorinda Matto
de Turner published Aves sin nido, which portrayed the
misery of the life of the descendants of the Incas. The
Mexican científicos looked patronizingly at the Amerindian
peons and attempted to elevate them through education
and paternalism. By the turn of the century, however,
positivism and the influence of social Darwinism spawned
more direct attacks on the alleged genetic weakness of
the Latin American population. Carlos Octavio Bunge
in Argentina, Raimundo Nina Rodrigues and Euclides da
Cunha in Brazil, Alcides Arguedes in Bolivia and others
lamented the mestizo heritage in somber, pseudoscien-
tific words and elevated racism to a point where it was
tacitly recognized as valid if not embraced openly by
Latin American elites.

RALEA. Breed, or ilk; like a Negro, of the Negro race.

RANCHERIA. A small palenque; a village of runaway slaves,
or maroons.

RANCHEROS. 1) Small independent landowners in Mexico,
usually in the North and often of mestizo origin. 2)
Mexican mestizos employed as foremen on haciendas
and other administrative positions, especially in the
northern part of the country where cattle raising dominated. Even during the colonial period, rancheros
were granted the right to live on hacienda land in exchange for services rendered to the landowner.

RANCHITOS. Slum areas of Caracas. Shantytowns filled mostly with immigrants from the rural areas of Venezuela.

RAPAZ ("Boy") see DOUTOR

RASS. A schoolboy word in Jamaica for the buttocks, in use on the island since at least the early 1790's.

RAS TAFARI MOVEMENT. A black-power oriented religious-political sect in Jamaica identified with Haile Selassie, King of Kings and Emperor of Ethiopia, whom the Rastafarians have adopted as a messiah although no contact existed between Jamaica and Ethiopia during Selassie's lifetime. In recent years the movement has grown in influence and been exported to other islands and to the United States by West Indian migrants. It has become militantly anti-white as well as involved in internecine factionalism on political grounds. It is vehemently anti-white, and advocates that Jamaican blacks abandon the Caribbean and return to Africa. See also NYA-BINGHI.

RATTA CASTLE. An old house, falling apart, in the slums of urban Jamaica.

RAZA CHILENA. "The Chilean race," the title of a book by Nicolas Palácios (1904), and the theme of Chilean superiority owing to its racial descent from gothic Spaniards and Araucanian Indian women.

RAZA DE BRONCE, LA see ARGUEDES, ALCIDES

RECLAMES DE PIXE. "Shouts of tar," a Bahian slang term for someone "black as pitch."

RECOPILACION OF 1680 see REDUCCIONES

RED EBOE. An insulting term (Jamaica) for a mulatto. The word "red" is used in the sense that the word "yellow" is used elsewhere, to denote cowardice.

RED LEGS. A Caribbean expression for a poor white. Comparable to the United States term "redneck."

REDUCCIONES. Mission villages of Amerindians, established by the Spanish Crown authorities after the 1570's and required by law under the Recopilación of 1680 in order to protect the Indian population from violence and abuse and to isolate them from influences deemed harmful to their morals. This attempt to enforce residential segregation was based upon the dual model of the "Repúblicas de Indios" and "Republicas de Españoles" and was imposed in cities as well as in rural villages. In Peru, Indians were restricted to special districts in urban areas, such as Lima's Cercado.

REECE, H. W. The only Bajan politician in the early 1900's to publicly acknowledge his "coloured" status, and a leading member of the Barbados House of Assembly.

REEVES, SIR CONRAD. A mulatto boy in Barbados who rose to become, in the 1930's, Chief Justice of the Supreme Court of the colony.

REGIMENT OF BROWNIES AND DARKIES. The name given to the Sixth Argentine Regiment during the nineteenth century. The troops, who Borges credits for the victory at the Battle of Cerrito, were mulattoes and blacks, but the officers called them "brownies and darkies" (in Spanish) so as not to offend them. In Martín Fierro, black troops are called "men of humble color."

REI MOMO see BOIS-BOIS

REJETER. The act of adjuring Voodoo practices or an adjurer of Voodoo.

REMOVAL. The Spanish colonial policy of resettling Indians to achieve a sharp distinction between indigenous and European communities. Gerhard has shown that the policy was employed as early as 1550, not after 1600 as is commonly supposed.

RENT-A-NANNY. Jamaican black power phrase for the approach of the official government tourist agency, which the militants accuse of Uncle Tomism and subservience to foreign whites.

REPARTIMIENTO. A Spanish colonial institution introduced as a reform of the older encomienda system of compulsory labor. In the new system, Crown officials replaced encomenderos in the role of principal agents for

labor recruitment. Harris argues that repartimiento
was probably the cheapest form of labor ever invented,
since the system required no initial investment of capital, and sick or maimed laborers could be discarded
without the expenditure of any resources to care for
them. Wages, when paid, were grotesquely low, and
the permission given to the workers to farm their own
milpas (garden plots) for subsistence simply removed
responsibility from the landowner to provide even the
barest essentials for life. Ultimately, the system was
replaced by debt peonage.

REPUBLICA DE INDIOS. Spanish policy toward the New
World recognized two juridical entities; the República
de españoles, (or Spanish republic) and the Indian republic. Mestizaje, of course, blended the two worlds;
Spanish and mestizo vagrants took up residence in Indian villages, and race intermixture further clouded
the legal distinctions.

REQUINTERON. A fanciful product of a union between a
Spaniard and a woman who is one-fourth mulatto, in
colonial Peru. Mörner suggests that such categories
reflect more the almost pathological interest in gene-
ology in the eighteenth century and that century's ex-
oticism and rococo than a serious effort to define the
social reality of the Indies.

RESGUARDOS. A Colombian term for communally-held Indian lands, this legal category was created in Nueva
Granada by decree in 1593. As in Mexico, nineteenth-
century reformers tried to break up the communal lands
in favor of private landholdings, but after 1890 the Colombian government took steps to maintain them. In
the 1950's, an estimated 90,000 Amerindians lived on
84 resguardos.

RETINTO. A Peruvian term for a very dark-skinned person (literally, "re-dyed").

RIVER YY (or YI) PALENQUE. A settlement of twenty
Uruguayan slaves and their families who fled Montevideo in 1803 and established a fugitive colony on an
island in the River Yy, 100 miles northwest of the
capital. Attacked by Spanish troops, they were overcome and returned to slavery.

ROCHA, MANUEL RIBEIRO DA. An eighteenth-century

Brazilian priest who attacked the slave trade and proposed abolition of slavery. See also COUTINHO, AZEVEDO.

RODNEY, WALTER. A Guyanese historian who was expelled, in 1968, from the University of the West Indies (and from Jamaica) for speaking about black power and for making contacts with the Rastafarians, whom he called his "brethern."

ROMERO, SYLVIO (1851-1914). A Brazilian literary critic and self-described Social Darwinist, avidly seeking to modernize his country through the adoption of technology, and convinced that Brazil's habitat was debilitating and that racial mixture posed anxious problems for the country's future.

ROOSEVELT, THEODORE. While in Brazil for an expedition to the Amazon and to the interior of the Mato Grosso in 1913-14, the former President of the United States enthusiastically endorsed the "whitening" thesis which held that the Negro in Latin America would disappear, within a few generations, through absorption into the white race. Roosevelt's article, published in Outlook magazine in 1914, was translated and published on the front page of Rio de Janeiro's Correio da Manhã.

ROOTS. The unprecedentedly successful television series (based on the book by Alex Haley) aired in 1977 about the saga of a black family from its African origins to the late nineteenth century. Although it was equally popular in Europe, the series was not shown widely in Latin America, and it was not shown at all on Brazilian television despite that country's high degree of interest in programming originating in the United States. (The TV teleplay "Holocaust," for example, was shown successfully in 1979.) The series was shown to private audiences throughout the country under the auspices of the United States Information Service, but without Portuguese subtitles. Critics suggested that the message of Roots hit too close to home, in spite of official assertions that no race problem exists.

ROSCA. Rural Bolivian term for the landowning oligarchy or elite.

ROXO DE CABELO BOM. "People of good hair." A racial

category used in rural Brazil showing the pejorative connotation of Negroid hair: <u>cabelo bom</u> in this case means straight hair of fine texture.

RUDIES. Jamaican "Rude Boys," or urban brawlers who rove in gangs, as do the Rastas, or Rastafarians.

RUIZ BELVIS, SEGUNDO (1829-1867). A Puerto Rican landowner who freed his slaves and became a fervent abolitionist. After denouncing the colonial regime in 1886 he fled into exile in Chile, where he died.

RYUKYUANS OF BOLIVIA. An Asiatic ethnic minority which has produced one of the highest rates of intermarriage of any Oriental group in Latin America--almost 75 percent.

-S-

SACATRA. A term for a light mulatto in the French islands, according to the scheme of classification imposed in the eighteenth century by the French colonizers.

SACSAHUAMAN CITADEL. A massive fortress of hewn stone, standing several hundred feet above the city of Cuzco, Peru. The citadel engaged as many as 20,000 laborers conscripted by the Incas, and took 90 years to complete.

SAHAGUN, BERNARDINO DE (1499-1590). A Spanish Franciscan who arrived in Mexico eight years after the Spanish conquest, and whose <u>Florentine Codex,</u> originally written in Nahuatl, offers detailed documentation on Aztec culture before most of it was destroyed by the conquistadores and their bureaucratic descendants.

ST. BARTS, ST. BARTHELEMY. A small island in the Caribbean, ceded by the French to Sweden in 1784 in exchange for the right to establish a commercial center at Göteborg, and sold back to France in 1877. The inhabitants are mostly descendants of Norman and Breton farmers.

ST. JOHN SLAVE REVOLT. A major rising on the island of St. John, Virgin Islands, in 1733. The rebels held

St. John for nearly six months, and destroyed half of its 98 plantations.

SAINTOIS. East Indians residing in Martinique, part of a migration stream from South India and French Africa of 70,000 or more coolie laborers in the nineteenth and early twentieth centuries. Most of the immigrants died; many emigrated to Trinidad or the Guianas. About 5,000 were left on Martinique in the early 1960's, most as laborers in the sugar fields of the north or working as sweepers in the city. They remain the pariahs of the island, and have virtually no opportunity for upward social mobility.

SALABANDA   see   MAYOME SYNCRETISM

SALACION. A Cuban term referring to the technique by which the Afro-Cuban sorcerer, using a potion of salt and other items, casts a spell over his victim. The term is used in the mid-twentieth-century Cuban expression: "Blanco es una profesiòn, mulato es un oficio, negro es una salaciòn" ("White is a profession; mulatto is a status; negro is bewitched").

SALCEDO, DIEGO. A Spanish soldier who was captured and drowned in 1511 on Puerto Rico as a test of the Spaniards' immortality. His death helped precipitate the Taino rebellion.

SALTA ATRAS. A term used by some Latin American intellectuals to describe the impact of miscegenation and mestizaje. See also TENTE EN EL AIRE.

SALT-WATER CREOLES. A Jamaican term for slaves born on shipboard during the passage from Africa.

SAMBO-MOSQUITOS. The term applied to describe the Afro-Indian inhabitants of the Central American Mosquito coast south from Nicaragua. Here, blacks brought by English slaveowners as well as escaped slaves from Jamaica and the Spanish settlements of the interior intermarried with the Sumus Indian of the region. The British allied with them, supplying them with arms and liquor in exchange for protection against the Spanish, who attempted to drive the fewer than 1,000 English settlers from the region.

SAMBOS. A Uruguayan spelling of zambos, people of mixed Amerindian and Negro parentage.

SAN BASILIO. A fugitive slave community, or palenque, located near the city of Cartagena, Nueva Granada after 1599. It was headed by a slave leader, Domingo Bioho, who called himself King Benkos and led attacks on nearby Spanish settlements. Unable to subdue the cimarrones, the Spanish Governor offered amnesty and freedom in exchange for cessation of hostilities. But within five years (in 1619) a new slave revolt in Cartagena moved the new Governor, García Girón, to rescind the promise of his predecessor, and Benkos was arrested and hanged.

SAN BERNADINO. A German colony in Paraguay, established in 1881. See also NUEVA GERMANIA.

SANG-MELE. A "non-white," being one part black and 127 parts white, but still considered "colored" by legal definition in colonial Saint-Domingue under the French. See also REQUINTERON.

SAN PEDRO REVOLT OF 1548. The first known slave revolt in Central America, in Honduras.

SANTA CRUZ DE LA REAL. A Panamanian palenque granted autonomy by Madrid in 1582. See PANAMANIAN CIMARRONES.

SANTERIA. A Cuban-Yoruba candomblé. See CHANGO.

SANTIAGO DEL PRINCIPE. A Panamanian palenque granted autonomous status by Madrid in 1597. See PANAMANIAN CIMARRONES.

SANTO DOMINGO STATUTE OF 1785 see CODIGO NEGRO CAROLINO

SANTO DOMINGO UPRISING OF 1532. An insurrection, led by ladinos and Muslim-influenced gelofes, slaves from the region between Senegal and Sierra Leone, which led to restrictions by Spanish officials on the categories of bondsmen who could be shipped to the New World in order to guarantee docility and order.

SARARA. A light-skinned Brazilian mulatto, usually a

woman, with reddish kinky hair and aquiline nose. The
sararà has been characterized by Jorge Amado and
others as sensual and unusually attractive to white men.

SARMIENTO, DOMINGO FAUSTINO. Argentine president
and author of a number of books touching on racial
themes. Sarmiento's identification of the rustic, mestizo gaucho with primitivism and backwardness typified
the elite's obsession with Europeanizing Argentina through
the importation of Anglo-Saxon immigrants and modern
forms of technology. One of his major statements on
race was his Conflictos e armonías de las razas en
América (1883).

SARRACENOS NEGROS. Literally, "black Muslims," a
Portuguese term in the fifteenth century for African
slaves who, after 1462, were sold to Spanish merchants at Cádiz for shipment to the interior of Spain.

SAYAÑERO. A colono working for the right to cultivate
crops on the hacienda rather than for wages. His plot
is called a sayaña. The term is used in Bolivia and
Peru.

SCHOELCHER, VICTOR (1804-1893). A French politician
and abolitionist primarily responsible for the abolition
of slavery in the French colonies in 1848. A member
of the Société des Amis des Noirs, he lived in the
French Antilles from 1837 to 1847 and published his
Abolition of Slavery in 1840.

SEAGA, EDWARD. A Jamaican of Syrian parentage who
studied sociology at Harvard, then returned to Jamaica
to study under the West Indian sociologist, M. G. Smith.
His contacts with the poor led him into politics, where
he developed a loyal urban constituency within the Jamaican Labour Party. His enemies call him a boss
who uses black thugs to enforce his control. His supporters credit him with an astute political sense and
an awareness of the needs of his district.

SEINEN-KAI. A juvenile association among young Japanese
residing in Latin America.

SELASSIE, EMPEROR HAILE see RAS TAFARI MOVEMENT

SELVAJE. "Savage," a term used indiscriminately for

Indian by condescending members of the white or mestizo elite of South American Spanish-speaking republics. The term, contrasted with gente de razón--"people of reason," used for whites--connotes paganism and lack of civilized behavior.

SEMI-LIBERATION. The act of freeing a slave legally but requiring either additional service or that the freed slave leave and never return. Both conditions often led to reinslavement. In Paraguay, slaves manumitted by their owners were often taken into custody for being unable to pay the required Crown tax of 3 pesos; they then were released to Church and local officials in "protection" (amparo), and thus return to a disguised form of slavery.

SEÑOR. A term connoting social status as well as being the equivalent for "Mister." In the colonial period only encomenderos, or land-owners, could use the title.

SERINGALISTAS. Rubber prospectors in the Brazilian Amazon, either working independently or as agents for rubber firms. There rough frontiersmen have been accused of widespread mistreatment of Amerindian peoples not only in Brazil but in Colombia, Venezuela, and all of the countries bordering on the Amazon basin.

SERRANIA DE CORO REVOLT. An insurrection of Venezuelan slaves in 1795 which led to the establishment of a maroon colony in the mountains. The fugitive settlement, however, was crushed by Spanish troops before it could prepare fortifications for its defense.

SERVIDUMBRE DISFRAZADA. "Disguised slavery," a term used to describe contract labor and other forms of legal servitude in Cuba and elsewhere in the nineteenth century.

SEXAGENARIAN LAW. A national law passed by the Brazilian parliament in 1885 which unconditionally granted freedom to all slaves over the age of sixty-five and conditionally freed those over the age of sixty. Cynics note that slaves at this age were usually poor workers, and represented little loss to slaveowners.

SEXISM, RACIAL CONNOTATIONS OF. In much of Latin America, especially in the Caribbean and Brazil, the

mulatto woman has been portrayed as the ideal extra-
marital sexual companion for white men. Donald Pierson, writing in the (innocent?) 1940's, notes that Bahian
males pronounce the word morena "with a tone indicative of admiration, affection, desire." Another popular
saying in Brazil, quoted by Gilberto Freyre, goes:
"White women are for marrying, blacks for serving,
mulatas for fornication."

SEXUAL PROHIBITIONS. In Chile, after 1550, and in Central America, escaped black slaves who engaged in sexual relations with Indian women were punished by castration. The practice persisted even though a decade
before, Carlos I had specifically banned the practice.

SHAMAN see ZAHORIS

SHANGO see CHANGO; BANTU-YORUBA TRANSFER

SHON. The Papiamento word for "master," after the colonial period used by slaves to address persons of
authority and ultimately, it evolved into a term of affection.

SHOUTERS. A revivalist sect, in Trinidad, banned in 1917
but surviving in clandestine fashion, which is a clear
example of Afro-Protestant syncretism. The cult's
African features are reminiscent of Bahian candombles
and some aspects of Haitian Voodoo.

SILVA, EDSON NUNES DA. An Afro-Brazilian who studied
at the University of Nottingham in England in the mid-
1940's and who returned to Brazil to write several books
on the role of the black in Brazilian society, although
his work is largely unknown.

SINGH, BOYSIE. The most celebrated Trinidadian criminal,
whose career in the 1940's followed Chicago-style lines
as American capitalist culture (according to Bickerton)
filtered through American troops stationed in Port of
Spain, facilitated the transformation of petty hoodlums
into professional gangsters.

SINHA INOCENCIA. A famous Bahian story teller, a black
slave woman of the late nineteenth century, known for
her tales and songs mixing Portuguese with Nagô.

SINHU-RENGA see BANTU RELIGIOUS INFLUENCE

SIRIVINACO. A Quechua practice of trial marriage, where the couple live together for a year or until a child is born before officially announcing their engagement.

SIX RACES, THE. A commonly-used expression in Guyanese public rhetoric: the nation's blacks, Portuguese, Indians, mestizos, "whites" and amerindians. "Whites" presumably are citizens of English extraction.

SLAVE INSURRECTION OF 1522. The first known revolt of African slaves in the New World occurred on Santo Domingo, where slaves working on land owned by Diego Columbus, the explorer's son, led slaves from nearby plantations in an uprising before Christmas. Nine whites were killed before the Europeans, heading an armed force of Spaniards and Indians, could crush the insurrection.

SLAVE MARRIAGE. Recent scholarship on Brazil and elsewhere suggests that stable consensual union rather than religious ceremony defined marriage in the nineteenth century. Slaves on non-plantation settings were found to have less stable sexual unions than those on fazendas.

SLAVE ORIGINS IN AFRICA. The majority of slaves transported to the New World came from the lands south of the Senegal River and north of Portuguese Angola. Slaves taken from the North were often of Muslim faith, or at least influenced by Muslim culture. The lack of a common language facilitated efforts by their new masters to force them to speak Spanish or Portuguese or French or English, but tribal culture survived even under the adverse conditions of the passage to the Americas.

SLAVE REVOLTS. Risings among slaves in the Spanish and Portuguese colonies occurred regularly, including the following: Hispaniola (1522); Mexico (1537, 1546, 1570, 1608, 1670, 1725, 1735); Honduras (1548); Colombia (1531, 1550, 1598, 1599-1600, 1732); Venezuela (1552, 1560, 1560-1600, 1732-33, 1749, 1795); Ecuador (1556, 1650); Panama (1552-1582, 1755); Peru (1578, 1763-64); Chile (1647, 1804); Cuba (1533, 1713, 1726); Argentina (1795); Uruguay (1803).

"SLY MONGEESE." A pejorative term used by Grenadians to describe Bajans (Barbadians).

SMALL GANGS see GANGS

SNAKECOE. One of the small number of villages in the Carib reservation on Dominica. The reservation is 3,700 acres. Anthropologists claim that only a few dozen "pure" Caribs were left by the early 1970's.

SOCIAL CONCEPT OF RACE. By the end of the colonial period in Latin America, terms connoting race--such as Indian--had acquired sociocultural meaning. An "Indian" was a member of an Indian community, but if he travelled to the city, became Europeanized in manner, and adopted Spanish as his daily language, he became accepted as an "indígena." In Brazil, a similar pattern emerged: racial terms became interchanged with class descriptions. The word caboclo, formerly a strictly racial classification, now was applied to all rural peasants. In Spanish America, the word "indígena" became interchangeable with "campesino," or poor peasant.

SOCIEDADE BENEFICENTE 13 DE MAIO. An Afro-Brazilian cultural and self-help organization formed in 1915 and briefly successful, mainly as a social group.

SOCIEDAD DE CASTAS. Society of Castes, the system of social stratification by which inhabitants of Spain's New World colonies were carefully classified and restricted economically and socially within the group to which they had been assigned. There was some vertical social mobility, however, and non-whites could purchase certificates of racial purity to facilitate social acceptance. The word "casta," strictly speaking, is a medieval term which does not mean "caste" in the Hindu sense. Mörner shows that the concept of the Society of Castes helped transfer the hierarchic, estate-based corporate society of Spain to its multiracial New World empire.

SOCIEDADE CONTRA ESCRAVIDÃO. The Brazilian anti-slavery society founded in 1880 by abolitionist Joaquim Nabuco.

SOCIETES CONGO. Collective name for Afro-Haitian cultural and religious associations. See also NATIONS.

SOCIO-RACIAL CLASSIFICATIONS, Most, of these classifications particularly those developed in eighteenth-century Spanish America, reflected disdain, as Aguirre Beltrán shows. A partial list includes the following:
Spaniard + Indian = mestizo

Mestizo + Spanish woman = castizo
Castizo + Spaniard = Spaniard
Spaniard + mulatto women = morisco
Morisco woman + Spaniard = albino
Spaniard + albino woman = torna atrás
Indian + torna atrás woman = lobo
Lobo + Indian woman = cambujo
Cambujo + mulatto woman = albarazado
Albarazado + mulatto woman = barcino
Barcino + mulatto woman = coyote
Coyote woman + Indian = chamiso
Chamiso woman + mestizo = coyote mestizo
Coyote mestizo + mulatto woman = ahé te estás
Spaniard + mulatto woman = cuarterón de mulatto
    (Peru)
Spaniard + cuarterona de mulatto = quinterón
Spaniard + Quinterona de mulatto = requinterón

SOCORINO. An extinct Indian group indigenous to the east-
    ern region of Santa Cruz, Bolivia.

SODRE, JERONYMO. A Bahian physician and member of
    the Brazilian parliament who raised the call for aboli-
    tion at the national level in 1879, nine years before it
    actually was achieved.

¿SOMOS INDIOS? "Are we Indians?"--used in Peru and
    Ecuador to mean "Do you take us for fools?"

SOULOUSQUE, FAUSTIN. The black dictator of Haiti who,
    in 1849, invaded the newly independent Dominican Re-
    public but whose troops were driven back by the mulatto
    rural caudillos led by Pedro Santana.

SOUTHERN ROUTE. By 1601, with more and more slaves
    being shipped from the coasts of southern Africa, Buen-
    os Aires (and ultimately Montevideo) became the chief
    port of arrival in the New World, since the trip to the
    old centers of Veracruz and Cartagena was too long and
    too many slaves died. Many of these slaves were tak-
    en overland to Peru, Bolivia, Chile, and Paraguay,
    where they were sold as mining or agricultural laborers.

SOUZA DANTAS, RAIMUNDO. Brazil's only black ambas-
    sador, sent by the Kubitschek administration to Ghana
    in the late 1950's.

SPARROW. The leading Calypsonian of Trinidad in the

1960's, also known as the "Mighty Sparrow," and the "Road March King."

STAR-APPLE. A tropical fruit tree, planted in the West Indies to provide a staple food for slaves. Trinidad, then, with only forty years of slavery, has proportionately fewer star-apple trees than Jamaica or Barbados. See also BREADFRUIT.

STARS AND STARLETS. The men and women chosen at Carnaval time in Cuba (as well as elsewhere) as the outstanding beauties of the festivities, and, as Booth has observed, typically light-skinned and Caucasoid in features, even after the Revolution. This is paralleled by the Brazilian practice of always selecting white women to represent Brazil in international beauty pageants, lest, as the social writer of the Jornal do Brasil wrote in 1964, the rest of the world came to think that "our society is comprised of a bunch of pickaninnies."

STEDMAN'S NARRATIVE. A late eighteenth-century book published in Europe, filled with drawings depicting the horrors of slavery in Surinam. Stedman was a Dutch officer sent to Surinam to help crush the slave rebellion of 1773, and was no abolitionist; but his notes and sketches reveal horrors which explain why the greatest threat a British planter could make to a slave was to promise to "sell him to a Dutchman." (The author, an English traveller in 1807, noted that Dutchmen held even a greater threat: to sell his slave to a free black.") "The colony of Surinam," Stedman wrote, "is reeking and dyed with the blood of African Negroes."

STEREOTYPES, RACIAL. Stereotypes attributing behavior characteristics and even moral qualities abound throughout North and South America. Argentine whites, for example, refer to Brazilians as macacos, or monkeys. Of "los negros," an Argentine of German ancestry replied: "(They) are the humble people who live in straw huts around the city. They do manual labor. They are all pure Argentine people. Their style of life is characterized by laziness; if they earn fifty, they spend sixty. Their children beg for bread in the streets when parents are too lazy to work....They live from day to day and they do not seem to worry."

SUJETOS. Small villages in colonial Mexico reserved for

Indians, in the spirit of the policy of segregation of Spanish and Indian places of residence. Larger village units were called cabeceras.

SUNDIDE. The Yoruba sacrificial blood-bath, in Haitian voodoo substituted by the ritual killing of a chicken. See also MACUMBA.

SU-QUION. A woman, in Haitian legend, who sheds her skin during the voodoo ritual and passes by in the night as a hellion or fireball.

SUTTA. An Aymará term used in the Yungas for the head of a community or ayllu. See also JILACATA.

SWIDDEN AGRICULTURE. Slash-and-burn agriculture, used by the Mayas as well as by pre-modern agricultural populations (including Brazilian peasants) through the present day, and one of the factors cited for the Maya's eventual economic decline.

SYLBARIS, LUDGER. A black prisoner held in an underground solitary confinement cell in St. Pierre, Martinique--and the only survivor in the population of 30,000 when Mt. Pelée erupted and poured incandescent gas and lava into the city and harbour.

SYNCRETISM. The union or fusion of two or more value or religious systems. Anthropologists believe that the initial phase of New World syncretism, expressed in the fusion of African and Catholic ritual and beliefs as well as between African and Amerindian practices, has given way to a less spontaneous form of interaction infused with political overtones. For Brazil, syncretism produced a hybrid set of religious practices neither African nor European in their nature. See also CANDOMBLES; PAGELANCE.

SYRIAN HOUSES. Two-story Trinidadian houses made of concrete blocks, the top floor repeating the lower. Many were built in the 1940's by Syrio-Lebanese merchants in Port-of-Spain.

-T-

TABERNILLA, FRANCISCO. Batista's Army Chief of Staff

and a black. Batista himself was a light mulatto, and some of the officers promoted by him during the 1930's were black, an unprecedented step for Cuba.

TACKY, "THREE-FINGERED JACK." A seven-foot tall Jamaican slave leader, reputedly a chief before his capture in Africa. He led a slave rebellion in the 1770's, but it was crushed, leading some slaves to commit suicide rather than to meet the fate planned for them by angered slave owners.

TAINO INDIANS. A branch of the Arawak tribe. About 70,000 Tainos inhabited Puerto Rico at the time of the arrival of the Spaniards in 1493. They were relatively passive, in contrast to the warlike Caribs. The word Taino probably is derived from the Arawak word "nitaynos," the tribal nobility.

TAINO REBELLION. An insurrection on the island of Puerto Rico by the Taino tribe in 1511, under the leadership of chieftain Agüeybana II, in response to the harsh working conditions imposed in the mines on Indian laborers.

TALKEE. A safe-conduct pass required for slaves during the Jamaican maroon wars of the 1700's.

TALKIE-TALKIE. A limited local dialect used by nationalistic Surinamers seeking to uproot the Dutch heritage. See also PAPIAMENTO.

TAPIA. A building material, made of mud and dung, used to make the walls of shacks inhabited by the poor in Trinidad. The Tapia group black power intellectuals, led by Dr. Lloyd Best, chose the material for its name as a symbol of their link with the dirt-poor of the island.

TAPUIA. A synonym for caboclo in the Brazilian Amazon region.

TATA. "Father," the term of respect used by Aymara peasants in Bolivia to address landowners or visiting persons of higher status groups. See also YOCALLA.

TATU, JECA. A fictional Brazilian caboclo, the invention of São Paulo modernist writer Monteiro Lobato, who used the character--in 1914--to portray the elite's view of the racially-mixed Brazilian as lethargic, superstitious, and ignorant. Later, Lobato himself reversed his original negative view of "Jeca" and redrew his character as a symbol for the need for reformers to recognize social necessities.

TAWANTINSUYU. Inca name for the Incan Empire, initiated by Pachacuti Inca Yupanqui, the ninth emperor of the Inca royal house. It administered conquered populations with an efficient bureacracy, and varied its severity in keeping with the degree to which the new vassals accepted their status. The Incas transported the children of chieftains of the conquered tribes to Cuzco, their capital, and indoctrinated them. They raided conquered tribes for skilled artisans and workers, and used the technique of forced resettlement as a form of social control. See also INCAS.

TEATRO EXPERIMENTAL DO NEGRO. Rio de Janeiro's Black Experimental Theater, founded in 1944 in an attempt to provide jobs for black actors and to combat stereotypes of Afro-Brazilians as Sambos. The Theater's organizers sponsored a national Afro-Brazilian Congress in Rio de Janeiro in 1950, and a newspaper, Quilômbo.

TECTECUTZIN, TEULES. Names for Aztec middle-level nobles, roughly equivalent in status within Aztec society to the Spanish encomenderos, holders of royal encomiendas.

TEHUELCHE INDIANS. The inhabitants of present-day Patagonia, in Argentina, discovered by Fernando Magalhães (Magellan) on his voyage of circumnavigation. The explorer named the land Patagonia because of the natives' large leather boots (patagón is slang for a large, clumsy foot, in Spanish). Two Tehuelches were tricked into sailing with the fleet and were to be given as gifts to King Charles, but they died aboard ship, unused to the cramped conditions in which they were kept.

TEM SANGUE. "Has blood," a rural Brazilian expression used to mean that a person has Negro ancestry. An analagous term is tem pinta ("is touched with the tarbrush").

TENCHUGUMI. A secret organization among Japanese-Brazilians during World War II whose name translated as

"Executors of God's punishment." It terrorized Japanese silk farmers and destroyed some of their lands on the grounds that they were aiding the war effort of the United States, to whom the silk was exported. The organization, however, was very limited in scope and impact.

TENTE EN EL AIRE. A term used by some racist intellectuals (Galindo Villa of Mexico, for example) to characterize unions between non-whites of the same intermediate color: mestizo with mestizo, or mulatto with mulatto. The phrase literally means "stay in the air," suggesting that racial quality will neither be improved nor weakened. See also SALTA ATRAS.

TERESA, QUEEN. A Cabinda queen who had been caught in adultery and sold into slavery. Shipped to Brazil, she was purchased by a landowner who beat her violently until she submitted and became an "excellent slave." The story is related by the French traveller L. F. Tollenare.

TERRAS NOVAS. Blacks taken as slaves from the Lower Guinea River and the Niger River Delta.

TERREIRO. An autonomous candomblé community serving religious and social functions within Brazilian society. Pre-eminently Afro-Brazilian. See also COMUNIDADE OBA-BIYI.

TESTIMONIOS. Memoir literature and oral history, very widely read in Cuba. Subjects range from the didactic "oral essays" of Fidel Castro to Miguel Barnet's "Autobiography of a Runaway Slave."

TEULES see TECTECUTZIN

"THIEVES." The name used by Grenadians to describe Trinidadians.

THOMAS, CLIVE. A Guyanan political economist and member of the black power movement of the 1960's. See also BLACK POWER.

THOMPSON, DUDLEY. A black Jamaican lawyer, counsel to Jomo Kenyatta during the Mau Mau uprising, who was defeated by Edward Seaga by the Kingston residents of the lower class (and black) legislative district. Whites hostile to growing sentiments of black nationalism in Jamaica pointed to the victory as a sign of the lack of rapport of the militants with the "masses." See also SEAGA, EDWARD.

THUNDER. The official newspaper of Cheddi Jagan's socialist movement in pre-independence Guyana, pro-black and pro-land reform.

TIAHUANACOS. A pre-modern people living south of Lake Titicaca on the Bolivian plateau who, around 600 A.D., began to expand their territory by conquest, at the same time the Huaris further to the north undertook similar expansion. The Tiahuanaco state spread to encompass all of southern Peru from Arequipa to present-day Chile. Little remains of their culture, however, except for massive ceremonial ruins in the Lake Titicaca area, adorned by statuesque granite monoliths not unlike the statuary of unknown origin found today on Easter Island in the Pacific.

TIETE. A São Paulo social club which refused, in 1978, to admit black youths to play on its juvenile soccer team. The event helped provoke the May 13th movement, organized among members of "Black São Paulo" (see BLACK RIO) to protest racial discrimination in Brazilian society.

TIMOTE INDIANS. Arawak-speaking peoples inhabiting present-day Venezuela, known for their well-developed culture and stone-walled residences. Their agriculture utilized irrigation and other technologically-advanced methods.

TIRA-TEIMA. A Brazilian family's "black sheep," a person with more pronounced Negroid racial characteristics who was often shunned by other family members less he or she betray their pretensions to acceptance as whites.

TIROLIEN, GUY (1917-   ). A Guadelupe poet whose work emphasizes the African roots of Caribbean culture.

TITHES see DIEZMOS

TLACOPIPILTZIN. Sons of Aztec rulers. Their grandsons were known as pipiltzintl.

TOME-AÇU. A Japanese colony in the Amazon which during the Second World War was used to intern Japanese settlers in the interests of national security.

TONTOS, LOS. A pejorative word for "backward" village Indians in Mexico, in contrast to citified persons (los correctos).

TORRES, ALBERTO. A Brazilian jurist, writer, and republican political figure who endorsed the environmentalist school of anthropology being developed by Franz Boas in the United States at the turn of the century, and refuted some of the racist theories which had convinced the elite of Brazil's dim future. A nationalist, Tôrres argued that the Brazilian upper class needed to embrace Brazilian culture and find Brazilian solutions to national problems.

TOUSSAINT L'OUVERTURE, PIERRE DOMINIQUE (c. 1749-1803). A leader of the Haitian slave rebellion in 1791, he was an ex-slave whose French master had allowed him to educate himself and acquire funds to earn his manumission. Crossing into Santo Domingo, he joined Spanish forces who were fighting the French and rose to command a militia of blacks against both the Spanish and British who were seeking to take control. When Spain ceded Santo Domingo to France in 1795, two years after the abolition of slavery, Toussaint was made commander-in-chief of French forces in the colony, and assumed dictatorial powers. In 1801 he decreed the emancipation of slaves throughout the island but at the same time allowed for further importation of bondsmen from Africa. Toussaint's forces were attacked by an invading army of 23,000 men sent by Napoleon, and finally defeated. Toussaint died in a French prison in 1803, but the remaining French forces surrendered to General Jean-Jacques Dessalines, who declared Haiti's independence on January 1, 1804.

TRIANGULAR TRADE. Slave dealers in Holland, France, England, and Portugal sent cargos of guns, liquor, and clothing to Africa, exchanging them for slaves who were then shipped--on the so-called "middle voyage"--to the West Indies and South America. The ships were then reloaded with sugar, molasses, rum, dyes, and other tropical products for sale in Europe.

TRIGUEÑO. Wheat-colored, a Colombian term for a light mestizo. Also used in Cuba.

TRINIDADIAN SLAVERY. As compared to the institution of slavery on other Caribbean islands (Barbados, or St. Kitts, for example), slavery on Trinidad was relatively short-lived. This fact, plus the more pronounced Spanish-French legacy, influenced patterns of settlement and general race relations as well. There was no English "squirearchy," for example, and the white elite was multi-national in origin (English, Spanish, French, Portuguese). What Lewis calls a "national spirit" only began to emerge in Trinidad and Tobago after the First World War.

TRINITARIA, LA. A secret society of Spanish-speaking creoles in Saint-Domingue in the late 1830's whose members resisted rule from independent black Haiti. Led by Juan Pablo Duarte and others (many of them mulattoes), the society won independence for San Domingo, of the Dominican Republic, in 1844, although its leaders were exiled when caudillos took control of the country.

TRISTÃO, NUNO. One of Prince Henry the Navigator's chief admirals, whose voyages along the African coast in the 1440's brought the Portuguese into contact with slave traders and general sources of supply. In 1443 he was granted by King Affonso a monopoly on all slave traffic south of Cape Bojador. He reached the Senegal River in 1444 and helped another Portuguese, Dinis Dias, discover Cape Verde in 1445. Tristão was killed, however, on a slave raid in the Senegal River region, and the monopoly passed to the Lagos Company, which by 1445 was trading activity with Muslim suppliers of slaves along the coast.

TRUCHO. A Panamanian expression for an animal or person with a leg, ear or other body part missing. Used to describe mutilated slaves.

TRUNK FLEET. A Jamaican term for a line of porters, usually women, who walked carrying heavy loads on their heads.

¿TU ABUELA DONDE ESTA? Literally, "where is your

grandmother?" a remark directed at socially pretentious
persons to remind them of their probable black ancestry.

TUCKER, SIR HENRY see FORTY THIEVES

TUGURIOS. Slum settlements in Spanish American urban
centers, almost always more non-white than the over-
all population.

TULA. A leader of the 1795 slave revolt on Curaçâo who,
with his colleague Carpata, was captured and executed.
He was also known as "Rigud," from the name of the
Haitian mulatto general who led a slave uprising there.

TULSIS FAMILY. A fictional family of East Indian background in Trinidad, portrayed by V. S. Naipaul's A
House for Mr. Biswas.

TUMBADERO. A flogging post on Cuban sugar plantations.
See also NOVENARIO.

TUPAC AMARU (1545-1574). The last Inca emperor, executed brutally with his family (his body was pulled
apart by horses) in retaliation for the killing of a mis-
sionary. His death led to several rebellions among
Peruvian Indians in later years.

TUPAC AMARU II (1740-1781). A wealthy mestizo and descendant of Tupac Amaru who led the descendants of
the Inca peoples in the Peruvian Andes in a bloody,
large-scale rebellion against Spanish domination in 1780-
81. Calling himself the reborn Inca, he succeeded in
uniting Indians behind the rebellion but in turn united
the non-Indian population against the uprising. He was
captured and executed by the Spaniards in 1781 although
the revolt continued for several more years.

TUPAC AMARU, ANDRES (? -1783). Purported son of Tupac Amaru II, and leader of the Indian insurrection after 1781. For a time he fought in alliance with a creole guerrilla, Rodriguez. Troops from La Plata crushed
the revolt in 1783 and executed its leaders.

TUPAC CATARI (? - 1783). Self-declared Inca Viceroy of
Peru in 1781 under the name Tupac Catari. Leading
80,000 Indians in a three-month siege of La Paz for

three months, he was finally subdued by Spanish troops
from La Plata.

TUPAC INCA YUPANQUI, FELIPE VELASCO (?-1783).
"Cousin" of Tupac Amaru II, the leader of a short-
lived continuation of the Indian rebellion in 1783 until
his capture and execution.

TUPIAN.   Also known as TUPI-GUARANI, a language group
spoken by Amerindian groups of "Amazon" culture. See
also GUARANI.

TURBAS REPUBLICANAS.   Gangs of dispossessed and impoverished Puerto Ricans, most of them mestizos, who
roamed both countryside and urban districts and attacked
members of the upper class during the initial period of
United States military occupation. Resentful of the landowners, whom they blamed for their economic woes,
they were manipulated by republican leaders and aided to
some degree by the police, who were sympathetic to them.

TURCOS.   Name given indiscriminately to persons of Arab
background who have migrated the Latin America. Many
"Turcos" are Lebanese but others have come from all
parts of the Near East, including Turkey itself. Prevailing stereotypes portray the Turco as swarthy, with
a pronounced nose, and given to sharp business practices. Turco, like judío, can be used as a form of personal insult. They are supposed to be quickly roused
to anger, and to be suspicious and clannish.

TWO HUNDRED FAMILIES.   The social elite of Haiti, mostly mulattoes, tracing its roots back to the revolutionary
era. The elite is eminently Francophile and prejudiced
against black peasantry, especially culturally.

TZOMPANTLI.   A wooden rack on which Aztecs displayed
the skulls of sacrificed victims.

TZUTUHIL PEOPLES.   Pre-Colombian Amerindian inhabitants of present-day Guatemala.

-U-

UGARANO.   An Indian group of Zamucoan language, dwelling
in the Chacs district ceded by Bolivia to Paraguay in
the 1930's.

UMBANDA. A Brazilian candomblé, its name of Kimbundo origin, though derived etymologically from Sanskrit.

"UM POUCO DA RAÇA." "A little color," a term used in Brazil in the 1940's and before to describe a mulatto of good social standing who marries a women of lighter skin.

UÑANUE, HIPOLITO (1755-1833). A Peruvian physician and racial theorist who helped codify (in a book on the subject published in 1805) the up-to-then unwritten categories of racial mixtures within Peruvian society: cuarterones, quinterones, and so on.

UNIÃO NEGRA BRASILEIRA. A substitute for the Frente Negra Brasileira after the latter was outlawed along with all other Brazilian political parties in 1938 by Getúlio Vargas under the dictatorial Estado Nôvo. The União--a "cultural" association in contrast to the political format of the Frente Negra--failed to win widespread support, and it dissolved.

UNIÃO NEGRA BRASILEIRA. The "Black Brazilian Union," a group organized in the late 1920's and linked to the São Paulo-based Frente Negra Brasileira.

UNIFIED BLACK MOVEMENT AGAINST RACIAL DISCRIM-
INATION IN BRAZIL. A militant group formed among Afro-Brazilian intellectuals in São Paulo in 1979, in protest over a number of incidents of overt racial discrimination. The group held a public demonstration on the steps of São Paulo's Municipal Theater on May 13, 1979--the anniversary of abolition in 1888--which was attacked for its militancy. Branches of the movement have been established in Rio de Janeiro, Belo Horizonte, and Pôrto Alegre.

UNITED BLACK ASSOCIATION FOR DEVELOPMENT. A black power organization in Belize, off-and-on suppressed by government officials in the mid-1970's for seditious writings in its newspaper, Amandala.

UNPOLLUTED BIMS. A derisory reference to the Barbadians, or Bajans, mocked for being more British than the British, representatives of a tropical England which passed away elsewhere in the world in 1914. The phrase is Patrick Leigh-Fermor's.

URU. An Amerindian group of Puguinan language, inhabitants today of the swampy islands (some man-made of
woven reefs) in Lake Titicaca. In spite of the cold
(owing to the high altitude) and gradual pollution of the
lake (which limits fishing and bird-hunting), the Urus
remain on their island prison. Foreign Protestant missions have taught some of the Urus weaving and other
simple handicrafts to sell to tourists, but the general
standard of living remains extremely low.

URUBU. A black vulture--the symbol of the Flamengo soccer club of Rio de Janeiro, the team of the city's
blacks. Anthropologists point to the link between the
adoption of the symbol and the blacks' self-conscious
self-image.

USPANTECA. A pre-Columbian tribe of Amerindians, in
present-day Guatemala.

UTAHUAHUA, UTAWAWA, UTAGUAGUA. Aymará variations
for a landless peasant who lives with a colono's family
and works for no wages, as if he were "adopted." In
the Bolivian altiplano, mestizo and white families "adopt"
Indian children who serve as unpaid servants, and, according to Heath, are rarely allowed to marry.

UTANI. An Aymará youth at the time of his marriage,
when he is accepted into the community as a sharehold-
er of its corporate land.

-V-

VADIAGEM. Marginalization of the free population of Brazil, mostly peasants of racially-mixed parentage, as a
result of widespread reliance during the colonial period
and well into the nineteenth century on slave labor.
Once slaves were freed in 1888, they too joined the
miserable, unemployed or underemployed segment of
the population and drifted into the status of sharecroppers, or the urban poor, or beggars. Pointing to the
racial dimension of the problem, the phenomenon of
vadiagem was also known as caboclização, literally,
"caboclo-izing."

VAGOS. In Spanish America, vagrants. By the sixteenth
century vagrancy had become a major social problem,
and most were mestizos or mulattoes. The policy of

residential segregation which sought to isolate Amerindian peoples on missions and on plantations in part responded to the fear that vagrants would stir up or otherwise contaminate social equilibrium. Vagrants, for their part, were attracted to the countryside, where they could cultivate the land or exploit unsophisticated peasants. See also VADIAGEM.

VALDIVIA ATTACK OF 1556. A band of Araucanian Indians attacked the Spanish settlement of Valdivia in 1556 and took its inhabitants as prisoners. It is reported that, never having seen a black person, they tied one slave woman to a tree and attempted to rub off her skin pigmentation. Rout (citing Mellafe) claims that they then skinned her alive and stuffed her skin with straw, adding that "(such) incidents emphasize the fact that Afro-Indian relations were often characterized by a good deal of antipathy."

VARAYOC. The collective term by which lower-rank Amerindian officials who dealt with Peruvian Spanish colonial administration came to be known. Dobyns and Doughty observe that the name, appropriately, is half-Spanish and half-Quechua. Vara is Spanish ("staff") and yoc is Quechua ("bearer").

VARONES. Slave men. See HEMBRAS.

VAUDOU RADA. One of the two main voodoo cults in Haiti, characterized by its attempts to maintain links to African culture. The other, the Vaudou Petro, is entirely creole.

VAVAL. The local name for Carnaval in the French Antilles.

VAZ, TRISTÃO. The Portuguese conquerer of the Madeira Islands, with João Gonçalves Zarco, in 1419-20, in the service of Prince Henry, Duke of Viscu, later known as the "Navigator." The acquisition set the stage for Portuguese penetration of the African coast and the beginnings of Portuguese colonization in Africa.

VECINOS LADINOS. Term used in colonial Mexico for mestizos living among Indians residents of the pueblos de índios.

VENEZUELAN SLAVE REVOLT OF 1749. A planned rising

slaves in Caracas in concert with <u>cimarrones</u> living in the mountains set for the feast of St. John the Baptist, which was discovered by authorities and crushed before it could take place. See also ESPINOSO, MANUEL.

VICTORIANISM. A solicitousness among the elites of the British Caribbean for the social welfare of the non-white masses, based on the presumption that the "wise guidance" of the white race under the Empire could "elevate" the backwards peoples of the region.

"VIEJAS, FEAS Y NEGRAS." "Old, ugly, and black," a callous Spanish expression used by white men to describe women not to their taste, especially prostitutes.

VIENTRE LIBRE. The declaration of freedom for all slaves in Cuba and Puerto Rico born after September 29, 1868, decreed by the Spanish Cortês under the provisional government of Francisco Serrano.

VILA RECONCAVO. A Bahian town studied by Henry Hutchinson in order to analyze the differences in race relations in Brazil and in the United States. His conclusion stresses the inflexibility of the "line" between white and Negro in the U.S. whereas in Vila Recôncavo the line is "recognized rather than drawn."

VIRACOCHA INCA (c. 1400-1438). The eighth Inca ruler, and the leader of the Empire's great military expansion. Viracocha was the Inca Sun God; when the conquistadores arrived many Inca priests believed the Spaniards to be his incarnation.

VISITADORES DE IDOLATRIA. Agents of the Catholic Inquisition who travelled among highland Indian communities in the sixteenth and seventeenth centuries seeking out religious devotion, often torturing Indians publicly for having placed food offerings at mountain shrines or for following other practices deemed pagan. Since highlands Indians were legally exempted from the Inquisition, this practice was justified as a measure to protect the Indians from deviltry and the influence of Satan.

"VOCE SABE COM QUEM ESTA FALANDO?" "Do you know with whom you are speaking?" An authoritarian phrase with racist overtones frequently repeated in Brazil in order to intimidate or dominate a person of a lower status group, such as a doorman or domestic.

VON IHERING, HERMANN. A German physical anthropologist who migrated to Brazil in the 1880's and founded the Museu Paulista, a center for the study of Amerindian culture, in 1893. See also GOELDI, EMILIO.

VOODOO, VODUN. An Afro-Haitian adaptation of African religion to Catholicism. Voodoo has become the medium through which rural peasants have been able to express themselves and preserve their African roots, and is based on the structure of the large extended family-- the laku--governed by patriarchal rule. Voodoo, in the absence of a stronger European-dominated culture in Haiti, has evolved as a "living religion" and has become, in the words of Roger Bastide, a kind of "national creed." Its origin is Dahomean, and it is linked to the "preserved Voodoo" cults of South America, especially to candomblé. See also CANDOMBLE; PRESERVED RELIGIONS.

VOZ DA RAÇA, A. The newspaper of the Frente Negra Brasileira, first published on March 18, 1933, and unprecedentedly militant for Brazil. See also CLARIM DA ALVORADA.

-W-

WALCOTT, DEREK (1930-). A working-class Trinidadian poet born on St. Lucia, a founder of the Trinidad Theater Workshop, and a strident critic of racism and privilege.

WALKING BUKRA see POOR CARIBBEAN WHITES

WAPPEN-BAPPEN. Name for a slum dwelling in urban Jamaica. See also RATTA CASTLE.

WARI see HUARI

WAR OF THE NEGROES. The battle between cimarrones and Spanish military forces on Hispaniola (Santo Domingo) in the years between 1545-1548 were given this name. The "war" ended when the most important fugitive, Diego de Campo, was captured by the Spaniards and defected to their side. He then led the Spanish forces against his fellow cimarrones and crushed them.

WASHINGTON, EDWARD EMMANUEL (1929-). A United

States-born black supremacist, the head of a group
known as the House of Israel, in Guyana, and a fugitive from justice in his native country. Washington
heads a para-military branch of the government party
of Prime Minister Forbes Burnham, and has been accused of using his followers to break up anti-Government
rallies with force. Since he preaches that he is God,
he has been called a black Rev. Jim Jones. After Rev.
Jones directed the mass suicides at Jonestown, Guyana,
in 1978, membership in Washington's cult swelled to an
estimated eight thousand, mostly young black men between the ages of 16 and 25.

WASUSUS. A Nambicuara tribe in the Brazilian Amazon
which was forcibly resettled by the government's Indian agency, FUNAI, to the Nambicuara reservation on
the savanna. Faced with catastrophe (the tribe, accustomed to a jungle environment), FUNAI reversed its
decision in 1977 and resettled the tribe near its original
home.

WATERMELON RIOT see PANAMA RIOT

WEST INDIAN DIASPORA. Gordon Lewis and others have
pointed to the dispersion of the black West Indian population as a diaspora not unlike that of the Jews. Independence was seen as a possible antidote for a people, even whose literature (Zobel's Fête à Paris, Sel-
von's The Lonely Londoners, and Thorner's Tropico en
Manhattan) is seen as a literature of exile.

WEST INDIAN MIGRATION TO CENTRAL AMERICA AND
CUBA. Seeking jobs, blacks from the West Indies settled during the nineteenth century and early twentieth
century elsewhere in the Caribbean region, creating
problems of culture contact (they were Protestant and
black migrating to places predominately Catholic and
mestizo). In Costa Rica they remained isolated, in
the eastern part of the country; in Panama they spread
generally throughout the countryside and became assimilated into Panamanian culture. While they have sought
to gain acceptance within their new societies, many
have retained their cultural identity, especially in more
recent decades.

WHITE-A-MIDDLE. Term used by blacks to ridicule mulattoes who put on the airs of whites. Used in the
British Caribbean.

WHITE CARIBBEAN ELITE. Knight finds that the major
difference between the leading colonial families in the
British Caribbean--the Codrington, Drax, Pickering
and Hothersall families in Barbados, Warner and Jeaf-
ferson in St. Kitts, Warner and Kaynell in Antigua,
Stapleton and Pinney in Nevis, and Price, Dawkins,
Tharp, and Beckford in Jamaica--and their North American counterparts in New England, Canada, and Virginia,
was their adaptation. They lived as Englishmen, and
retained as many ties to England as possible, even
though they prospered as Caribbean planters and merchants.

WHITE-MESTIZO PERCENTAGES. Although each Latin
American country defines racial group differently--and
some, like Brazil after 1960, have ceased classifying
its citizens according to any racial categories, the following percentages approximate the combined totals of
whites and mestizos in the hemisphere: Argentina (99%),
Canada (98%), Uruguay (98%), Costa Rica (90%), United
States (89%), Cuba (80%), Brazil (70%), Chile (61%),
Dominican Republic (58%), Venezuela (55%), El Salvador
(49%), Guatemala (46%), Mexico (40%), Bolivia (31%),
Peru (27%), Ecuador (26%), Haiti (2%).

WILD INDIANS. Trinidadian term for Amerindians.

WILLIAMS, ERIC C. Prime Minister of Trinidad in the
1960's, and leader of the nation's blacks, who represent 43 percent of the island's population. East Indians,
about 38 percent of the population, have supported by
the Democratic Party, led in the early 1970's by Dr.
Rudranath Capildeo.

WISI. Black magic, from Dahomean origins, practiced by
(and guarded against by) the Bush Negroes of French
and Dutch Guiana. Benevolent, or white, magic is
called obia.

WORTHY PARK PLANTATION. A Jamaican plantation studied intensively by Craton and Greenland, who find that,
during slave days, "the distinction between African and
Creole slaves was almost as important as that between
slaves and free and between black and white."

WRAPPER COOLIE. An East Indian in the Caribbean who
uses a loin cloth instead of European trousers.

-X-

XARIONO. An "Amazon" culture Indian group indigenous to central Santa Cruz, Bolivia.

XAYMACA. "Land of springs," the Arawak name for the island of Jamaica.

XIVARO. The original spelling of jíbaro, a white rural peasant in Puerto Rico known for their bellicosity as well as their hospitality when not threatened by outsiders.

-Y-

YAM NIGGERS see BREADFOOT NIGGERS

YANACONA, YANA-CONA. Indians in the fifteenth century who left their communities to be servants to Spaniards or creoles. By the next century, so many had left the countryside that some were extradited back to their ayllus as mitayos.

YANAPEROS. Peasants in rural Bolivia who worked one or two days on the lands of their patrons, and who enjoyed the use, in turn, or proportionately less land than traditional squatters.

ÑANGA. The best-known cimarrón in Mexican history, known as Ñyanga or Ÿanga, a self-described Congolese prince who led a band of highwaymen and bandits during the early seventeenth century, attacking mule trains on the causeway linking Mexico City with the port of Veracruz. He was assisted by another articulate fugitive slave, Francisco Angola, a ladino.

YANKEES OF THE SOUTH. English translation of a phrase used during the 1930's and 1940's to refer to the Argentines, regarded as pushy and overly aggressive.

YARURO INDIANS. A tribe residing on the tributaries of the Orinoco River in an aquatic, nomad-like fashion in which they lived on fish, turtles and plants.

YATIRIS. Aymara medicine men, in Bolivia.

YAWS, YAWY. This disease was probably brought to the

Caribbean from Africa by Portuguese slaves. The term is also used as a generic description for a broad range of related illnesses.

YBYTYIMI. A Japanese agricultural colony in Paraguay, established in 1936 by the Japanese government.

YEMANJA. The Nigerian deity of freshwaters who, in Brazil, has become the goddess of the sea and of chaste love.

YOCAHU. Supreme god of the Taino Indians, the most important tribe inhabiting Puerto Rico at the time of the Spanish conquest.

YOCALLA. "Boy," a demeaning term used for Indian peasants of any age in Bolivia. See also TATA.

YORUBA CULTURE. In the New World, predominant in Cuba, Trinidad, Northeast Brazil (Bahia, Pernambuco, Alagoas), and Southern Brazil (from Pôrto Alegre to to Pelotas in Rio Grande do Sul).

-Z-

ZAHORIS. Witches, in Central American folk cultural cults. Also called brujos, or shaman.

ZAMBO. A person of Afro-Indian origin. In Spain, the word denoted a knock-kneed or cross-eyed person, and is therefore a term of ridicule.

ZAMBO BANDITS see ESMERALDAS

ZAMBO DE MESTIZO. An Afro-Indian living with his Indian parent, in contrast to a zambo de mulato, the official designation in Church and civil records of the colonial period in Costa Rica for an Afro-Indian living with a Negroid relation.

ZAMUCOAN. A language family native to the Chaco region of Bolivia and Peru.

ZAPES. Slaves taken from Upper Guinea, shipped mostly to Santo Domingo.

ZAPOTEC. An Amerindian culture native to the present-day state of Oaxaca, Mexico, dating back at least to 300 A.D.

ZARABANDA. A hybrid Cuban form of folk-magic, produced from cross-influences between Congo and Yoruba cultures. Zarabanda is regarded as the equivalent of the Yoruba war-god, Ogun.

ZARCO, JOÃO GONÇALVES. Conquerer of the Madeira Islands. See also TRISTÃO.

ZAZE. The Angolan name for the Yoruba thunder-god. See also BANTU-YORUBA TRANSFER.

ZEMIS. Arawak icons, resembling grotesque anthropomorphic figures, and collected by village chiefs as a measure of authority and influence. Carib religion, less elaborately ritualistic, had no Zemis.

ZE POVINHO. A 1930's Brazilian cartoon character, "Joe of the People," portrayed as lazy, illiterate, and a lout. He was depicted as a light-skinned caboclo, the artist's way of emphasizing his lack of overt racial prejudice, although his behavior was rigidly stereotypical.

ZION. A revivalist cult in the British West Indies which promised redemption through a part-Biblical, part-cult approach to the other-worldly.

ZOBOS. A "caste" of persons in Spanish America of mixed African and Amerindian parentage. Also called zambos and chinos.

ZOMBIE. An African word brought to the New World by practitioners of Voodoo, representing the deity of the python.

ZONITE. A citizen of the United States who resides in the Canal Zone. Virtually all are Caucasian, and extremely conservative politically as well as anti-Panamanian.

ZUMAS. An independent tribe of aboriginal peoples in Honduras, believed descended from the Caribs or the Mayas.

ZUMBI see PALMARES

SELECTED BIBLIOGRAPHY

This bibliography of books and articles has been arranged by region. See the following contents list for entries on specific countries:

GENERAL

1 "Africa en América." Casa de las Americas, 6:36-37 (May August 1966), Special Issue.

2 American Universities Field Staff. A Select Bibliography: Asia, Africa, Eastern Europe, Latin America. Cumulative Supplement, 1961-1971. New York, 1973.

3 Ballagas, Emílio. Mapa de la poesía negra americana. Buenos Aires: Editorial Pleamar, 1946.

4 Bastide, Roger. African Civilization in the New World. New York: Harper & Row, 1971.

5 _____. "Present Status of Afro-American Research Latin America." Daedalus. 103 (Spring 1974), 111-23.

6 Berghe, Pierre L. Van den. Race and Racism: A Comparative Perspective. New York: John Wiley, 1967.

7 Biddiss, Michael. "The Universal Races Congress of 1911." Race, 13:1 (July 1971), 37-46.

8 Bowser, Frederick P. "The African in Colonial Spanish America: Reflections on Research and Achievements and Priorities." Latin American Research Review. 7:1 (Summer 1972), 77-94.

9 Boyd, Antonio Olliz. "The Concept of Black Esthetics as seen in Selected Works of Three Latin American Writers: Machado de Assis, Nicolás Guillén and Adalberto Ortiz." Diss. Stanford University, 1974.

10 Bradford, Sax. Spain in the World. Princeton, N.J.: Van Nostrand Company, 1962.

11 Bryan, Patrick. "The African in Latin America." Bulletin of the African Studies Association of the West Indies, 4 (December 1971), 40-55.

12 Campbell, Ernest Q. ed. Racial Tensions and National Identity. Nashville, Tenn.: Vanderbilt University Press, 1970.

13 _____, ed. Racial Tensions and National Identity. Nash-
    ville: Vanderbilt University Press, 1972.

14 Carlson, Donald Arthur. "Great Britain and the Abolition of
    the Slave Trade to Latin America." Diss. University of
    Minnesota, 1964.

15 Carvalho Neto, Paulo de. "El folklore de la lucha negra." El
    Folklore de las Luchas Negras. Mexico City: Siglo XXI,
    1973, pp. 65-122.

16 Clarke, John H., ed. Marcus Garvey and the Vision of Africa.
    New York: Vintage Books, 1974.

17 Cobb, Martha K. "Africa in Latin America: Customs, Cul-
    ture and Literature." Black World. 21: 10 (August 1972),
    4-19.

18 _____. "An Appraisal of Latin American Slavery through
    Literature." Journal of Negro History, 58 (1974), 460-
    69.

19 Cohen, David W. and Jack P. Green. Neither Slave nor Free:
    The Freedman of African Descent in the Slave Societies of
    the New World. Baltimore: Johns Hopkins University
    Press, 1972.

20 Comas, Juan. Bibliografia selectiva de las culturas indígenas
    de América. Mexico: Pan American Institute of Geography
    and History, 1953.

21 _____. "Recent Research in Race Relations, Latin Amer-
    ica." International Social Science Bulletin, 13: 2 (1961),
    271-299.

22 Conrad, Alfred and John R. Meyer. The Economics of Slavery
    and other Studies in Econometric History. Chicago: Al-
    dine Publishing Company, 1964.

23 Cordeiro, Daniel Raposo; S. V. Bryant; H. N. Piedracueva; and
    B. H. Stein, eds. A Bibliography of Latin American Bib-
    liographies: Social Sciences and Humanities. Metuchen,
    N. J.: Scarecrow Press, 1979.

24 Costa Pinta, Luis Aguiar de. "Negros y blancos en América
    Latina." Comunidades, 4: 11 (May-August 1969), 115-135.

25 Coulthard, G. R., "Antecedentes de la negritud en la literatura
    hispano-americana." Mundo Nuevo, 11 (May 1967), 73-77.

26 _____. "Negritude, Reality and Mysticism." Caribbean
    Studies, 10 (April 1970), 42-51.

27 Cox, Oliver. Caste, Class and Race. New York: Monthly
    Review Press, 1964.

28 Crosby, Alfred W., Jr. The Columbian Exchange: Biological
    and Cultural Consequences of 1492. Westport, Conn.:
    Greenwood Press, 1973.

29 Curtin, Philip D. The Atlantic Slave Trade: A Census. Mad-
    ison: University of Wisconsin Press, 1969.

30 Dallas, R. C. The History of the Maroons. London: T. N.
    Longman and O. Rees, 1803.

31 Dash, Michael. "Marvelous Realism--The Way out of Negri-
    tude." Black Images, 3:1 (Spring 1974), 80-95.

32 Dathorne, O. R. "Africa in West Indian Literature." Black
    Orpheus, (Ibadan, Nigeria) 16 (October 1964), 42-54.

33 Davis, David Brion. The Problem of Slavery in Western Cul-
    ture. Ithaca: Cornell University Press, 1966.

34 Deal, Carl W., ed. Latin America and the Caribbean: A Dis-
    sertation Bibliography. Ann Arbor: University Microfilms
    International, 1978.

35 DeCamp, David. "The Field of Creole Language Studies." La-
    tin American Research Review, 3: 3 (Summer 1968), 25-
    46.

36 De Costa, Miriam, ed. Blacks in Hispanic Literature: A Col-
    lection of Critical Essays. Port Washington, N.Y.: Ken-
    nikat Press, 1976.

37 Depestre, René. "Les métamorphoses de la negritud en Amér-
    ique." Présence Africaine, 75 (1970), 19-33.

38 Diggs, I. "Color in Colonial Spanish America." Journal of
    Negro History, 38 (October 1953), 403-427.

39 _____. "Zambo-Peluca." Phylon, 13 (March 1952), 43-47.

40 Drake, St. Claire. "The Black Diaspora in Pan-African Per-
    spective." The Black Scholar, 7: 1 (September 1975), 2-
    14.

41 Duncan, Kenneth and Jan Rutledge, eds. Land and Labour in
    Latin America. London: Cambridge University Press,
    1978.

42 Elkins, Stanley M. Slavery: A Problem in American Institu-
    tional and Intellectual Life. Chicago: University of Chi-
    cago Press, 1959.

43 Engerman, Stanley L. and Eugene D. Genovese, eds. Race and Slavery in the Western Hemisphere: Quantitative Studies. Princeton: Princeton University Press, 1974.

44 Fanon, Frantz. Black Skin, White Masks. New York: Grove Press, 1967.

45 Ferguson, J. Halcro. Latin America: The Balance of Race Redressed. London: Oxford University Press for the Institute of Race Relations, 1961.

46 Foner, Laura and Eugene D. Genovese, ed. Slavery in the New World: A Reader in Comparative History. Englewood Cliffs, N.J.: Prentice-Hall, 1969.

47 Franchesi, Victor. "El hombre blanco en la poesia negra." Loteria, 4: 44 (June 1959), 134-39.

48 Franco, José L. Afroamérica. Havana: Junta Nacional de Argueología y Etnología, 1961.

49 Frazier, E. Franklin. Race and Culture Contacts in the Modern World. New York: Alfred A. Knopf, 1957.

50 Freilich, Morris. "Serial Polygyny, Negro Peasants, and Modern Analysis." American Anthropologist, 63:5 (October 1961), 955-975.

51 Frucht, Richard. Black Society in the New World. New York: Random House, 1971.

52 Garvey, Marcus. "The Negro's Greatest Enemy." Current History, 18 (1923), 951-7.

53 Genovese, Eugene. "Materialism and Idealism in the History of Negro Slavery in the Americas." Journal of Social History, 1: 4 (Summer 1968), 371-95.

54 _____. The World the Slaveholders Made. New York: Pantheon Books, 1969.

55 Gerhard, Peter. "Congracaciones de indios en la Nueva España antes de 1570." Histôria Mexicana, 26 (January-March 1977), 347-395.

56 Greene, Jack P., ed. The Role of the Black and Free Mulatto in Societies of the New World. Baltimore: Johns Hopkins University Press, 1971.

57 Greenfield, Sidney M. On the Founding and Diffusion of the Slave Plantation in the New World. Milwaukee: University of Wisconsin Latin American Center, 1968.

156 / Bibliography

58 _____ . Slavery and the Plantation in the New World. Milwaukee, Wisc.: University of Wisconsin Latin American
Center, 1969.

59 _____ . "Slavery and the Plantation in the New World."
Journal of Inter-American Studies and World Affairs, 11:
1 (January 1969), 44-57.

60 Griffith, Patrick. "C.L.R. James and Pan-Africanism: An
Interview." Black World, 21: 1 (November 1971), 4-13.

61 Guillot, Carlos Federico. Negros rebeldes y negros cimarrones: Perfil afroamericano en la historia del Nuevo Mundo
durante el siglo XVI. Buenos Aires: Editores Farina,
1961.

62 Hanke, Lewis. Aristotle and the American Indians: A Study
of Race Prejudice in the Modern World. Chicago: Reg-
nery, 1959.

63 _____ . The Selected Writings of Lewis Hanke. Tempe:
Arizona State University, 1979.

64 Harris, Marvin. Patterns of Race in the Americas. New
York: Walker & Company, 1964.

65 Herskovits, Melville J. "African Gods and Catholic Saints in
New World Negro Belief." American Anthropologist, 39
(1937), 635-643.

66 _____ . "The Ahistorical Approach to Afroamerican Studies:
A Critique." American Anthropologist, 62: 4 (August 1960),
559-568.

67 _____ . The Myth of the Negro Past. Boston: Beacon
Press, 1958.

68 _____ . The New World Negro. Bloomington: Indiana University Press, 1966.

69 _____ . On Some Modes of Ethnographic Comparison. Netherlands West Indies: n.p., 1956.

70 Hoetink, Harry. "Colonial Psychology and Race." Journal of
Economic History, 21 (1961), 629-41.

71 _____ . Slavery and Race Relations in the Americas: Comparative Notes on Their Nature and Nexus. New York:
Harper & Row, 1973.

72 Hooker, James R. George Padmore's Path from Communism
to Pan-Africanism. New York: Praeger, 1970.

73 Jackson, Richard L. The Black Image in Latin American

Literature. Albuquerque: University of New Mexico Press, 1976.

74 _____. "Black Phobia and the White Aesthetic in Spanish American Literature." Hispania, 58: 3 (September 1975), 467-80.

75 _____. "Black Song Without Color: The Black Experience and the Negritude of Synthesis in Afro-Spanish American Literature." Inter-American Review of Bibliography, 26: 2 (April-June 1976).

76 _____. "Mestizaje vs. Black Identity: The Color Crisis in Latin America." Black World, 24: 9 (July 1975), 4-21.

77 James, C. L. R. A History of Pan-African Revolt. 2nd ed. Washington, D.C.: Drum and Spear Press, 1969.

78 Joel, Miriam. African Traditions in Latin America. Cuernavaca: CIDOC, 1972.

79 Jones, R. C. "Negroes in Latin America." Sociology and Social Research, 30 (September 1945), 45-51.

80 July, Robert. "Nineteenth-Century Negritude: Edward W. Blyden." Journal of African History, 5 (1964), 73-86.

81 Kamen, Henry. "El Negro en Hispano-América, 1500-1700." Anuario de Estudios Americanos, 28 (1971), 121-137.

82 Katz, Friedrich. The Ancient American Civilizations. London: Oxford University Press, 1972.

83 King, James F. "The Colored Castes and American Representation in the Cortes of Cádiz." Hispanic American Historical Review, 33 (1953), 526-637.

84 _____. "The Latin American Republics and the Suppression of the Slave Trade." The Hispanic American Historical Review, 24 (August 1944), 387-411.

85 Lancaster, C. M. "Gourds and Castanets: The African Finger in Modern Spain and Latin America." Journal of Negro History, 28 (January 1943), 73-85.

86 Lanternari, Vittorio. The Religions of the Oppressed: A Study of Modern Messianic Cults. New York: Mentor Books, 1965.

87 Latin America, A Bibliography of Books in English. Washington, D.C.: Anaquel Press, multi-volume series, 1979.

88 Latin American Studies Center. Black Latin America. Los Angeles: California State University, Los Angeles, 1977.

89 Leff, Nathaniel H. "Long-term Viability of Slavery in a Backward Closed Economy." Journal of Interdisciplinary History, 5 (Summer 1974), 103-8.

90 Long, Richard A. Handbook of African and African-American Studies. New York: Negro Universities Press, 1969.

91 Mannix, Daniel P. and Malcolm Cowley. Black Cargoes: A History of the Atlantic Slave Trade. New York: Viking, 1962.

92 Mason, Philip. Race Relations. London: Oxford University Press, 1970.

93 Matheus, John F. "African Footprints in Hispanic American Literature." Journal of Negro History, 23 (1938), 265-289.

94 Mathieson, W. L. British Slavery and Its Abolition, 1823-1838. New York: Octagon Books, 1967.

95 Melafe, Rollando. La esclavitud en hispanoamérica. Buenos Aires: Eudeba, 1964.

96 Mörner, Magnus. "The History of Race Relations in Latin America Some Comments on the State of Research." Latin American Research Review, 1: 3 (Summer 1966), 28-34.

97 _____, ed. Race and Class in Latin America. New York: Columbia University Press, 1970.

98 _____. Race Mixture in the History of Latin America. Boston: Little Brown and Company, 1967.

99 _____, and Charles Gibson. "Diego Muñoz Camargo and the Segregation Policy of the Spanish Crown." Hispanic American Historical Review, 42: 4 (November 1962), 558-568.

100 Morse, Richard M. Negro-White Relations in Latin America. New Haven: Ninth Yale University Conference on the Teaching of Social Sciences, 1964.

101 NACLA. NACLA's Bibliography on Latin America. New York: North American Congress on Latin America, March 1973.

102 Normano, João F. "Japanese Emigration to Latin America." Population, 2: 4 (1938), 77-99.

103 Owens, William A. Slave Mutiny: The Revolt on the Schooner Amistad. New York: John Day Company, 1953.

104 Patterson, H. Orlando. The Sociology of Slavery. London: MacGikkon and Kee, 1967.

105   Pescatello, Ann, ed.   The African in Latin America.   New
      York: Alfred A. Knopf, 1976.

106   Pike, Ruth.   "Sevillian Society in the Sixteenth Century: Slaves
      and Freedmen."   Hispanic American Historical Review,
      47 (1957) 344-359.

107   Pitt-Rivers, Julian.   "Race, Color, and Class in Central
      America and the Andes."   Daedalus, 96: 2 (Spring 1967),
      542-559.

108   _____.   Race Relations in Mexico, Central America, and
      the Andes.   London: Oxford University Press, 1969.

109   Price, A. Grenfell.   White Settlers in the Tropics.   New
      York: American Geographical Society Special Publication
      No. 23, 1939.

110   Price, Richard, ed.   Maroon Societies: Rebel Slave Com-
      munities in the Americas.   New York: Anchor/Double-
      day, 1973.

111   Riemens, Hendrik.   L'Europe devant l'Amérique Latine.   La
      Haye: n.p., 1962.

112   Rivera, Julius.   Latin America: A Sociocultural Interpreta-
      tion.   2nd ed.   New York: Irvington Publishers, 1978.

113   Romero, F.   "The Slave Trade and the Negro in South Amer-
      ica."   Hispanic American Historical Review, 24 (August
      1944), 368-86.

114   Rubin, Vera.   "Approaches to the Study of National Charac-
      teristics in a Multi-Cultural Society."   International Jour-
      nal of Social Psychiatry, 5:1 (Summer 1969), 20-6.

115   Ruiz Del Vizo, Hortensia.   Black Poetry of the Americas.
      Miami: Ediciones Universal, 1972.

116   Saco, José Antonio.   Historia de la esclavitud de la raza af-
      ricana en el Nuevo Mundo y en especial en los países
      américo-hispanos.   4 vols.   Havana: Cultural, S.A.,
      1938.

117   Santos, Eduardo.   Pan-Africanismo.   Lisbon: Ediçāo do Autor,
      1968.

118   Scelle, Georges.   La traité négrière aux Indes de Castille:
      Contrats et traités d'assiento.   2 vols.   Paris: L. La-
      rose et L. Tanin, 1906.

119   Schemann, Ludwig.   Gobineau: eine biographie.   2 vols.
      Strassburg: n.p., 1916.

120 Senghor, Leopold Sedar. "The Problematics of Negritude."
    Black World, 20: 10 (August 1971), 4-24.

121 Simpson, George Eaton. "Afro-American Religions and Re-
    ligious Behavior." Caribbean Studies, 12: 2 (July 1972),
    5-30.

122 Singham, A. W. The Hero and the Crowd in a Colonial Policy.
    New Haven: Yale University Press, 1968.

123 Sio, Arnold A. "Interpretations of Slavery: The Slave Status
    in the Americas." Comparative Studies in Society and
    History, 7: 3 (April 1965), 289-308.

124 The Situation of the Indian in South America. New York:
    World Council of Churches, 1972.

125 Smith, T. Lynn. "Studies of Colonization and Settlement."
    Latin American Research Review, 4: 1 (1960), 93-123.

126 Solaún, Mauricio and Sidney Drones. Discrimination Without
    Violence: Miscegenation and Racial Conflict in Latin
    America. New York: John Wiley, 1973.

127 Sternberg, Hilgard O'Reilly. A Geographer's View of Race
    and Class in Latin America. Berkeley: University of
    California Press, 1970.

128 Steward, Julian H., ed. Handbook of South American Indians.
    New York: Cooper Square Press, 1963- .

129 _____, and Faron, Louis C. Native Peoples of South Amer-
    ica. New York: McGraw-Hill, 1959.

130 Stycos, J. M. Human Fertility in Latin America: Sociologi-
    cal Perspective. Ithaca: Cornell University Press, 1968.

131 Tannenbaum, Frank. Slave and Citizen: The Negro in the
    Americas. 1946; rpt., New York: Vintage Books, 1963.

132 Tavâres, Regina A. and Hadjine Lisbôa. Influencias africanas
    en la América Latina. Rio de Janeiro: CLAPCS, 1963.

133 Thompson, Edgar T. The Plantation: A Bibliography. Wash-
    ington, D.C.: Pan American Union, Social Science Mon-
    ographs IV, 1957.

134 _____, ed. Race Relations and the Race Problem: A Defin-
    ition and an Analysis. (1939), New York: Greenwood
    Press, 1968.

135 R.W. Thompson. Germans and Japs in South America. Lon-
    don: Faber and Faber Limited, 1942. (Originally pub-
    lished as Voice from the Wilderness, 1940.)

136 Tigner, James. "Japanese Immigration into Latin America: An Overview." Paper presented to the Pacific Coast Council on Latin American Studies, California State University, Fullerton, October 1978.

137 Tiryakian, Josefina Cintrón. "Campillo's Pragmatic New System: A Mercantile and Utilitarian Approach to Indian Reform in Spanish Colonies of the Eighteenth Century." History of Political Economy, 10:2 (1978), 233-257.

138 Toplin, Robert B., ed. Slavery and Race Relations in Latin America. Westport, Conn.: Greenwood Press, 1974.

139 Vigil, Ralph H. "Negro Slaves and Rebels in the Spanish Possessions, 1503-1558." The Historian, 33: 4 (August 1971), 637-655.

140 Wagley, Charles. The Latin American Tradition. New York: Columbia University Press, 1962.

141 _____. "On the Concept of Social Race in the Americas." Contemporary Cultures and Societies of Latin America. Ed. Dwight B. Heath and Richard N. Adams. New York: Random House, 1965, pp. 542-566.

142 _____, and Marvin Harris. Minorities in the New World: Six Case Studies. New York: Columbia University Press, 1958.

143 Whitten, Norman E. Black Frontiersmen: A South American Case. Cambridge, Mass.: Schenkman Publishing Co., 1974.

144 _____, and John F. Szwed, eds. Afro-American Anthropology: Contemporary Perspectives. New York: The Free Press, 1970.

145 Willeford, Mary Jo. "Negro New World Religions and Witchcraft." Bim, 12:48 (January-June 1969), 216-22.

146 Willey, Gordon R. An Introduction to American Archaeology. Englewood Cliffs, N.J.: Prentice Hall, 1966.

147 Williams, Eric E. Capitalism and Slavery. New York: Russell & Russell, 1961.

148 Wingo, L. "Recent Patterns of Urbanization Among Latin American Countries." Urban Affairs Quarterly, 2: 3 (1967), 81-109.

149 Wright, Philip. "War and Peace with the Maroons." Caribbean Quarterly, 16: 1 (1970), 5-27.

150 Wyndham, H. A. The Atlantic and Emancipation. London:

Oxford University Press for the Royal Institute of International Affairs, 1937.

151 Zavala, Sílvio. The Defense of Human Rights in Latin America, Sixteenth to Eighteenth Centuries. Paris: UNESCO, 1964.

152 Zea, Leopoldo. "Negritud e indigenismo." Cuadernos Americanos, 197 (November-December 1974), 16-30.

153 Zelinsky, Wilbur. "The Historical Geography of the Negro Population of Latin America." The Journal of Negro History, 34 (April 1949), 153-221.

154 Zolberg, Aristide R. "Frantz Fanon: A Gospel for the Damned." Encounter, 27 (November 1966), 56-63.

NORTH AMERICA AND CARIBBEAN

GENERAL CARIBBEAN

155 Andic, Fuat and T. G. Mathews, eds. The Caribbean in Transition: Papers on Social, Political, and Economic Development. San Juan: Institute of Caribbean Studies, University of Puerto Rico, 1965.

156 Baa, Enid M., comp. Theses on Caribbean Topics, 1778-1968. San Juan: ICS (Caribbean Bibliographic Series, No. 1), 1970.

157 Blanshard, Paul. Democracy and Empire in the Caribbean: A Contemporary Review. New York: Macmillan, 1947.

158 Brathwaite, E. K. "African Presence in Caribbean Literature." Daedalus, 103 (Spring 1974), 73-109.

159 Canton, Berthe E. "A Bibliography of West Indian Literature." Current Caribbean Bibliography, 7, (1957), 1-56.

160 Carmichael, A. C. Domestic Manners and Social Condition of the Whites, Coloured, and Negro Population of the West Indies. New York: Negro University Press, 1969.

161 Clarke, John Henrik. "Slave Revolt in the Caribbean." Black World. 22: 4 (February 1973), 12-24.

162 Clermont, Norman. Bibliographie annotée de l'anthropologie physique des Antilles. Montreal: Centre de Recherches Caraïbes, 1972.

163 Cohen-Stuart, B. A. Women in the Caribbean; An Annotated
     Bibliography. Leiden: CARAF, 1979.

164 Coleman, Ben. "Black Themes in the Literature of the Car-
     ibbean," The Rican: A Journal of Contemporary Puerto
     Rican Thought, 3 (Spring 1973), 49-54.

165 Comitas, Lambros. Caribbeana 1900-1965: A Topical Bibli-
     ography. Seattle: University of Washington Press for
     the Research Institute for the Study of Man, 1968.

166 Conzemius, Eduard. "Ethnographical notes on the Black Carib
     (Garif)." American Anthropologist, 30 (1928), 183-205.

167 Cortada, Rafael L. "A Bibliography of Comparative Slave
     Systems: The United States and the Greater West In-
     dies." Current Bibliography on African Affairs, 2: 9
     (September 1969), 9-21.

168 Coulthard, G. R. "Negritude--Reality and Mystification."
     Caribbean Studies, 10: 1 (1970), 42-51.

169 _____. Race and Colour in Caribbean Literature. London:
     Oxford University Press for the Institute of Race Rela-
     tions, 1962.

170 _____. "Parallelisms and Divergencies Between Negritude
     and Indigenismo." Caribbean Studies, 8:1 (April 1968),
     31-55.

171 _____. Race and Colour in Caribbean Literature. London:
     Oxford University Press, 1962.

172 Crahan, Margaret and Franklin Knight, eds. Africa and the
     Caribbean: The Legacies of a Link. Baltimore: Johns
     Hopkins University Press, 1979.

173 Cross, Malcolm and Arnaud Marks, eds. Peasants, Planta-
     tions and Rural Communities in the Caribbean. Guilford,
     Surrey: University of Surrey, 1979.

174 Cundall, Frank. Bibliography of the West Indies. New York:
     Johnson Reprint Corporation, 1971. Reprint of 1909 ed.

175 DeKadt, Emanuel. Patterns of Foreign Influence in the Carib-
     bean. London: Royal Institute of International Affairs, 1972.

176 Dodge, Peter. "Comparative Racial Systems in the Greater
     Caribbean." Social and Economic Studies, 16 (1967),
     249-261.

177 Drake, Sandra Elizabeth. "The Uses of History in the Car-
     ibbean Novel." Diss. Stanford University, 1977.

178 Edmondson, Locksley. Black Power, Africa and the Carrib-
       bean. Kampala: Makere University College, 1968.

179 _____. "Comparative Caribbean Orientations Toward the
       African Connection." Paper presented to the Symposium
       on the Political Economy of the Black World, U. C. A. L.,
       May 11, 1979.

180 Gerber, Stanford N., ed. The Family in the Caribbean. Rio
       Piedras: Institute of Caribbean Studies, University of
       Puerto Rico, 1968.

181 Gibson, Margaret Alison. "Ethnicity and Schooling: A Carib-
       bean Case Study." Diss. University of Pittsburgh, 1976.

182 Goddard, Lawford Lawrence. "Social Structure and Migration:
       A Comparative Study of the West Indies." Diss. Stanford
       University, 1976.

183 González, Nancie L. Solien. Black Carib Household Structure:
       A Study of Migration and Modernization. Seattle: Uni-
       versity of Washington Press, 1969.

184 Green, Helen B. "Caribbean Blacks and West African Blacks:
       A Study in Attitude Similarity and Change." Revista In-
       teramericana de Psicologia, 4: 3-4 (1970), 189-201.

185 Guerin, Daniel. The West Indies and Their Future. London:
       Dennis Dobson, 1961.

186 Henriques, Fernando. "Colour and Contemporary Society in
       the Caribbean." Journal de la Société Américanistes,
       58 (1969), 207-221.

187 Henry, Frances. "Social Stratification in an Afro-American
       Cult." Anthropological Quarterly, 38: 2 (April 1965), 72-
       78.

188 Hoetink, Harry. The Two Variants in Caribbean Race Rela-
       tions: A Contribution to the Sociology of Segmented So-
       cieties. Tr. Eva M. Hooykaas. New York: Oxford Uni-
       versity Press, 1967.

189 Holly, James Theodore and J. Dennis Harris. Black Separa-
       tism and the Caribbean. Ann Arbor: University of Mich-
       igan Press, 1970.

190 Horowitz, M. Peoples and Culture of the Caribbean. New
       York: Natural History Press, 1971.

191 Horton, V. P. Oswald, ed. Chinese in the Caribbean. Kings-
       ton: Jamaica: Souvenir, 30th Anniversay of the Chinese
       Republic, 1941.

192 Institute of International Relations. University of the West Indies. The Caribbean Yearbook of International Relations. Leyden, The Netherlands: Sijhoff Publishing Co., 1975.

193 James, C. L. R. West Indians of East Indian Descent. Port-of-Spain: Ibis Publications. 1969.

194 Kerton, Robert Richard. "Labor Theory and Developing Countries: The Individual's Supply of Effort in the Caribbean." Diss. Duke University, 1969.

195 Lamur, H. E. and J. D. Speckman, eds. Adaptation of Migrants from the Caribbean in the European and American Metropolis. Amsterdam: University of Amsterdam, 1978.

196 Lekis, Lisa. "The Origin and Development of Ethnic Caribbean Dance and Music," Diss. University of Florida, 1956.

197 Leigh-Fermor, Patrick. The Traveller's Tree. London: John Murray, 1950.

198 Lier, R. A. J. van. The Development and Nature of Society in the West Indies. Amsterdam: Indisch Instituut, 1960.

199 Lowenthal, David. "Black Power in the Caribbean Context." Economic Geography, 48 (January 1972), 116-134.

200 _____. "Conflict and Race in the Caribbean," Integrated Education, 9:53 (September-October 1971), 42-48.

201 _____. "Post-Emancipation Race Relations: Some Caribbean and American Perspectives." Journal of Inter-American Studies, 13:3-4 (July-October 1971), pp. 367-377.

202 _____. "Race and Color in the West Indies." Daedalus, 96: 2 (Spring 1967), 580-626.

203 _____. A Study of the Development of Race Relations in the Caribbean. New York: Oxford University Press, 1966.

204 _____. West Indian Societies. London: Oxford University Press, 1972.

205 _____, and Lambros Comitas. Consequences of Class and Color: West Indian Perspectives. Garden City, N.Y.: Anchor Press, 1973.

206 MacDonald, John Stuart and Leatrice D. MacDonald. "Transformations of African and Indian Family Traditions in the Souther Caribbean." Comparative Studies in Society and History, 15: 2 (March 1973), 171-198.

207 Marks, Arnaud F. and Theo. Oltheten, eds.   The Caribbean: History, Dependence and Development.   Leiden: CARAF, 1979.

208 Mathews, Thomas.   "Los estudios sobre historia econômica del Caribe (1585-1910)."   Historiografía y bibliografía americanistas, 15: 3 (December 1971), 445-476.

209 May, Robert Evan.   "The Southern Dream of a Caribbean Empire, 1854-1861."   Diss. University of Wisconsin, 1969.

210 Mintz, Sidney W.   Caribbean Transformation.   Chicago: Aldine, 1974.

211 Morris, Jan.   "Black Thoughts from the Caribbean."   Encounter, 40 (April 1973), 27-31.

212 Naipaul, V. S.   The Middle Passage.   London: Andre Deutsch, 1962.

213 Niehoff, Arthur and Juanita.   East Indians in the West Indies. Milwaukee Public Museum: Publications in Anthropology, No. 6, 1960.

214 Ober, Frederick A.   Our West Indian Neighbors.   New York: James Pott and Co., 1907.

215 Oltheten, Theo.   Inventory of Caribbean Studies: An Overview of Social Scientific Publications on the Caribbean by Antillean, Dutch and Surinamese Authors, 1945-1978/79. Leiden: CARAF, 1979.

216 Proudfoot, Malcolm J.   Population Movements in the Caribbean.   Port-of-Spain: Caribbean Commission, 1950.

217 Raphael, Lennox.   "West Indians and Afro-Americans."   Freedomways (New York), 4 (1964), 438-45.

218 Révert, E.   Le monde caraïbe.   Paris: Les Editions françaises, 1958.

219 Rodman, Selden.   The Caribbean.   New York: Hawthorn Books, 1968.

220 Rubin, Vera, ed.   Caribbean Studies: A Symposium.   Jamaica: Institute of Social and Economic Research, 1957.

221 Schuler, Monica.   "Ethnic Slave Rebellions in the Caribbean and the Guianas."   Journal of Social History, 3 (1970), 274-85.

222 Schwarz-Bart, André.   A Woman Named Solitude.   New York: Atheneum, 1973.

223   Sheridan, Richard B. "Africa and the Caribbean in the Atlantic Slave Trade." American Historical Review, 77:1 (February 1972), 15-35.

224   Simpson, George E. Religious Cults of the Caribbean: Trinidad, Jamaica, and Haiti. Rio Piedras: Institute of Caribbean Studies, University of Puerto Rico, 1970.

225   _____, and P. Hammond. "The African Heritage in the Caribbean," Caribbean Studies: A Symposium. Ed. Vera Rubin. Seattle: University of Washington Press, 1960, pp. 48-53.

226   Smith, Michael G. "The African Heritage in the Caribbean," Caribbean Studies: A Symposium. Ed. Vera Rubin, Seattle: University of Washington Press, 1960, pp. 34-45.

227   Sturtevant, William C. The Significance of Ethnological Similarities Between Southeastern North America and the Antilles. Yale University Publications in Anthropology, no. 64, 1960.

228   Szulc, Tad, ed. The United States and the Caribbean. Englewood Cliffs, N.J.: Prentice-Hall, 1971.

229   Trollope, Anthony. The West Indies and the Spanish Main. London: Chapman and Hall, 1860.

230   Waddell, D. A. G. The West Indies and the Guianas. Englewood Cliffs, N.J.: Prentice-Hall, 1967.

231   Wilgus, A. Curtis, ed. The Caribbean. 17 vols. Gainesville: University of Florida Press, 1951-1967.

232   Williams, Eric E. From Columbus to Castro: The History of the Caribbean, 1492-1969. London: Andre Deutsch, 1970.

233   _____. The Negro in the Caribbean. Washington, D.C.: Associates in Negro Folk Education, 1942.

234   _____. "Race Relations in Caribbean Society," Caribbean Studies: A Symposium, Ed. Vera Rubin. Seattle: University of Washington Press, 1960, pp. 54-59.

235   Wilson, Basil. "Toward Pan-Africanism: The Caribbean: Rumbles Left and Right," Black World, 29: 10 (August 1970), 23-26.

236   Wilson, Peter J. Crabantics: The Social Anthropology of English-speaking Negro Societies of the Caribbean. New Haven: Yale University Press, 1973.

237 Wood, Donald. "Kru Emigration to the West Indies." Paper
    presented to the Society for Caribbean Studies, Surrey,
    U.K., April 1978.

238 Worcester, Donald E. and Wendell G. Schaeffer. "The Carib-
    bean Area, 1600-1700," Growth and Culture of Latin
    America. New York: Oxford University Press, 1956,
    pp. 182-201.

CUBA

239 Aguirre, Benigno. "Differential Migration of Cuban Social
    Races." Latin American Research Review, 11:1 (1976),
    103-124.

240 Aimes, Hubert H. S. The History of Slavery in Cuba, 1511-
    1868. New York: Octagon Books, 1967.

241 Alienes y Urosa, Julián. Caracteristicas fundamentales de la
    economia Cubana. Havana: Banco Nacional de Cuba,
    1950.

242 Alvarez Mola, Martha Verónica and Pedro Martínez Pérez.
    "Algo acerca del problema negro en Cuba hasta 1912."
    Universidad de la Habana, 179 (May-June 1966), 79-93.

243 Amaro, Nelson and Carmelo Mesa-Lago. "Inequality and
    Classes." Revolutionary Change in Cuba. Pittsburgh:
    University of Pittsburgh Press, 1971, 347-353.

244 Amor, Sister Rose Teresa. "Afro-Cuban Folk Tales as In-
    corporated into the Literary Tradition of Cuba." Diss.
    Columbia University, 1969.

245 Arozarena, Marcelino. Canción negra sin color. Havana:
    Cuadernos Unión, 1966.

246 Arrendondo, Alberto. El negro en Cuba. Havana: Editorial
    Alfa, 1939.

247 Bascom, William R. "The Focus of Cuban Santería." South-
    western Journal of Anthropology, 6: 1 (Spring 1950), 64-
    68.

248 Bekarevich, Anatolii. Cuba. Moscow: Nauka, 1970.

249 Bernel, Emilia. La raza negra en Cuba. Santiago: Prensas
    de la Universidad de Chile, 1937.

250 Betancourt, Juan René. El negro, ciudadano del futuro. Ha-
    vana: Cardenas y Cia., c. 1955.

251 Bibliografia cubana. 1969/62. Havana: Consejo Nacional de
Cultura.

252 Blassingame, John W. "Bibliographical Essay: Foreign Writers View Cuban Slavery." The Journal of Negro History,
57 (October 1972), 415-24.

253 Boorstein, Edward. The Economic Transformation of Cuba.
New York: Monthly Review Press, 1968.

254 Booth, David. "Cuba, Color and the Revolution." Science &
Society, 40:2 (Summer 1976), 129-172.

255/56 Bouachea, Rolando, and Nelson P. Valdes, eds. Cuba in
Revolution. Garden City, N.Y.: Anchor Books, 1972.

257 Calixto, García. "El negro en la narrativa cubana." Diss.
City College of New York, 1973.

258 Carneado, José Felipe. "La discriminación racial en Cuba no
volverá jamás." Cuban Socialistas, (January 1962), 54-
67.

259 Casal, Lourdes. "Images of Cuban Society Among Pre-and
Post-Revolutionary Novelists." Diss. New School for
Social Research, 1975.

260 Centro Nacional de Investigaciones Cientificas. Informe, 1969.
Havana: Universidad de La Habana, 1969.

261 Chapeaux, Pedro Deschamps. "Cimarrones urbanos." Revista de la Biblioteca Nacional José Martí, 2 (1969), 145-
164.

262 Clytus, John. Black Man in Red Cuba. Coral Gables, Florida: University of Miami Press, 1970.

263 Cook, M. "Cuban Approach to the Race Problem Compared
with That in the United States." Free World, 6 (September 1943), 268-72.

264 Corwin, Arthur F. Spain and the Abolition of Slavery in Cuba,
1817-1886. Austin: University of Texas Press, 1967.

265 Cuba. Ministerio de Relaciones Exteriores. Cuba: Country
Free of Segregation. Havana: Dirección de Información
circa 1965-66.

266 Cuba Resource Center. Blacks in Cuba. New York, January
1973.

267 Cuban Economic Research Project. A Study on Cuba. Coral
Gables, Fla.: University of Miami Press, 1965.

268 Deschamps Chapeaux, Pedro. "El negro en la economía ha-
    banera del siglo XIX." Revista de la Facultad de Cien-
    cias Económicas. (Havana), 10: 1 (January-April 1968),
    53-59.

269 Dominguez, Jorge I. Cuba: Order and Revolution. Cam-
    bridge, Mass.: Harvard University Press, 1978.

270 Entralgo, Elías. "Los fenómenos raciales en la emancipación
    de Cuba." Round Table on the Origins of the Spanish
    American Emancipation Movement. Caracas: Academia
    Nacional de la Historia, 1961.

271 Fagan, Richard R., R. A. Brody, and T. J. O'Leary. Cubans
    in Exile: Disaffection and the Revolution. Stanford, Cal.:
    Stanford University Press, 1968.

272 Fermoselle López, Rafael. "The Blacks in Cuba; A Bibli-
    ography." Caribbean Studies, 12: 3 (October 1972), 103-
    112.

273 Fraginals, Manuel Moreno. The Sugar Mill. New York:
    Monthly Review Press, 1979.

274 Geoffrey, E. F. "Race, Sex, and Revolution in Cuba." In-
    terracial Marriage. Ed. I. R. Stewart and L. Abt. New
    York: Grossman Publishers, 1973, pp. 293-308.

275 Guerra y Sánchez, Ramiro. Cuban Counterpoint. Tr. Harriet
    de Onis. New York, 1947.

276 _____. Sugar and Society in the Caribbean. Tr. Marjory
    M. Urquidi. New Haven: Yale University Press, 1963.

277 Guillén, Nicolás. Cuba, amor y revolucion. Lima: Editorial
    Causachun, 1972.

278 Hall, Gwendolyn M. Social Control in Slave Plantation Soci-
    eties: A Comparison of St. Dominque and Cuba. Balti-
    more: Johns Hopkins University Press, 1971.

279 Jiménez Pastrana, J. Los chinos en las luchas por la liber-
    ación cubana (1847-1930). Havana: n.p., 1963.

280 Klein, Herbert S. Slavery in the Americas: A Comparative
    Study of Virginia and Cuba. London: Oxford University
    Press, 1967.

281 Knight, Franklin W. Slave Society in Cuba during the Nine-
    teenth Century. Madison: University of Wisconsin Press,
    1970.

282 MacGaffey, Wyatt et al. Cuba: Its People, Its Society, Its
    Culture. New Haven: HRAF Press, 1962.

283 Macmaster, Richard Kerwin. "The United States, Great Britain and the Suppression of the Cuban Slave Trade 1835-1860." Diss. Georgetown University, 1968.

284 Martí, Jose. La question racial. Havana: Lex, 1959.

285 Martinez-Alier, Verena. Marriage, Class and Colour in Nineteenth Century Cuba. London: Cambridge University Press, 1974.

286 Masferrer, Marianne and Carmelo Meso-Lago. "The Gradual Integration of the Black in Cuba: Under the Colony, the Republic, and the Revolution." Slavery and Race Relations in Latin America. Ed. Robert B. Toplin. Westport, Conn.: Greenwood Publishing Company, 1974, pp. 348-384.

287 Montejo, Esteban. The Autobiography of a Runaway Slave. Ed. Miguel Barnet. New York: Pantheon, 1968.

288 More, Carlos. "Le peuple noir a-t-il sa place dans la révolution cubaine?" Présence Africaine, 52 (1964), 177-230.

289 Nelson, Lowry. Rural Cuba. Minneapolis: University of Minnesota Press, 1951.

290 North, Joseph. "Negro and White in Cuba." Political Affairs, (July 1963) 34-45.

291 Ortiz, Fernando. La Africanía de la música folklórica de Cuba. Havana: Ministerio de Educación, 1950.

292 _____. Hampa afro-cubana, los negros esclavos; Estudio sociologico y de derecho público. Havana: Revista Bimestre Cubana, 1916.

293 Pereda Valdés, Ildefonso. Lo negro y lo mulato en la poesía cubana. Montevideo: Ediciones Ciudadela, 1970.

294 Portuondo, José Antonio. "El negro, heroe, bufón y persona en la literatura cubana colonial." Unión, 7: 4 (December 1968), 30-36.

295 Revolutionary Cuba; A Bibliographical Guide, 1966-1968. 3 vols. Coral Gables, Fla.: University of Miami Press, 1967-1970.

296 Ring, Harry. How Cuba Uprooted Race Discrimination. New York: Pioneer Publications, 1961.

297 Romero, Fernando. "Afro-Cuban Studies and the Negro in Martí's Homeland." Bimonthly Review, 47 (1941), 395-411.

172 / Bibliography

298 Seers, Dudley, ed. Cuba: The Economic and Social Revolution. Chapel Hill: The University of North Carolina Press, 1964.

299 Smith, Harold F. "A Bibliography of American Travellers' Books About Cuba Published Before 1900." The Americas, 22: 4 (April 1966), 404-412.

300 Thomas, Hugh. Cuba, or the Pursuit of Freedom. New York: Harper & Row, 1971.

301 Trelles y Govin, Carlos. Bibliografía social cubana. Havana: Biblioteca Nacional José Martí, 1969.

302 Valdés, Nelson P. "Inventorio bibliográfico sobre Cuba." Aportes, 11 (January 1969), 66-75.

303 Verger, Pierre. "Nigeria, Brazil, and Cuba." Nigeria Magazine, 66 (October 1960), 113-123.

304 Winn, Peter. "The State and the Arts." New York Times Book Review June 10, 1979, 13-39.

305 Zeitlin, Maurice. Revolutionary Politics and the Cuban Working Class. Princeton, N.J.: Princeton University Press, 1967.

DOMINICAN REPUBLIC

306 Debien, Gabriel. "Les esclaves marrons à Saint-Domingue en 1764." Jamaican Historical Review, 61 (1966) 9-20.

307 Franco Pichardo, Franklyn J. Los negros, los mulatos y la nación dominicana 2nd ed. Santo Domingo: Editora Nacional, 1970.

308 Hoetink, Hermannus. El pueblo dominicano, 1850-1900. Apuntes para una sociología histórica. Santiago, Dominican Republic: n.p., 1971.

309 Houdaille, J. "Trois paroisses de Saint-Dominque au XVIIIe siècle. Etude démographique." Population 18: 1 (1963), 93-110.

310 James, C. L. R. The Black Jacobins: Toussaint L'Ouverture and the San Domingo Revolution. 2nd ed. New York: Random House, 1963.

311 Larrazabal Blanco, Carlos. Los negros y la esclavitud en Santo Domingo. Santo Domingo: Julio D. Postigo e Hijos, 1967.

312 Vaissiere, Pierre de. Saint-Domingue, 1629-1789: La So-
     ciété et la vie créole sous l'ancien régime. Paris: Per-
     rin, 1909.

313 Viau, Alfred. Noirs, mulâtres, blancs ou rien que du sang.
     Ciudad Trujillo: Montalvo, 1955.

314 Walker, Malcolm Trafford. "Power Structure and Political
     Behavior in a Community of the Dominican Republic."
     Diss. Columbia University, 1970.

HAITI

315 Aubourg, M. "Survivances dahaméennes dan le folklore haï-
     tien." Bulletin du Bureau d'Ethnologie, 4: 29 (November
     1963), 30-36.

316 Augustin, J. J. Life in a Haitian Valley. New York: Ryer-
     son Press, 1937.

317 Bissainthe, Max. Dictionnaire de bibliographie haitienne:
     premier supplément. Metuchen, N.J.: Scarecrow Press,
     1973.

318 Breathett, George. "Religious Protectionism and the Slave in
     Haiti." Catholic Historical Review, 55: 1 (April 1969),
     26-39.

319 Bourguignon, Erika. "The Persistence of Folk Beliefs: Some
     Notes on Cannibalism and Jombis in Haiti." Journal of
     American Folklore, 72: 283 (January-March 1959), 36-46.

320 Cole, Hubert. Christophe, King of Haiti. New York: Viking
     Press, 1967.

321 Courlander, Harold. The Drum and the Hoe, Life and Lore
     of the Haitian People. Berkeley: University of California
     Press, 1960.

322 _____, and Remy Bastien. Religion and Politics in Haiti.
     Washington, D.C.: Institute for Cross-Cultural Research,
     1966.

323 Davis, Harold Palmer. Black Democracy: The Story of Haiti.
     New York: Dodge Publishing Company, 1936.

324 Deren, Maya. Divine Horsemen: The Voodoo Gods of Haiti.
     New York: Delta Books, 1972.

325 Efron, E. "French and Creole Patois in Haiti." Caribbean
     Quarterly, 3 (1954), 199-214.

326 Franklin, James. The Present State of Haiti. Westport,
    Conn.: Negro University Press, 1970.

327 Herskovits, Melville J. Life in a Haitian Valley. New York:
    Alfred A. Knopf, 1937.

328 James, C. L. R. The Black Jacobins. 2nd ed. New York:
    Vintage Books, 1963.

329 Leyburn, James G. The Haitian People. New Haven: Yale
    University Press, 1941.

330 Logan, Rayford. Haiti and the Dominican Republic. London:
    Oxford University Press, 1968.

331 Macleod, Murdo J. "The Haitian Novel of Social Protest."
    Journal of Inter-American Studies, 4: 2 (April 1962), 207-
    221.

332 Métraux, Alfred. Voodoo in Haiti. Tr. H. Chareteris. New
    York: Oxford University Press, 1959.

333 Mintz, Sidney W. and Vern Canoe. "A Selective Social Science
    Bibliography of the Republic of Haiti." Revista Interamer-
    icana de Ciencias Sociales, 2: 3 (1963), 405-419.

334 Murray, Gerald Francis. "The Evolution of Haitian Peasant
    Land Tenure: A Case Study in Agrarian Adaptation to
    Population Growth." Diss. Columbia University,
    1977.

335 Paul, Emmanuel C. Panorama du Folklore Haïtien: Présence
    Africaine en Haiti. Port-au-Prince: Imprimerie de l-Etat,
    1962.

336 Price-Mars, Jean. "Africa in the Americas." Tomorrow
    (New York), 3: 1, (1954), 75-84.

337 _____. "Les Survivances africaines dans la communauté
    haïtienne." Etudes dahoméennes, 6 (1945?), 5-10.

338 Romain, Jean Baptiste. L'Anthropologie physique des Haitiens.
    Haiti: Imp. Seminaire Adventiste, 1971.

339 Rotberg, Robert I. Haiti: The Politics of Squalor. Boston:
    Houghton Mifflin Company, 1971.

340 St. John, Spenser. Hayti, or, the Black Republic. New York:
    Scribner and Welford, 1889.

341 Simpson, George Eaton. "Haiti's Social Structure." American
    Sociological Review, 6: 5 (1941), 640-9.

342 Spitzer, Daniel Charles. "A Contemporary Political and
     Socio-Economic History of Haiti and the Dominican Re-
     public." Diss. University of Michigan, 1972.

343 Syme, Ronald. Toussaint: The Black Liberator. New York:
     William Morrow, 1971.

344 Thoby-Marcelin, Philippe. The Pencil of God. Tr. Leonard
     Thomas. Boston: n. p., 1951.

345 Vincent, Sténo. En posant les jalons. Port-au-Prince: n. p.,
     1939.

346 Wilson, Edmund. Red, Black, Blonde and Olive: Studies in
     Four Civilizations: Zuni, Haiti, Soviet Russia, Israel.
     New York: Oxford University Press, 1956.

347 Wingfield, Roland and V. J. Parenton. "Class Structure and
     Class Conflict in Haitian Society." Social Forces. 43,
     (1965), 338-48.

348 Young, C. W. "Some Aspects of Haiti's Population and Na-
     tional Territory Significant in Census Considerations."
     Estadística, 25 (1949) 516-19; 26: 69-86; 27: 204-16;
     and 28: 388-99.

JAMAICA

349 Abrahams, Peter. Jamaica: An Island Mosaic. London,
     H. M. S. O., 1957.

350 Andrade, Jacob A. P. M. A Record of the Jews in Jamaica
     from the English Conquest to the Present Time. Kingston:
     The Jamaica Times Ltd., 1941.

351 Anthony-Welch, Lillian D. "A Comparative Analysis of the
     Black Woman as Transmitter of Black Values, Based on
     Case Studies of Families in Ghana and Among Jamaicans
     and Afro-Americans in Hartford, Connecticut." Diss.
     University of Massachusetts, 1976.

352 Bagley, Chris. "The Social Context of Cognitive Style: A
     Class, Sex, and Ethnic Comparison of 10 year olds
     in Jamaica and Britain." Paper presented to the
     Society for Caribbean Studies, Surrey, U. K., April
     1978.

353 Banbury, R. Thomas. Jamaica Superstition; Or the Obeah
     Book. Kingston, Jamaica: 1894.

354 Barrett, Leonard E. The Rastafarians: A Study in Messianic
     Cultism in Jamaica. Rio Piedras: Institute of Caribbean
     Studies, University of Puerto Rico, 1968.

355 _____ . The Sun and the Drum: African Roots in Jamai-
     can Folk Tradition. Kingston, Jamaica: Heinemann Ed-
     ucational Books, Ltd. , 1976.

356 Beckwith, Martha W. Black Roadways: A Study of Jamaican
     Folk Life. Chapel Hill: University of North Carolina
     Press, 1929.

357 Bennett, Louise and Una Wilson, eds. Anansi Stories and
     Dialect Verse. Kingston, Jamaica: The Pioneer Press,
     1946.

358 Bigelow, John. Jamaica in 1850, or the Effects of Sixteen
     Years of Freedom on a Slave Colony. New York: George
     P. Putnam, 1851.

359 Blake, Judith, J. Mayone Stycos, and Kingsley Davis. Fam-
     ily Structure in Jamaica: The Social Context of Repro-
     duction. New York: Free Press, 1961.

360 Brathwaite, Edward. Folk Culture of the Slaves in Jamaica.
     London: New Beacon Books, 1970.

361 _____ . "Jamaican Slave Society, a Review." Race, 9
     (1967-8), 331-42.

362 Broom, Leonard. "The Social Differentiation of Jamaica."
     American Sociological Review, 19 (1954) 115-25.

363 Brymner, D. "The Jamaica Maroons: How They Came to
     Nova Scotia--How They Left It." Transactions of the
     Royal Society of Canada. (second series) 1 (1895), 81-
     90.

364 Campbell, Horace. "Jamaica: The Myth of Economic Devel-
     opment and Racial Tranquility." The Black Scholar, 4
     (February 1973), 16-24.

365 Cassidy, Frederic. Jamaican Talk: Three Hundred Years of
     English Language in Jamaica. London: Macmillan, 1961.

366 Craton, Michael and Garry Greenland. Searching for the In-
     visible Man: Slaves and Plantation Life in Jamaica. Cam-
     bridge, Mass.: Harvard University Press, 1978.

367 Cronon, Edmund David. Black Moses: The Story of Marcus
     Garvey and the Universal Negro Improvement Association.
     Madison: University of Wisconsin Press, 1964.

368 Cundall, Frank. Jamaica Negro Proverbs and Sayings. Kingston, Jamaica: n.p., 1910.

369 Curtin, Philip D. Two Jamaicas: The Role of Ideas in a Tropical Colony, 1830-1865. Cambridge, Mass.: Harvard University Press, 1955.

370 Dalby, David. "Ashanti Survivals in the Language and Traditions of the Windward Maroons of Jamaica." African Language Studies, 12 (1971), 31-51.

371 DeLisser, Herbert G. Twentieth Century Jamaica. Kingston, Jamaica: n.p., 1913.

372 Duncker, Sheila J. "The Free Coloured and Their Fight for Civil Rights in Jamaica, 1800-1830." M.A. Thesis. University of London, 1961.

373 Eisner, Gisela. Jamaica, 1830-1930: A Study in Economic Growth. Manchester: University Press, 1961.

374 Ellis, Robert A. "Color and Class in a Jamaican Market Town." Sociology and Social Research. 41, (1957), 354-60.

375 Emerick, Abraham. Obeah and Duppyism in Jamaica. Woodstock, Mass.: privately printed, 1915.

376 Furness, A. E. "The Maroon War of 1795." Jamaican Historical Review, 5 (1965), 30-49.

377 Guy, Henry A. Men in Prison. Kingston: privately published, 1962.

378 Hart, Richard. "Cudjoe and the First Maroon War in Jamaica." Caribbean Historical Review, 1 (1950), 146-179.

379 Henriques, Fernando. Family and Colour in Jamaica. 2nd ed. London: MacGikken and Kee, 1968.

380 Higman, Barry W. "Household Structure and Fertility in Jamaican Slave Plantations: A Nineteenth Century Example." Population Studies, 27 (1973), 527-550.

381 _____. "The Slave Family and Household in the British West Indies, 1800-1834." Journal of Interdisciplinary History, 6 (1975), 261-287.

382 _____. Slave Population and Economy in Jamaica, 1807-1834. Cambridge: Cambridge University Press, 1976.

383 Kerr, Madeline. Personality and Conflict in Jamaica. London: Liverpool University Press, 1963.

384 Kitzinger, Sheila. "The Rastafarian Brethern of Jamaica."
      Comparative Studies in Society and History, 9: 1 (October
      1966), 33-39.

385 Knox, Graham A. J. Class and Color in Jamaica, 1838-1962.
      Washington, D.C.: Howard University Press, 1966.

386 Kopytoff, Barbara K. "The Incomplete Polities: An Ethno-
      historical Account of the Jamaica Maroons." Diss. Uni-
      versity of Pennsylvania, 1972.

387 Le Page, R. B. and David DeCamp. Jamaican Creole. Lon-
      don: Macmillan, 1960.

388 Lewin, Olive. "Jamaican Folk Music." Caribbean Quarterly,
      14 (March-June 1968), 49-56.

389 Livingstone, W. P. Black Jamaica: A Study in Evolution.
      London: Sampson Low, 1899.

390 Low, W. A. "Record from an Eighteenth Century Jamaican
      Estate." Journal of Negro History, 59 (April 1974), 168-9.

391 MacMillan, W. M. Warning from the West Indies. London:
      n.p., 1935.

392 Mathews, C. S. "Marcus Garvey Writes from Jamaica on the
      Mulatto Escape Hatch." Journal of Negro History, 59
      (April 1974), 170-6.

393 Nettleford, Rex M. Mirror, Mirror: Identity, Race and Pro-
      test in Jamaica. Kingston, Jamaica: William Collins
      and Sangster, 1970.

394 _____. "National Identity and Attitudes to Race in Jamaica."
      Race, 7: 1 (July 1965), 59-72.

395 _____. "The Performing Arts in Jamaica." Black World,
      23: 9 (July 1974), 40-47.

396 Norris, Katrin. Jamaica: The Search for Identity. London:
      Oxford University Press, 1972.

397 Olivier, Sydney H. The Myth of Governor Eyre. London:
      Hogarth Press, 1933.

398 _____. White Capital and Coloured Labour. Westport,
      Conn.: Negro University Press, 1910.

399 Paget, Hugh. "The Free Village System in Jamaica." Carib-
      bean Quarterly, 1: 4, 12-19.

400 Palmer, Ransford W. The Jamaican Economy. New York:
      Frederick A. Praeger, 1968.

401 Patterson, Horace Orlando. The Children of Sisyphus. Kingston, Jamaica: Bolivar Press, 1964.

402 _____. "Jamaica Today." New Left Review, 31 (1965), 35-44.

403 _____. "Slavery, Acculturation and Social Change: The Jamaican Case." British Journal of Sociology, 17: 2 (June 1966), 151-164.

404 _____. "Slavery and Slave Revolts: A Sociohistorical Analysis of the First Maroon War, Jamaica, 1655-1740." Social and Economic Studies, 19: 3 (September 1970), 289-305.

405 _____. The Sociology of Slavery: An Analysis of the Origins, Development and Structure of Negro Slave Society in Jamaica. New Jersey: Fairleigh Dickinson University Press, 1967.

406 Purchas-Tulloch, Jean Andrea. "Jamaica Anansi: A Survival of the African Oral Tradition." Diss. Howard University, 1976.

407 Reckford, Mary. "The Jamaica Slave Rebellion of 1831." Past and Present, 40 (July 1968), 108-125.

408 Roberts, George W. The Population of Jamaica. Cambridge: University Press for the Conservation Foundation, 1957.

409 Robinson, Carey. The Fighting Maroons of Jamaica. London: William Collins and Sangster, 1969.

410 Russell, Thomas. The Etymology of Jamaican Grammar. London (?): n.p., 1868.

411 Salkey, Andrew. The Late Emancipation of Jerry Stover. London: Hutchinson, 1968.

412 Schlesinger, Benjamin. "The Jews of Jamaica: A Historical View." Caribbean Quarterly, 12:1 (March 1967), 46-53.

413 Scott, Clarissa S. "Cultural Stability in the Maroon Village of Moore Town, Jamaica." M.A. Thesis. Florida Atlantic University, Boca Raton, 1968.

414 Semmel, Bernard. The Governor Eyre Controversy. London: MacGibbon and Kee, 1962.

415 _____. "The Issue of 'Race' in the British Reaction to the Morant Bay Uprising of 1865." Caribbean Studies, 2:3 (October 1962), 3-15.

416 _____. Jamaican Blood and Victorian Conscience: The

Governor Eyre Controversy. Boston: Houghton Mifflin
Company, 1963.

417 Sires, R. V. "Negro Labor in Jamaica in the Years Following Emancipation." Journal of Negro History, 25 (October 1940), 484-97.

418 Smith, M. G. Dark Puritan. Kingston: UWI, Department
of Extra-Mural Studies, 1963.

419 _____, Roy Augier and Rex Nettleford. The Rastafari
Movement in Kingston, Jamaica. Kingston: Institute of
Social and Economic Research, University of the West
Indies, 1960.

420 Smith, R. W. "Legal Status of Jamaican Slaves Before the
Anti-Slavery Movement." Journal of Negro History, 30
(July 1945), 293-303.

421 Stewart, J. A View of the Past and Present State of the Island of Jamaica. Edinburgh: Oliver and Boyd, 1823.

422 Watson, E. L. "Patterns of Black Protest in Jamaica: The
Case of the Rastafarians." Journal of Black Studies, 4
(March 1974), 329-43.

423 Williams, Joseph J. Psychic Phenomena of Jamaica. New
York: The Dial Press, 1934.

424 Wynter, Sylvia. The Hills of Hebron: A Jamaican Novel.
London: Jonathan Cape, 1962.

TRINIDAD-TOBAGO

425 Augelli, John P., and Harry W. Taylor. "Race and Population Patterns in Trinidad." Annals Association of American Geographers, 50 (1960), 123-38.

426 Bahadoorsingh, Krishna. Trinidad Electoral Politics: The
Persistance of the Race Factor. London: Institute of
Race Relations, 1968.

427 Bell, Robert R. "Marriage and Family Differences Among
Lower-Class Negro and East Indian Women in Trinidad."
Race, 12, (1970-1), 59-73.

428 Bickerton, Derek. The Murders of Boysie Singh. London:
Arthur Barker Ltd., 1962.

429 Bonaparte, Tony H. "The Influence of Culture on Business in
a Pluralistic Society: A Study of Trinidad, West Indies."
American Journal of Economics and Sociology, 28 (1969),
285-301.

430 Carr, Andrew T. "A Rada Community in Trinidad." Caribbean Quarterly, 3: 1 (1953), 36-54.

431 Cross, Malcolm. "Labour Movements and Colonial Policy in Trinidad: The Experience of the 1930's." Paper presented to the Society for Caribbean Studies, Surrey, U.K., April 1978.

432 Darbeau, Dave. "The Chains Are Bursting." East Dry River Speaks, 3 (1970), entire issue.

433 Elkins, W. F. "Black Power in the British West Indies: The Trinidad Longshoremen's Strike of 1919." Science and Society, 33: 1 (Winter 1969), 71-76.

434 _____. "Marcus Garvey, the Negro World, and the British West Indies: 1919-20." Science and Society, 36 (Spring 1972), 63-77.

435 Green, Helen B. Socialization values in the Negro and East Indian Subcultures of Trinidad. Diss., University of Connecticut, 1963.

436 _____. "Three Values of Lower-class Negroes in Trinidad with Comparison to East Indian Values." Congress of the Interamerican Society of Psychology (Florida) 9 (1964), 661-666.

437 _____. "Values of Negro and East Indian School Children in Trinidad." Social and Economic Studies, 14: 2 (June 1965), 204-216.

438 Malik, Yogendra K. East Indians in Trinidad: A Study in Minority Politics. London: Institute of Race Relations, 1971.

439 Martin, T. "Revolutionary Upheaval in Trinidad, 1919: Views from British and American Sources." Journal of Negro History, 58 (July 1973), 313-26.

440 Naipaul, V. S. An Area of Darkness. London: Andre Deutsch, 1964.

441 _____. A House for Mr. Biswas. London: Andre Deutsch, 1961.

442 _____. The Loss of El Dorado: A History. London: Andre Deutsch, 1969.

443 _____. The Mimic Men. London: Andre Deutsch, 1967.

444 _____. The Suffrage of Elvira. London: Andre Deutsch, 1958.

182 / Bibliography

445 Nicholls, David G. "East Indians and Black Power in Trinidad." Journal of the Institute of Race Relations, 12: 4 (April 1971), 443-459.

446 Ottley, Carlton Robert. A Historical Account of the Trinidad and Tobago Police Force from the Earliest Times. Trinidad: privately published, 1964.

447 Oxaal, Ivar. Black Intellectuals Come to Power: The Rise of Creole Nationalism in Trinidad and Tobago. Cambridge, Mass.: Schenkman, 1968.

448 _____. Race and Revolutionary Consciousness: A Documentary Interpretation of the 1970 Black Revolt in Trinidad. Cambridge, Mass.: Schenkman, 1971.

449 Rodman, Hyman. Lower-class Families: The Culture of Poverty in Negro Trinidad. New York: Oxford University Press, 1971.

450 Ryan, Selwyn Douglas. "Decolonization in a Multi-Racial Society: A Case Study of Trinidad and Tobago." Diss., York University, 1967.

451 _____. "The Struggle for Afro-Indian Solidarity in Trinidad and Tobago." Trinidad and Tobago Index, 4 (September 1966), 3-28.

452 Saxe, Allen. "Urban Squatters in Trinidad: The Poor in a Mass Society." M.A. Thesis. Brandeis University, 1968.

453 Simpson, George E. "The Shango Cult in Nigeria and in Trinidad." American Anthropologist, 64: 6 (December 1962), 1204-1219.

454 Thomas, J. J. The Theory and Practice of Creole Grammar. Port of Spain, Trinidad: n.p., 1869.

455 Warner, Maureen. "African Feasts in Trinidad." Bulletin of the African Studies Association of the West Indies, 4 (December 1971) 85-94.

456 Williams, Eric E. History of the People of Trinidad and Tobago. New York: Praeger, 1964.

457 Wood, Donald. Trinidad in Transition: The Years After Slavery. London: Oxford University Press for the Institute of Race Relations, 1968.

458 Yawney, Carole D. "Drinking Patterns and Alcoholism Among East Indians and Negroes in Trinidad." M.A. Thesis. McGill University, 1968.

OTHER BRITISH WEST INDIES

459 Abrahams, Roger D. "The Shaping of Folklore Traditions in the British West Indies." Journal of Inter-American Studies, 9: 3 (July 1967), 456-480.

460 _____, and Richard Bauman. "Sense and Nonsense in St. Vincent: Speech Behavior and Decorum in a Caribbean Community." American Anthropologist, 73: 3 (June 1971), 762-772.

461 Allen, Michael. "Differential Responses to Crisis in the Sugar Industry by Plantocratic Elites in Barbados and Martinique, 1960-1977." Paper presented to the Society for Caribbean Studies, Surrey, U.K., April 1978.

462 Aufhauser, R. "Profitability of Slavery in the British Caribbean." Journal of Interdisciplinary History, 5 (Summer 1974), 45-67.

463 Augier, F. Roy, and Shirley C. Gordon. Sources of West Indian History. London: Longmans, Green, 1962.

464 Ayearst, Morley. The British West Indies: The Search for Self-Government. New York: New York University Press, 1960.

465 Bermuda Library, Hamilton, Bermuda Islands. Bermudiana; Bibliography. Hamilton, 1971.

466 Bryans, Robin. Trinidad and Tobago: Isles of the Immortelles. London: Faber and Faber, 1967.

467 Campbell, A. A. St. Thomas Negroes: A Study of Personality and Culture. American Psychological Association, Psychological Monographs, 55: 5 (1943).

468 Cox, Edward Locksley. "The Shadow of Freedom: Freedmen in the Slave Societies of Grenada and St. Kitts, 1763-1833." Diss. The Johns Hopkins University, 1977.

469 Craton, Michael. "Changing Patterns of Slave Families in the British West Indies." Journal of Interdisciplinary History, 10:1 (Summer 1979), 1-36.

470 _____. A History of the Bahamas. London: Collins, 1962.

471 Crowley, David. "I Could Talk Old-Story Good: Creativity in Bahamian Folklore." University of California Publications, 10, April 1966.

472 Dann, Graham M. S., ed. Everyday Life in Barbados. Leiden: CARAF, 1979.

473 Davy, John. The West Indies Before and Since Slave Eman-
     cipation Comprising the Windward and Leeward Island's
     Military Command: Founded on Notes and Observations
     Collected During a Three Years' Residence. London:
     Frank Cass, 1971.

474 Dunn, Richard S. Sugar and Slaves: The Rise of the Planter
     Class in the English West Indies, 1624-1713. Chapel Hill:
     University of North Carolina Press, 1972.

475 Easton, David K. "A Bibliography on the Federation of the
     British West Indies." Current Caribbean Bibliography,
     5 (1966), 1-14.

476 Ehrlich, Allen S. "History, Ecology, and Demography in the
     British Caribbean: An Analysis of East Indian Ethnicity."
     Southwestern Journal of Anthropology, 27: 2 (Summer
     1971), 166-180.

477 Eltis, D. "Traffic in Slaves Between the British West Indian
     Colonies, 1807-1833." Economic History Review, 25 (Feb-
     ruary 1972), 55-64.

478 Firbank, Ronald. Prancing Nigger. n.p., 1921.

479 Fisher, R. A. "Note on Divide and Conquer: Letter from
     Valentine Morris, Governor of St. Vincent in the British
     West Indies, dated March 25, 1777 on Fomenting Discord
     Between Runaway Negroes and Carib Indians." Journal
     of Negro History, 30 (October 1945), 437-38.

480 Fortune, Stephen Alexander. "Merchants and Jews: The
     Economic and Social Relationships Between the English
     Merchants and Jews in The British West Indian Colonies,
     1650-1740." Diss. University of California, 1976.

481 Frisbie, Charlotte J. "Aspects of Slave Life in Barbados:
     Music and Its Cultural Context." Caribbean Studies, 11:
     4 (January 1972), 5-46.

482 Froude, James Anthony. The English in the West Indies.
     London: Longmans, 1888.

483 Goggin, John M. "The Seminole Negroes of Andros Island,
     Bahamas." Florida Historical Quarterly, 24 (1946), 200-
     206.

484 Goode, William J., ed. Colonial and Colored United, Pro-
     gramme of Action: History of the Pan-African Congress.
     Manchester: Panal Services, 1947.

485 Goveia, Elsa V. Slave Society in the British Leeward Islands
     at the End of the Eighteenth Century. New Haven: Yale
     University Press, 1965.

486 _____ . A Study on the Historiography of the British West Indies to the End of the Nineteenth Century. Mexico, D. F.: Pan American Institute of Geography and History, 1956.

487 Green, W. A. "West Indies and British West African Policy in the Nineteenth Century--A Corrective Comment." Journal of African History, 15: 2 (1974), 247-59.

488 Greenfield, Sidney M. English Rustics in Black Skin: A Study of Modern Family Forms in a Pre-Industrialized Society. New Haven: College and University Publishers, 1966.

489 Guerin, Daniel. The West Indies and Their Future. London: Humanities Press, 1961.

490 Handler, Jerome S. A Guide to Source Materials for the Study of Barbados History, 1627-1834. Carbondale: Southern Illinois University Press, 1971.

491 _____, and Frederick W. Lange. Plantation Slavery in Barbados. Cambridge, Mass.: Harvard University Press, 1978.

492 Harlow, Vincent. A History of Barbados, 1625-1685. Oxford: Oxford University Press, 1926.

493 Harrison, David. "The Social Effects of Tourism on a Small Caribbean State: The Case of St. Vincent." Paper presented to the Society for Caribbean Studies, Surrey, U. K., April 1978.

494 James, C. L. R. Party Politics in the West Indies. San Juan, Trinidad: n. p., 1962.

495 League of Coloured Peoples. Memorandum on the Recommendations of the West Indian Royal Commission. London: L. C. P., 1940.

496 Lewis, Gordon K. The Growth of the Modern West Indies. New York: Modern Reader Paperbacks, 1968.

497 Lewis, Matthew G. Journal of a West India Proprietor. London: n. p., 1834.

498 Lowenthal, David. "Barbuda: The Past of a Negro Myth." Comparative Perspectives on Slavery in New World Plantation Societies. Ed. Vera Rubin and Arthur Tuden. New York: n. p., 1977, pp. 510-534.

499 Lynch, Louis. The Barbados Book. London: Andre Deutsch, 1964.

500 Merrill, Gordon E. The Historical Geography of St. Kitts
     and Nevis, the West Indies. Mexico, D. F.: Pan-Amer-
     ican Institute of Geography and History, 1958.

501 Otterbein, Keith F. The Andros Islanders. Kansas: Uni-
     versity of Kansas Press, 1966.

502 Oxaal, Ivar. "Race, Pluralism and Nationalism in the British
     Caribbean." Journal of Biosocial Science, Supplement
     No. 1 (July 1969), 153-62.

503 _____, and Wendell Bell. Decisions of Nationhood: Po-
     litical and Social Development in the British Caribbean.
     Denver: University of Denver Press, 1964.

504 Parsons, E. C. "Spirituals and Other Folklore from the Ba-
     hamas." Journal of American Folklore, 41 (October
     1928), 457-470.

505 Peach, Ceri. West Indian Migration to Britain: A Social
     Geography. London: Oxford University Press for the
     Institute of Race Relations, 1968.

506 Phillips, Andrew Peter. "The Development of a Modern La-
     bor Force in Antigua." Diss., University of California,
     Los Angeles, 1964.

507 Pitman, F. W. "Slavery on the British West India Plantations
     in the Eighteenth Century." Journal of Negro History, 11
     (October 1926).

508 Price, Edward T. "The Redlegs of Barbados." Yearbook As-
     sociation of Pacific Coast Geographers, 19 (1957), 35-39.

509 Ragatz, Lowell J. The Fall of the Planter Class in the Brit-
     ish Caribbean, 1763-1833. [1928] New York: Octagon
     Books, 1963.

510 _____, comp. A Guide for the Study of British Caribbean
     History, 1763-1834, including the Abolition and Emancipa-
     tion Movements. Washington, D.C.: Government Print-
     ing Office, 1932.

511 Rodney, Walter. The Groundings with My Brothers. London:
     Bogle-L'Ouverture Publications, 1969.

512 Rose, E. J. B., et al. Colour and Citizenship: A Report on
     British Race Relations. London: Oxford University Press
     for the Institute of Race Relations, 1969.

513 Russell, Richard J., and McIntire, William G. Barbuda Re-
     connaissance. Baton Rouge: Louisiana State University
     Press, 1966.

514 Saul, S. B. "The British West Indies in Depression, 1880-1914." Inter-American Economic Affairs, 12:3 (Winter 1958), 3-25.

515 Schuler, Monica. "Akan Slave Rebellions in the British Caribbean." Savacou, 1: 1 (June 1970), 8-31.

516 Spadoni, Robert Bernard. "National Identity Formation and Diffusion in the Commonwealth of the Bahamas: A Politico-Geographic Appraisal." Diss. University of Northern Colorado, 1977.

517 Sturge, Joseph and Thomas Harvey. The West Indies in 1837: Being the Journal of a Visit to Antigua, Montserrat, Dominica, St. Lucia, Barbados, and Jamaica. London: Frank Cass and Company, 1968.

518 Thomas, J. J. Froudacity: West Indian Fables by James Anthony Froude. London: New Beacon Books, 1969.

519 Thomas-Hope, Elizabeth. "British Subjects in a Foreign Land: West Indians in Central America and Cuba, 1840-1940." Paper presented to the Society for Caribbean Studies. Surrey, U.K., April 1978.

520 Tyson, J. D. Report on the Condition of Indians in Jamaica, British Guiana and Trinidad, 1938-39. Simla: Government of India Press, 1939.

521 Updike, John. "Letter from Anguilla." New Yorker (June 22, 1968), 70-80.

522 Watson, Karl Stewart. "The Civilised Island, Barbados, A Social History, 1750-1816." Diss. The University of Florida, 1975.

523 Wesley, Charles H. "The Free Colored Population in the British Empire." Journal of Negro History, 19 (1934), 137-70.

524 Williams, Eric E. Slavery to Chaguaramas. Port of Spain: P.N.M. Publishing Co., 1959.

525 Young, Sir William. An Account of the Black Charaibs in the Island of St. Vincent. London: J. Sewell, 1795.

DUTCH ANTILLES (incl. SURINAM)

526 Adhin, Jan Hansdew. Development Planning in Surinam in Historical Perspective (with Special Reference to the 10 Year Plan). New York: W. S. Heinman, 1961.

527 Balen, W. J. van. Ons Gebiedsdeel Curaçao. Haarlem:
     H. D. Tjeenk Willink & Zoons, 1938.

528 Boxer, C. R. The Dutch Seaborne Empire 1600-1800. Lon-
     don: Hutchinson, 1965.

529 Buschkens, W. F. L. The Family System of the Paramaibo
     Creoles. The Hague: Nijhoff, 1974.

530 Diekmann, Miep. Een Doekje voor het Bloeden (Koninkrijsk-
     verband). The Hague: Leopold, 1970.

531 Dupuis, Jacques. "Les paradoxes de Curaçao." Cahier
     d'Outre-Mer, 22 (1969), 63-74.

532 Encyclopedie van de Nederlandse Antillen. Amsterdam: El-
     sevier, 1969.

533 Ensberg, Louise. Boeken over Suriname; bibliografie van
     boeken uit of bevattende een beschrijving van Suriname
     als geheel. n. p., 1969.

534 Gastmann, Albert L. Historical Dictionary of the French and
     Netherlands Antilles. Metuchen, N. J.: Scarecrow Press,
     1978.

535 _____. The Politics of Surinam and the Netherlands An-
     tilles. (Caribbean Monograph Series, No. 3) Rio Piedras:
     Institute of Caribbean Studies, University of Puerto Rico,
     1968.

536 Goslinga, Cornelis Ch. Curaçao and Guzmán Blanco. The
     Hague: Nijhoff, 1975.

537 _____. The Dutch in the Caribbean. Assen, Netherlands:
     Van Gorcum, 1971.

538 Graves, Anne Victoria Adams. "The Present State of the
     Dutch Creole of the Virgin Islands." Diss. University
     of Michigan, 1977.

539 Groot, Silvia W. de. Djuka Society and Social Change: His-
     tory of an Attempt to Develop a Bush Negro Community in
     Surinam, 1917-1926. Assen, Neth.: Van Gorcum, 1969.

540 _____. From Isolation Towards Integration: The Surinam
     Maroons and Their Colonial Rulers. The Hague: Nijhoff,
     1977.

541 _____. "Maroons, Migration and Wage Labour in 19th and
     20th Century Surinam." Paper presented to the Society
     for Caribbean Studies, Surrey, U. K., April 1978.

542 Herskovits, Melville J. On Some Modes of Ethnographic Com-
prison. Netherlands West Indies: n.p., 1956.

543 _____, and F. S. Herskovits. Rebel Destiny: Among the
Bush Negroes of Dutch Guiana. New York: McGraw-Hill,
1934.

544 _____, and F. S. Herskovits. Suriname Folk-lore. New
York: Columbia University Press, 1936.

545 Hiss, Philip H. Netherlands America. New York: Duell,
Sloan and Pearce, 1943.

546 _____. A Selective Guide to the English Literature on the
Netherlands West Indies, with a Supplement on British
Guiana. New York: Netherlands Information Bureau,
1943.

547 Hoetink, Harmannus. "Curaçao como sociedad segmentada."
Revista de Ciencias Sociales, 4 (1960), 179-92.

548 _____. "Diferencias en relaciones raciales entre Curaçao
y Suriname." Revista de Ciencias Sociales, 5 (1966),
499-514.

549 Ismael, Joseph. De immigratie van Indonesiërs in Suriname.
Leiden: Luctor et Emergo, 1949.

550 Keur, Dorothy L. "The Nature of Recent Change in the Dutch
Windward Islands." International Journal of Comparative
Sociology, 5: 1 (March 1964), 40-47.

551 Lamur, H. E. The Demographic Evolution of Surinam, 1920-
1970. The Hague: Nijhoff, 1973.

552 Lier, R. A. J. van. The Development and Nature of Society
in the West Indies. Amsterdam: Indisch Instituut, 1960.

553 _____. Frontier Society: A Social Analysis of the History
of Surinam. The Hague: Nijhoff, 1971.

554 _____. "Negro Slavery in Surinam." Caribbean Historical
Review. 3-4 (December 1954), 108-48.

555 Malefijt, Annemarie de Waal. The Javanese of Surinam: Segment of a Plural Society. Assen, Neth.: Van Gorcum,
1963.

556 Marks, Amand F. Male and Female and the Afro-Curaçaoan
Household. The Hague: Nijhoff, 1976.

557 _____, and Romer, R. A., eds. Family and Kinship in

190 / Bibliography

Middle America and the Caribbean. Curaçao: University
of the Netherlands Antilles, 1978.

558 Rens, L. L. E. "Analysis of Annals Relating to Early Jewish
     Settlement in Surinam." Vox Guyanae, 1:1 (May 1954),
     19-38.

559 van der Elst, Dirk Hendrik. "The Bush Negro Tribes of Sur-
     inam, South America: A Synthesis." Diss. Northwestern
     University, 1970.

560 Voorhoeve, Jan. Kriorodron: An Anthology of Creole Liter-
     ature in Surinam. New Haven: Yale University Press,
     1974.

561 _____, and Antoon Donicie. Bibliographie du Négro-anglais
     du Surinam Avec une Appendice sur les langues créole
     parlées a l'intérieur du pays. The Hague: Martinus Nij-
     hoff, 1963.

FRENCH ANTILLES (see also HAITI)

562 Abonnenc, E., Hurault, J., and R. Saban. Bibliographie de
     la Guyane française; Tome I: Ouvrages et articles de
     langue française concernant la Guyane et les territoires
     avoisinants. Paris: Éditions Larose, 1957.

563 Allaire, Louis. "Later Prehistory in Martinique and the Is-
     land Caribs: Problems in Ethnic Identification." Diss.
     Yale University, 1977.

564 Atwood, Thomas. The History of the Island of Dominica.
     London: Frank Cass and Company, 1971.

565 Banbuck, C. A. Histoire politique, économique et sociale de
     la Martinique, 1635-1789. Forte-de-France: Société de
     Distribution et de Culture, 1972.

566 Benoist, Jean, ed. Les Sociétés antillaises: études anthro-
     pologiques. Montreal: University of Montreal, Depart-
     ment of Anthropology, 1966.

567 Bois, Etienne P. Les amerindiens de la Haute-Guyane fran-
     çaise. Paris: College de la Société de Pathologie Exo-
     tique, 1967.

568 Bouckson, Germain, and Edouard Bertrand. Les Antilles en
     question, assimilation et conflits de culture dans les DOM.
     Fort-de-France: n.p., 1972.

569 Breton, André, with Andre Masson. Martinique charmeuse de
     serpents. Paris: Editions du Sagittaire, 1948.

570 Capécia, Mayotte. Je suis martiniquaise. Paris: Corréa, 1948.

571 Chauleau, Liliane. Histoire Antillaise. [Vol. 5 of Encyclopédie Antillaise, Emile Desormeaux, ed.] Point-à-Pitre: Desormeaux, 1973.

572 _____. La société a la Martinique au XVIIe siècle (1635-1713). Caen: Ozanne, 1966.

573 Corzani, Jack. Splendeur et misère: l'exotisme littéraire aux Antilles. (Etudes et Documents, no. 2.) Point-à-Pitre. Guadeloupe: Groupe Universitaire de Recherches Inter-Caribes, 1969.

574 Crouse, Nellis M. The French Struggle for the West Indies 1665-1713. New York: Columbia University Press, 1943.

575 Dease, Barbara Crockett. "Negritude and the Mythopoeic Quest in Black Literature of French Expression." Diss. The Florida State University, 1976.

576 Debien, Gabriel. "Les Antilles française (1963-1967). Bibliographie des publications 1963-1967." Revue française d'histoire d'outre-mer, 53: 192/193 (1966), 245-313.

577 _____. "Le marronage aux Antilles françaises au XVIIe siècle." Caribbean Studies, 6: 3 (October 1966), 3-43.

578 _____. "Sources de 'histoire de 'esclavage aux Antilles." Revue de la Société Haïtiene d'Histoire, de Géographie et de Géologie, 34: 111 (January-April 1967), 12-48.

579 Dubrueil, Guy. "La famille martiniquaise: analyse et dynamique, Anthropologica, 7: 1, (1965), 103-29.

580 Du Tertre, R. P. Histoire generale des Isles d'Amérique habitées par les français, 1667-1671. Fort-de-France: Société de Distribution et de Culture, 1972.

581 Eccles, W. J. France in America. New York: Harper & Row, 1972.

582 Fabre, Camille. Trois Siècles d'histoire de la côte sous le vent Vieux-Habitants. Guadeloupe: n.p., 1972.

583 Fouchard, Jean. Les marrons de la liberté. Paris: Editions de l'Ecole, 1972.

584 Gaston-Martin. Histoire de 'esclavage dans les colonies françaises. Paris: Presses Universitaires de France, 1948.

585 Gisler, Antoine. L'Esclavage aux Antilles françaises (XVIIe-

XIXe siècle): contribution au problème de 'esclavage. Fribourg, Switzerland: Editions Universitaires, 1965.

586 Goyheneche, E., and M. Nicolas. Des îles et des hommes. 2 vols. Fort-de-France: Editions des Horizons Caraïbes, 1956-1957.

587 Guadelupe. Boulogne: Deboise, 1972.

588 Horowitz, Michael M. Morne-Paysan: Peasant Village in Martinique. New York: Holt, Rinehart and Winston, 1967.

589 Hurault, Jean. Africains de Guyane: la vie matérielle et l'art des Noirs Réfugiés de Guyane. La Haye-Paris: Mouton, 1970.

590 _____. Les Noir Réfugiés boni de la Guyane Française. Dakar: n.p., 1961.

591 Hymans, Jacques Louis. "French Influences on Leopold Senghor's Theory of Négritude, 1928-1948." Race, 7 (1965-6), 365-70.

592 Jourdain, E. Du français aux parles créoles. Paris: Klincksieck, 1956.

593 Lacour, M. A. Histoire de la Guadeloupe, 4 vols. Paris: Maissoneuve et Larose, 1960.

594 McCloy, Shelby T. The Negro in the French West Indies. Lexington: University of Kentucky Press, 1966.

595 Martinau, Alfred and Louis Philippe May. Trois Siècles d'histoire antillaise (1635-1935). Paris: Le Roux, 1935.

596 Martinique. Paris: Delinas, 1972.

597 Mattioni, M., and Nicolas, M. Art précolombien de la Martinique. Fort-de-France: Musée Départemental de la Martinique, 1972.

598 Mirot, Sylvie. "Un document inédit sur le marronnage à la Guyane Francaise au XVIIIe siècle." Revue d'Histoire des Colonies, 41 (1954), 245-56.

599 Moskos, Charles C. The Sociology of Political Independence: A Study of Nationalist Attitudes Among West Indian Leaders. Cambridge, Massachusetts: Schenkman, 1968.

600 Murch, Arvin. Black Frenchmen: The Political Integration of the French Antilles. Cambridge, Mass.: Schenkman, 1971.

601 Nosel, José. "Les Etudiants à la Martinique." in "Problèmes universitaires des Antilles-Guyane française," Cahier de C. E. R. A. G. [Centre d'Etudes Regionales Antilles-Guyane], 18 (1969), pp. 36-71.

602 Petit Jean-Roget, Jacques. La Gaoulé, la révolte, de la Martinique en 1717. Fort-de-France: Société d'Histoire de la Martinique, 1966.

603 Petit Jean-Roget, Jacques. "Les juifs à la Martinique sous l'ancien régime." Revue d'Histoire des Colonies (1956), 138-58.

604 Piquion, René. Manuel de negritude. Port-au-Prince: Henri Duchamps, 1965.

605 Rennard, J. Histoire réligieuse des Antilles Françaises des origines à 1914. Paris: Larose, 1954.

606 Sartre, Jean-Paul. Black Orpheus. Tr. S. W. Allen. Paris: Presence Africaine, 1963.

607 Satineau, Maurice. Histoire de la Guadeloupe (1625-1789). Paris: Payot, 1928.

608 Schoelcher, Victor. Esclavage et colonisation. Paris: Presses Universitaires de France, 1848.

609 Smith, M. G. The Plural Society in the West Indies. Berkeley: University of California Press, 1965.

610 Zolberg, Aristide R. "Frantz Fanon: A Gospel for the Damned." Encounter 27 (November 1966), 56-63.

611 Zylberberg, Jacques. "Outline of the Sociology of Guadelupe." Civilisations, 16: 4 (1966), 478-499.

OTHER CARIBBEAN

612 Alvarez Nazario, Manuel. El elemento negroide en el Español de Puerto Rico. San Juan: Instituto de Cultura Puertoriquena, 1961.

613 Baralt, Guillermo Antonio. "Slave Conspiracies and Uprisings in Puerto Rico, 1796-1848." Diss. The University of Chicago, 1977.

614 Campbell, A. A. St. Thomas Negroes: A Study of Personality and Culture. Washington, D. C.: American Psychological Association, 1943.

615 Coll y Toste, Cayetano. Història de la esclavitud en Puerto

Rico. San Juan: Sociedad de Autores Puertoriqueños, 1969.

616 Díaz Soler, Luis M. Historia de la esclavitud negra en Puerto Rico (1493-1890). Madrid: Ediciones de la Uni- de Puerto Rico, 1953.

617 Hill, Marnesba D. and Harold B. Schleifer. Puerto Rican Authors: A Biobibliographic Handbook. Metuchen, N.J.: Scarecrow Press, 1974.

618 Janer, J. L. "Population Growth in Puerto Rico and Its Re- lation to Time Changes in Vital Statistics." Human Bi- ology, 17: 4 (1945), 267-313.

619 La Ruffa, Anthony L. San Cipriano: Life in a Puerto Rican Community. New York: Gordon and Breach, 1971.

620 Ledesma, Moises. Bibliografía cultural de Puerto Rico (ano- tada). New York: Plus Ultra Educational Publishers, 1970.

621 Lewis, Oscar and Douglas Butterworth. A Study of Slum Cul- ture: Background Studies for "La Vida." New York: Random House, 1969.

622 McCoy, James A. "The Bomba and Aguinaldo of Puerto Rico as They Evolved from Indigenous, African and European Cultures." Diss. Florida State University, 1968.

623 Maldonado-Denis, Manuel. Puerto Rico: A Socio-Historic Interpretation. New York: Random House, 1972.

624 Mathews, Thomas G. "The Question of Color in Puerto Rico." Slavery and Race Relations in Latin America. Ed. Robert B. Toplin. Westport, Conn.: Greenwood Publishing Com- pany, 1974, pp. 299-324.

625 _____, et al. Politics and Economics in the Caribbean. Rio Piedras: ICS, Special Study No. 3, 1966.

626 Megenney, W. W. "Black Puerto Rican: an Analysis of Ra- cial Attitudes." Phylon, 35 (March 1974), 83-93.

627 Mintz, Sidney. "Labor and Sugar in Puerto Rico and Jamaica, 1800-1850." Comparative Studies in Society and History, 1 (1959), 273-281.

628 Probinsky, Brent L. "A Political History of the Bahama Is- lands, 1967-1973: From Black Majority Rule to Indepen- dence." Latin Americanist (Gainesville, Florida), 13:4 (June 1978), 1-3.

629 Puerto Rican Research and Resources Center. The Puerto

Ricans: An Annotated Bibliography. Ed. Paquita Vivó. New York: Bowker, 1973.

630 Rodríguez Cruz, Juan. "Las relaciones raciales en Puerto Rico." Revista de Ciencias Sociales, 9: 4 (1965), 373-386.

631 Rogler, Charles. "Morality of Race Mixing in Puerto Rico." Social Forces, 25 (October 1946), 77-81.

632 _____. "The Role of Semantics in the Study of Race Distance in Puerto Rico." Social Forces, 22 (1943-4), 448-53.

633 _____. "Some Situational Aspects of Race Relations in Puerto Rico." Social Forces, 27 (1949), 72-77.

634 Smith, M. G. Kinship and Community in Carriacou. New Haven: Yale University Press, 1962.

635 Soler, Luiz Diaz. Historia de la esclavitud negra en Puerto Rico, 1493-1890. Madrid: n.p., n.d.

636 Tumin, Melvin M. Social Class and Social Change in Puerto Rico. Princeton: Princeton University Press, 1961.

637 Williams, Eric E. "Race Relations in Puerto Rico and the Virgin Islands." Foreign Affairs, 23 (January 1945).

MEXICO

638 Aguilera, Carmen. "Una posible diedad negroide en el panteón azteca." Estudios de Cultura Nahuatl, (Mexico City), 9 (1971), 47-56.

639 Aguirre Beltrán, Gonzalo. La población negra de México, 1519-1810: Estudio etnohistórico. México, D. F.: Ediciones Fuente Cultural, 1946.

640 _____. Problemas de la población indígna de la Cuenca de Tepelcatepec. Mexico: Instituto Indigenista Nacional, 1952.

641 _____. "The Slave Trade in Mexico." Hispanic American Historical Review, 24 (1944): 412-31.

642 _____. "Tribal Origins of Slaves in Mexico and Notes on the History of the Slave Trade." Journal of Negro History, 31 (July 1946), 269-352.

643 Almstedt, Ruth. Bibliography of the Diegueno Indians. Ramona, Calif.: Ballena Press, 1974.

196 / Bibliography

644 Anderson, Arthur J. O., Frances Berdan, and James Lockhart, eds. Beyond the Codices: The Nahua View of Colonial Mexico. Berkeley: University of California Press,
1976.

645 Andrade, Vicente de Paula. Ensayo bibliográfico mexicano
del siglo XVII. 2nd ed. México: J. Medina, 1971.

646 Anton, Ferdinand. Women in Precolumbian America. New
York: Abner Schram, 1973.

647 Arrom, Sylvia. "Women and the Family in Mexico City, 1800-
1857." Diss. Stanford University, 1978.

648 Ashburn, P. M. The Ranks of Death: A Medical History of
the Conquest of America. New York: Coward-McCann,
1947.

649 Barlow, Robert H. The Extent of the Empire of the Culhua
Mexica. Ibero-Americana, no. 28. Berkeley: University of California Press, 1949.

650 Béjar Navarro, Raúl. "Prejuicio y discriminación racial en
México." Revista Mexicana de Sociología, 31:2 (April-
June 1969), 417-433.

651 Beltrán, Gonzalo Aguirre. La población negra de México:
estudio etnohistórico. 2nd ed. México: Fondo de Cultura Económica, 1972.

652 Borah, Woodrow. "Race and Class in Mexico." Pacific Historical Review, 23 (1953): 331-42.

653 Boyd-Bowman, Peter. "Negro Slaves in Early Colonial Mexico." The Americas, 26:2 (October 1969), 134-151.

654 Brady, Robert L. "The Domestic Slave in Sixteenth-Century
Mexico." The Americas, 24:3 (January 1968), 281-289.

655 _____. "The Emergence of a Negro Class in Mexico, 1524-
1640." Diss. State University of Iowa, 1965.

656 Brundage, Burr C. A Rain of Darts: The Mexica Aztecs.
Austin: University of Texas Press, 1972.

657 Burland, Cottie A. The Gods of Mexico. New York: Capri-
corn Books, 1968.

658 Campos, Rubén M. "La tradición del negrito poeta." El
Folklore Literario de México. Mexico City: Secretaría
de Educación Pública, 1929.

659 Carroll, Patrick J. "Estudio sociodemográfico de personas

de sangre negra en Jalapa, 1791." Historia Mexicana, 23 (1973): 111-25.

660 _____. "Mandinga: The Evolution of a Mexican Runaway Slave Community: 1725-1827." Comparative Studies in Society and History, 19:4 (October 1977), 488-505.

661 Caso, Alfonso. The Aztecs: People of the Sun. Tr. Lowell Dunham. Norman, Oklahoma: University of Oklahoma Press, 1958.

662 Cervantes de Salazar, Francisco. México en 1554. Mexico City: n.p., 1939.

663 Chance, John K. and William B. Taylor. "Estate and Class in a Colonial City: Oaxaca in 1792." Comparative Studies in Society and History, 19 (October 1977), 454-487.

664 Cline, Howard F. "Mexican Community Studies." Hispanic American Historical Review, 32 (May 1952), 212-242.

665 _____. Mexico, Revolution to Evolution: 1940-1960. London: Oxford University Press, 1962.

666 _____. The United States and Mexico. Cambridge, Mass.: Harvard University Press, 1953.

667 Coe, Michael D. The Maya. New York: Praeger, 1956.

668 _____. Mexico. New York: Praeger, 1962.

669 Comas, Juan. "Indígenas de México." Revista Población, 1 (August 1953), 36-44.

670 Cone, Cynthia A. "Fields and Factories: Dynamics of Migration in Mexico." Diss. University of Minnesota, 1976.

671 Cook, Sherburne F. The Extent and Significance of Disease Among the Indians of Baja California, 1697-1773. Berkeley: University of California Press, 1937.

672 "The Incidence and Significance of Disease Among the Aztecs and Related Tribes." Hispanic American Historical Review, 26 (1946): 320-25.

673 _____, and Woodrow Borah. The Aboriginal Population of Central Mexico on the Eve of the Spanish Conquest. Berkeley: University of California Press, 1963.

674 _____, and _____. The Indian Population of Central Mexico, 1531-1610. Berkeley: University of California Press, 1960.

675 Cooper, Donald. Epidemic Disease in Mexico City, 1761-1813. Austin: University of Texas Press, 1965.

676 Covarrubias, Miguel. Indian Art of Mexico and Central America. New York: Alfred A. Knopf, 1957.

677 Dahl, V. C. "Alien Labor in the Gulf Coast of Mexico, 1880-1900." The Americas, 17: 1 (1960), 21-35.

678 Davidson, David. "Negro Slave Control and Resistance in Colonial Mexico, 1519-1650." Hispanic American Historical Review, 46 (1966) 235-53.

679 Davies, Nigel. The Aztecs: A History. London: Macmillan, 1973.

680 Diaz del Castillo, Bernal. The Discovery and Conquest of Mexico. Tr. A. P. Maudslay. New York: Farrar, Straus, and Cudahy, 1956.

681 Duran, Fr. Diego. The Aztecs: The History of the Indians of New Spain. Tr. Doris Heyden and Fernando Horcasitas. New York: Orion Press, 1964.

682 Dusenberry, William H. "Discriminatory Aspects of Legislation in Colonial Mexico." Journal of Negro History, 33 (1948), 284-302.

683 Edmondson, Munro S. A Triangulation on the Culture of Mexico. New Orleans: Tulane University: Middle American Research Inst., 1957. Publication 17, pp. 201-240.

684 Erasmus, Charles J., Solomon Miller, and Louis C. Faron. Contemporary Change in Traditional Communities of Mexico and Peru. Champaign: University of Illinois Press, 1967.

685 Falcón, Romana. El agrarismo en Veracruz, 1928-1935. Mexico City: El Colegio de México, 1977.

686 Friedrich, Paul. "Cacique: The Recent History and Present Structure of Politics in a Tarascan Village." Diss. Yale University, 1957.

687 Gamio, Manuel and Jose Vasconcelos. Aspects of Mexican Civilization. Chicago: University of Chicago Press, 1926.

688 _____. "Incorporating the Indian in the Mexican Population." Latin American Civilization. Ed. Harold A. Bierck. Boston: Allyn and Bacon, 1967, pp. 203-212.

689 García Quintana, Josefina. "Bibliografía náhuatl; 1966-1969." Estudios de Cultura Nahuatl, 9 (1971), 273-293.

690 Gibson, Charles. The Aztecs Under Spanish Rule: A His-

tory of the Indians of the Valley of Mexico, 1519-1810. Stanford: Stanford University Press, 1964.

691 _____. Tlaxcala in the Sixteenth Century. New Haven: Yale University Press, 1952.

692 Gordillo Ortíz, Octavio. "Bibliografía del descubrimiento y conquista de México y Centroamérica." In Congreso Mexicano-Centroamericano de Historia, Mexico City: 1972; Estúdios indigenistas; memoria del primer ..., vol. 2: Exploraciones y conquista en México y Centroamérica. México: Sociedad Mexicana de Geografía y Estadística, 1972. pp. 249-262.

693 Greenleaf, Richard E. "The Obraje in the Late Mexican Colony." The Americas, 23 (1967), 227-50.

694 _____, and Michael C. Meyer. Research in Mexican History: Topics, Methodology, Sources and a Practical Guide to Field Research. Lincoln: University of Nebraska Press, 1973.

695 Guthrie, Chester. "Riots in Seventeenth-Century Mexico." Greater America: Essays in Honor of Herbert Eugene Bolton. Ed. Adele Odgen. Berkeley: University of California Press, 1945, pp. 243-258.

696 Harkányi, Katalin. The Aztecs: Bibliography. San Diego, California: State College Library, 1971.

697 Hoberman, Louisa. "Bureaucracy and Disaster: Mexico City and the Flood of 1629." Journal of Latin American Studies, 6 (1974): 211-30.

698 Huerta Preciado, Maria Teresa. Rebeliones indígenas en el noreste de México en la época colonial. Mexico City: n.p., 1966.

699 Instituto Nacional Indigenista. Densidad de la población de habla indígena en la República Mexicana (por entidades federativas y municipios conforme al Censo de 1940). Mexico: I.N.I., 1950.

700 Israel, J. I. Race, Class and Politics in Colonial Mexico, 1610-1670. London: Oxford University Press, 1975.

701 Keen, Benjamin. The Aztec Image in Western Thought. New Brunswick: Rutgers University Press, 1971.

702 Koslow, Lawrence, ed. The Future of Mexico. Tempe, Arizona: Center for Latin American Studies, Arizona State University, 1977.

703 Kubler, George. The Art and Architecture of Ancient America:

The Mexican, Maya and Andean Peoples. Baltimore: Penguin Books, 1962.

704 Ladd, Doris S. The Mexican Nobility at Independence, 1780-1826. Austin: University of Texas Press, 1976.

705 Leon-Portilla, Miguel. Aztec Thought and Culture: A Study of the Ancient Nahuatl Mind. Tr. Jack Emory Davis. Norman: University of Oklahoma Press, 1963.

706 Lewis, Oscar. The Children of Sanchez: Autobiography of a Mexican Family. New York: Vintage Books, 1961.

707 _____. Life in a Mexican Village: Tepoztlan Restudied. Urbana: Illinois University Press, 1951.

708 Lord, Peter P. The Peasantry as an Emerging Political Factor in Mexico, Bolivia, and Venezuela. University of Wisconsin Land Tenure Center, Reprint No. 35. Madison: The Center, 1965.

709 Lopez Sarrelangue, Delfina Esmeralda. La nobleza indigena de Pátzcuaro en la época virreinal. Mexico City: n. p., 1965.

710 Love, Edgar F. "Legal Restrictions on Afro-Indian Relations in Colonial Mexico." Journal of Negro History, 55:2 (April 1970), 131-139.

711 _____. "Marriage Patterns of Persons of African Descent in a Colonial Mexico City Parish." Hispanic American Historical Review, 51: 1 (1971), 79-91.

712 _____. "Negro Resistance to Spanish Rule in Colonial Mexico." Journal of Negro History, 52:2 (April 1967), 89-103.

713 McAlister, Lyle N. "Social Structure and Social Change in New Spain." Hispanic American Historical Review, 43 (1963): 349-70.

714 Marshall, C. E. "The Birth of the Mestizo in New Spain." Hispanic American Historical Review, 19 (1939): 161-84.

715 Melgarejo, Antonio D. Los crímenes del Zapatismo. Mexico City: Editores Rojas, 1913.

716 Meyer, Michael C. and William Sherman. The Course of Mexican History. New York: Oxford University Press, 1979.

717 Morley, Sylvanus G. The Ancient Maya. Revised by G. W. Brainerd. Stanford: Stanford University Press, 1965.

718 Navarette, Carlos. "Fuentes para la historia cultural de los
     Zoques." Anales de antropología, 7 (April-June, 1970),
     207-246.

719 Padden, Robert C. The Hummingbird and the Hawk: Con-
     quest and Sovereignty in the Valley of Mexico, 1503-1541.
     New York: Harper & Row, 1970.

720 Paddock, John. "Tomorrow in Ancient Mesoamerica." Texas
     Quarterly, 2 (1959): 78-98.

721 Palmer, Colin A. "Negro Slavery in Mexico, 1570-1650."
     Diss. University of Wisconsin, 1970.

722 _____. Slaves of the White God: Blacks in Mexico. Cam-
     bridge: Cambridge University Press, 1976.

723 Paz, Octavio. The Labyrinth of Solitude: Life and Thought
     in Mexico. Tr. Lysander Kemp. New York: Grove
     Press, 1961.

724 Peterson, Frederick. Ancient Mexico. An Introduction to
     the Pre-Hispanic Cultures. London: Allen and Unwin
     Ltd., 1959.

725 Powell, Philip W. Soldiers, Indians and Silver. Tempe,
     Arizona: Center for Latin American Studies, Arizona
     State University, 1977.

726 Powell, T. G. "Mexican Intellectuals and the Indian Question,
     1876-1911." Hispanic American Historical Review, 48:1
     (February 1968), 19-36.

727 Raat, William D. "Los intelectuales, el positivismo y la
     questión indígena." História Mexicana, 20 (January-
     March 1971), 412-27.

728 Reed, Nelson. The Caste War of Yucatán. Stanford: Stan-
     ford University Press, 1964.

729 Rojas, Pedro. The Art and Architecture of Mexico, from
     10,000 B.C. to the Present Day. Reltham, Middlesex:
     Hamlyn Publishing Group, 1968.

730 Romanucci Schwartz, Lola. "Morality, Conflict and Violence
     in a Mexican Mestizo Village." Diss. Indiana Univer-
     sity, 1962.

731 Rounds, Christopher Robert. "From Hacienda to Ejido: Land
     Reform and Economic Development in Yautepec, Morelos,
     1920-1970." Diss. State University of New York at
     Stony Brook, 1977.

732 Sauer, C. O. The Aboriginal Population of Northwestern Mexico. Berkeley: University of California Press, 1935.

733 Sejourné, Laurette. Burning Water: Thought and Religion in Ancient Mexico. New York: Grove Press, 1960.

734 Simpson, N. Eyler. The Ejido: Mexico's Way Out. Chapel Hill: University of North Carolina Press, 1937.

735 Sotelo Inclán, Jesús. Raíz y razón de Zapata: Investigación histórica. Mexico City: Editorial Etnos, 1943.

736 Tannenbaum, Frank. The Mexican Agrarian Revolution. New York: Macmillan, 1929.

737 _____. Peace by Revolution: Mexico After 1910. New York: Columbia University Press, 1933; paperback edition, 1966.

738 Taracena, Alfonso. La tragedia Zapatista: Historia de la revolución del sur. Mexico City: Editorial Bolivar, 1932.

739 Taylor, William B. Drinking, Homicide, and Rebellion in Colonial Mexican Villages. Stanford: Stanford University Press, 1979.

740 Tjarks, Alícia. "Demographic, Ethnic and Occupational Structure of New Mexico, 1790." The Americas, 35:1 (July 1978), 35-88.

741 Tutino, John Mark. "Creole Mexico: Spanish Elites, Haciendas, and Indian Towns, 1750-1810." Diss. The University of Texas at Austin, 1976.

742 Uribe de Fernández de Córdoba, Susana. "Bibliografía histórica mexicana." Historia Mexicana, 16: 1 (July-September 1966), 93-153.

743 Vaillant, G. C. The Aztecs of Mexico. Baltimore: Penguin Books, 1950.

744 Valle, Rafael Heliodoro. Bibliografia Maya. [1937]. New York: B. Franklin, 1971.

745 Velázquez, María del Carmen. Documentos para la historia de México. Mexico City: n.p., 1963.

746 Von Hagen, Victor W. The Aztec: Man and Tribe. New York: New American Library, 1961.

747 Wagner, H. O. "Subsistence Potential and Population Density

of the Maya on the Yucatan Peninsula and Causes for the Decline in Population in the Fifteenth Century." Verhandlugen des 38 Internationalen Amerikanistenkongresses, Stuttgart-München 1968. Vol. 1. Munich. 1969, 179-96.

748 Wauchope, Robert. The Indian Background of Latin American History: The Maya, Aztec, Inca and Their Predecessors. New York: Alfred A. Knopf, 1970.

749 Weyl, Nathaniel and Sylvia. The Reconquest of Mexico: The Years of Lázaro Cárdenas. London: Oxford University Press, 1939.

750 Whetten, Nathan L. Rural Mexico. Chicago: University of Chicago Press, 1948.

751 _____, and R. G. Burnight. "Internal Migration in Mexico." Estadística, 16 (1956), 65-77.

752 Wolf, Eric R. "The Indian in Mexican Society." Alpha Kappa Delta: A Sociological Journal, 30 (Winter 1960), 3-6.

753 _____. Sons of the Shaking Earth. Chicago: University of Chicago Press, 1959.

754 Zavala, Sílvio Arturo. Los esclavos índios en Nueva España. Mexico City: Colegio Nacional, 1967.

755 Zorita, Alonso de. Life and Labor in Ancient Mexico. Tr. Benjamin Keen. New Brunswick: Rutgers University Press, 1963.

CENTRAL AMERICA

756 Adams, Richard N. Cultural Survey of Panama, Nicaragua, Guatemala, El Salvador and Honduras. Washington, D.C.: Pocket Books, 1960.

757 Anguizola, Gustave. "Negroes in the Building of the Panama Canal." Phylon, 29: 4 (Winter 1968), 351-359.

758 Arosemena Moreno, Julio. "Documentación relativa al negro en Panamá." Loteria, 14: 164 (July 1969), 49-60.

759 Asturias, Miguel Angel. Mulata de tal. Buenos Aires: Editorial Losada, 1963.

760 _____. Sociologia guatemálteca: el problema social del índio. Guatemala City: Universidade de Guatemala. [1923]. Tempe: Arizona State University, 1977.

761 _____. Viento fuerte. Buenos Aires: Editorial Losada,
1955.

762 Biesanz, John and Mavis Biesanz. The People of Panama.
New York: Columbia University Press, 1955.

763 Bishop, Hezekiah Adolfo. "Bidialectal Traits of West Indians
in the Panama Canal Zone." Diss. Columbia University
Teachers College, 1976.

764 Bryce-LaPorte, Roy. "Immigration, Nationality and Development: Blacks in Panama and Central America." Paper
presented to the Symposium on the Political Economy of
the Black World, U.C.L.A., May 11, 1979.

765 Castillero Calvo, Afredo. La sociedad panameña: História
de su formación e integración. Panama: Comisión de
Estudios Interdisciplinarios para el Desarrollo de la Na-
cionalidad, Editora Lemania, S.A., 1970.

766 Chinchilla Aguilar, Ernesto. La vida moderna en Centroamérica. Guatemala City: Ed. Jose de Pineda Ibarra,
1977.

767 Coelho, Ruy Galvão de Andrade. "The Black Carib of Honduras: A Study in Acculturation." Diss., Northwestern
University, 1955.

768 Conzimius, E. "Ethnographical Notes on the Black Carib."
American Anthropologist, 30 (April 1928), 183-205.

769 Cosminsky, Sheila. "Interethnic Relations in Punta Gorda,
British Honduras: A Preliminary Report." Brandeis
University, Waltham, Mass. (1966), mimeo.

770 Diez Castillo, Luis A. Los cimarrones y la esclavitud en
Panamá. Panamá: Editorial Litografica, 1968.

771 Dobles Segreda, Luis. Indice bibliográfico de Costa Rica.
11 vols. San José, C.R.: Impr. Lehmann, Associacíon
Costarricense de Bibliotecários, 1927-1968.

772 Duncan, Quince, and Meléndez, Carlos. El negro en Costa
Rica. San José: Editoral Costa Rica, 1972.

773 Funes, Matías. Oro y miseria, las minas de Rosário. Honduras: n.p., 1966.

774 García, Miguel Angel. Anuario bibliográfico hondureño, 1961-
1971. Tegucigalpa: Banco Central de Honduras, 1973.

775 González, Nancie L. Solien. Black Carib Household Structure.
Seattle: University of Washington Press, 1969.

776 _____. "Changes in Black Carib Kinship Terminology." Southwestern Journal of Anthropology, 16: 2 (Summer 1960), 144-159.

777 Hedrick, Basil C. and Anne K. Historical Dictionary of Panama. Metuchen, N.J.: Scarecrow Press, Inc., 1970.

778 Helms, Mary W. Asang: Adaptations to Culture Contact in a Miskito Community. Gainesville: University of Florida Press, 1971.

779 Jackson, Richard L. "La presencia negra en la obra de Rubén Darío." Revista Iberoamericana, 22 (1967) 395-417.

780 Jones, Chester Lloyd. Costa Rica and Civilization in the Caribbean. Madison: University of Wisconsin Press, 1935.

781 Kepner, Charles David. Social Aspects of the Banana Industry. New York: P. S. King and Son, Ltd., 1936.

782 Markman, Sidney D., comp. Colonial Central America: A Bibliography. Tempe, Arizona: Center for Latin American Studies, Arizona State University, 1977.

783 Meléndez, Carlos and Quince Duncan. El Negro en Costa Rica. San José: Editorial Costa Rica, 1972.

784 Minkel, Clarence W. and Ralph H. Alderman. A Bibliography of British Honduras, 1900-1970. East Lansing: Latin American Studies Center, Michigan State University, 1970.

785 Miralda, Paca Navas de. Barro. Guatemala: Editorial Ministerio de Educación Pública, n.d.

786 Moore, Richard E. Historical Dictionary of Guatemala. rev. ed. Metuchen, N.J.: Scarecrow Press, Inc., 1973.

787 Olien, Michael D. The Negro in Costa Rica: The Role of an Ethnic Minority in a Developing Society. Winston-Salem, N.C.: Wake Forest University Overseas Research Center, 1970.

788 Pérez-Venero, Mirna Miriam. "A Novelist's Erotic Racial Revenge." Caribbean Review. 4: 4 (October-December 1972), 24-27.

789 _____. "Raza, color y prejuicios en la novelistica panameña contemporánea de Tema Canalero." Diss., Louisiana State University, 1973.

790 Reina, Ruben E. Chinautla, a Guatemalan Indian Community. New Orleans: L.S.U. Press, 1960.

791 Seelye, A. Ned and María Guadalupe Mirón. "Phenotype

and Occupational Mobility in Guatemala City: A Preliminary Survey," Science Education 54:1 (January-March
1970), 13-16.

792 Sherman, William L. Forced Native Labor in Sixteenth-Century Central America. Lincoln: University of Nebraska
Press, 1979.

793 Sines, Jorge A., Edwin M. Shook and Michael D. Olien. Anthropological Bibliography of Aboriginal Panama. San
José, Costa Rica: Tropical Science Center, 1965.

794 Snarr, D. N. and E. L. Brown. "Social and Economic Change
in Central America and Panama; An Annotated Bibliography." International Review of Modern Sociology, 2 (March,
1972), 102-115.

795 Stephens, J. L. and Dean C. "Belize: A Story of Practical
Amalgamation; excerpts from Incidents of Travel in Cen-
tral America, Chiapas and Yucatán." Journal of Negro
History, 30 (October 1945), 432-6.

796 Tabar Cruz, Pedro. "La esclavitud del negro en Guatemala."
Antropología e Historia de Guatemala, 17: 1 (January
1965), 3-14.

797 Taylor, Douglas MacRae. The Black Carib of British Honduras. New York: Viking Fund Publications in Anthropology No. 17, 1951.

798 Vieytez, A. "La emigración salvadoreña a Honduras." Estudios Centro-Americanos, 254/255 (extra issue, El Con-
flicto Honduras-El Salvador). (1969), 399-406.

799 Whetten, Nathan L. Guatemala: The Land and the People.
New Haven: Yale University Press, 1961.

800 White, Leland Ross. "The Development of Racial and Ethnic
Relations in British Honduras during the Nineteenth Century." Diss. University of Missouri, 1969.

801 Zárate, A. O. Principales padrones de migración interna en
Guatemala. Guatemala: n.p., 1967.

SOUTH AMERICA

ARGENTINA

802 Chace, Russell Edward, Jr. "The African Impact on Colonial
Argentina." Diss. University of California, Santa Barbara, 1969.

803 Endrek, Emiliano. El mestizaje en Córdoba: Siglo XVIII y
     princípios del XIX. Córdoba: Universidad Nacional de
     Córdoba, 1966.

804 _____. El mestizaje en el Tucumán. Siglo XVII. Demo-
     grafía comparada. Tucumán, Argentina: n. p. , 1967.

805 Germani, Gino. Estructura social de la argentina. Buenos
     Aires: Bibliotica M. Belgrano, 1955.

806 Goldberg, Marta B. "La población negra y mulata de la ciu-
     dad de Buenos Aires, 1810-1840." Desarrollo Económico,
     16 (April-June 1976).

807 Johnson, Lyman L. "Manumission in Colonial Buenos Aires,
     1776-1810." Hispanic American Historical Review, 59:
     2 (May 1979), 258-279.

808 Masini, José Luis. La esclavitud negra en Mendoza: epoca
     independiente. Mendoza: Talleres Gráficos D'Accurzio,
     1962.

809 Molinari, Diego Luis. La trata de negros. 2nd ed. Buenos
     Aires: Facultad de Ciencias Económicas, Universidad de
     Buenos Aires, 1944.

810 Molinari, José Luis. "Los indios y los negros durante las
     invasiones al Rio de la Plata, en 1806 y 1807." Boletín
     de la Academia Nacional de Historia, 24: 2 (1963), 639-
     672.

811 Reina, Ruben E. Paraná: Social Boundaries in an Argentine
     City. Austin: University of Texas Press, 1973.

812 Rodríguez Molas, Ricardo. "Algunas aspectos del negro en la
     sociedad Rioplatense del siglo XVIII." Anuario del Insti-
     tuto de Investigaciones Históricas, 3: 3 (1958) 81-106.

813 _____. La música y la danza de los negros en el Buenos
     Aires de los siglos XVIII y XIX. Buenos Aires: Clío,
     1957.

814 Scheuss de Studer, Elena F. La trata de negros en el Río
     de la Plata durante el siglo XVIII. Buenos Aires: De-
     partamento Editorial, Universidad de Buenos Aires, 1958.

815 Scobie, James F. Argentina: A City and a Nation. New
     York: Oxford University Press, 1964.

816 _____. Revolution on the Pampas. Austin: University of
     Texas Press, 1964.

817 Sempat Assadourian, Carlos. El trafico de esclavos en Cór-

208 / Bibliography

doba, 1588-1610. Córdoba: Universidad Nacional de Córdoba, 1965.

818 _____. El tráfico de esclavos en Córdoba de Angola a Potosí: Siglos XVI-XVII. Córdoba: Universidad Nacional de Códoba, 1966.

819 Service, Elman R. and Helen Service. Tobatí, Paraguayan Town. Chicago: University of Chicago Press, 1954.

820 Solberg, Carl A. Immigration and Nationalism: Argentina and Chile, 1890-1914. Austin: University of Texas Press, 1970.

821 Somoza, J. L., and A. E. Lattes. Muestras de los dos primeros censos nacionales de población, 1869 y 1895. Buenos Aires: n.p., 1967.

822 Studer, Elena F. S. La trata de negros en el Rio de la Plata durante el siglo XVIII. Buenos Aires: n.p., 1958.

823 Wright, Ione and Lisa M. Nekhom. Historical Dictionary of Argentina. Metuchen, N.J.: Scarecrow Press, Inc., 1978.

BOLIVIA

824 Antezana Villagrán, J. El índio y la distribución de la tierra en Bolivia. La Paz: Universidad Interamericana, 1944.

825 Carter, William E. "The Ambiguity of Reform: Highland Bolivian Peasants and Their Land." Diss. Columbia University, 1963.

826 _____. Aymara Communities and the Bolivian Agrarian Reform. University of Florida Monographs, Social Sciences, No. 24. Gainesville: University of Florida, 1964.

827 Catálogo del libro potosino. Potosí: Universidad Boliviana Mayor "Tomás Frias," 1973.

828 Dandler-Hanhart, Jorge. "Local Group, Community and Nation: A Study of Changing Structure in Ucureña, Bolivia (1935-1952)." M.A. Thesis. University of Wisconsin, 1967.

829 Heath, Dwight B. Historical Dictionary of Bolivia. Metuchen, N.J.: Scarecrow Press, Inc., 1972.

830 LaBarre, Weston. The Aymara Indians of the Lake Titicaca Plateau, Bolivia. Menasha, Wisconsin: American Anthropological Association Memoir 68, 1948.

831 Leonard, Olen E. Bolivia: Land, People, Institutions. Washington, D. C. : Scarecrow Press, 1952.

832 _____. "La Paz, Bolivia: Its Population and Growth." American Sociological Review, 13: 4 (1948), 448-454.

833 Leons, Madeleine Barbara. "Changing Patterns of Social Stratification in an Emergent Bolivian Community." Diss. University of California at Los Angeles, 1966.

834 McBride, George. The Agrarian Indian Communities of Highland Bolivia. New York: Oxford University Press, 1921.

835 Reinaga, Fausto. Tierra y libertad: La revolución nacional y el indio. La Paz: Ediciones Rumbo Sindical, 1952.

836 Siles Guevara, Juan. "Bibliografía selecta de ciencias sociales bolivianas." Aportes, 17 (July 1970), 121-132.

837 Stearman, Allyn Mac Lean. "The Highland Migrant in Lowland Bolivia: Regional Migration and the Department of Santa Cruz." Diss. The University of Florida, 1976.

CHILE

838 Aránguiz Donoso, Horacio. Bibliografía histórica (1959-1967). Santiago de Chile: Universidad Catolica de Chile, Instituto de Historia, 1970.

839 Bizarro, Salvatore. Historical Dictionary of Chile. Metuchen, N. J. : Scarecrow Press, Inc. , 1972.

840 Bowman, Isaiah. Desert Trails of Atacama. New York: American Geographical Society, 1924.

841 Carmagnani, Marcello. "Colonial Latin American Demography: Growth of the Chilean Population, 1700-1830." Journal of Social History. 1: 2 (Winter 1967), 179-191, tables.

842 Chuaqui, Benedicto. Memorias de un emigrante. Santiago: Unión, 1957.

843 Faron, Louis C. Mapuche Social Structure. Urbana: University of Illinois Press, 1961.

844 Feliú Cruz, Guillermo. Chile visto a través de Agustín Ross. Santiago: n. p. , 1950.

845 Jefferson, Mark. Recent Colonization in Chile. New York: American Geographical Society, 1921.

846 Mellafe, Rolando. La introducción de la esclavitud negra en Chile. Santiago: Universidad de Chile, 1959.

210 / Bibliography

847 Munizaga Aguirre, Carlos. Vida de un araucano. Santiago: n.p., 1960.

848 Palacios, Nicolás. Raza chilena: Libro escrito por un chileno i para los Chilenos. Valparaíso: n.p., 1904.

849 Pike, Frederick B. "Aspects of Class Relations in Chile, 1850-1960." Hispanic American Historical Review, 42 (February 1963), 14-33.

850 Randolph, Jorge. Las guerras de Arauco y la esclavitud. Santiago: Sociedad Empresora Horizonte, 1966.

851 Sater, William F. "The Black Experience in Chile." Slavery and Race Relations in Latin America. Ed. Robert B. Toplin. Westport, Conn.: Greenwood Publishing Company, 1974, 13-50.

852 Smith, Edmond R. The Araucaniaus. New York: n.p., 1855.

853 Treutler, Paul. Andanzas de un alemán en Chile, 1851-1863. Santiago: Universidad de Chile, 1958. (originally published in German in 1882).

854 Vega, Nicolás. La immigración europea en Chile, 1882-1895. Paris: n.p., 1896.

855 Vergara, R. "Los censos de población de Chile." Proceedings of the American Scientific Congress (Washington, D.C.), 8 (1943), 95-108.

856 Vial Correa, Gonzalo. El africano en el reino de Chile: Ensayo histórico-jurídico. Santiago: Instituto de Investigaciones Históricas, Facultad de Ciencias Jurídicas y Sociales, Universidad Católica de Chile, 1957.

COLOMBIA

857 Ames, Barry. "The Negro in the Colombian Novel." Diss., Michigan State University, 1970.

858 Arango Cana, J. Inmigrantes para Colombia. Bogotá: n.p., 1951.

859 Arboleda, José Rafael. "The Ethnohistory of the Colombian Negroes." M.A. Thesis. Northwestern University, 1950.

860 _____. "Nuevas investigaciones afro-colombianas." Revista Javariana, 37 (1952), 197-205.

861 Arias Trujillo, Bernardo. Risaralda. Medellín: Editorial Bedout, 1960.

862   Arrazola, Roberto.   Palenque, primer pueblo libre de América.
      Cartagena: Ediciones Hernandez, 1970.

863   Bernal Villa, Segundo.   Guía bibliográfica de Colombia de in-
      terés para el antropólogo.   Bogotá: Ediciones Universi-
      dad de los Andes, 1969.

864   Bickerton, Derek and Aquilas Escalante.   "Palanquero: A
      Spanish-Based Creole of Northern Colombia." Lingua,
      24:3 (February 1970), 254-267.

865   Bierck, Harold A.   "The Struggle for Abolition in Gran Co-
      lombia." Hispanic American Historical Review, (1953),
      365-386.

866   Chandler, David L.   "Health Conditions in the Slave Trade of
      Colonial New Granada."   Ed. Robert B. Toplin.   West-
      port, Conn.: Greenwood Publishing Company, 1974, pp.
      51-88.

867   Davis, Robert H.   Historical Dictionary of Colombia.   Metuch-
      en, N.J.: Scarecrow Press, Inc., 1977.

868   Domínguez, Camila A.   Amazonia colombiana; bibliografía gen-
      eral preliminar.   Bogotá: Universidad Nacional de Co-
      lombia, Centro de Investigaciones para el Desarrollo,
      1973.

869   Escalante, Aguiles.   El Negro en Colombia.   Bogotá: Uni-
      versidad Nacional de Colombia, Facultad de Sociología,
      1964.

870   Fals Borda, Orlando.   "Indian Congregations in the New King-
      dom of Granada: Land Tenure Aspects, 1595-1850." The
      Americas, 13: 4 (1957), 331-51.

871   Friedemann, Nina S. and Jorge Morales Gómez.   "Estudios de
      negros en el litoral Pacífico Colombiano." Revista Co-
      lombina de Antropologia, 14 (1966/1969), 53-70.

872   Guzmán, Germán, Orlando Fals Borda, and Eduardo Umana
      Luna.   La violencia en Colombia: Estudio de un pro-
      ceso social.   Vol. 1: Monografías Sociológicas No. 12.
      Bogotá: Universidad Nacional, 1962.

873   Humphrey, N. D.   "Race, Caste, and Class in Colombia."
      Phylon, 13 (June 1952), 258-267.

874   Jaramillo Uribe, J.   "Esclavos y Señores en la sociedad co-
      lombiana del siglo XVIII." Anuario Colombiano de His-
      toria Social y de la Cultura, 1: 1 (1963), 3-62.

875   _____.   "La población indígena de Colombia en el mo-

mento de la Conquista y sus transformaciones poster-
iores." Anuario Colombiano de Historia Social y de la
Cultura, 1: 2 (1964), 239-93.

876 King, James F. Negro Slavery in the Viceroyalty of New
Granada. New York: Columbia University Press, 1939.

877 Knight, Rolf. "Why Don't You Work Like Other Men Do?
Labor Patterns and Sugar Plantations in the Cauca Valley, Colombia." Diss. Columbia University, 1968.

878 Melo, Jorge Orlando. Historia de Colombia. Vol. I. El
establicimiento de la dominación española. Bogotá: La
Carreta, 1978.

879 Palácios, Arnoldo. Las estrellas son negras. Bogotá: Editorial Revista Colombiana, 1971.

880 Palácios Preciado, Jorge. La trata de negros por Cartagena
de Indias: 1650-1750. Tunja, Col.: Ediciones La Rana
y El Aquita, 1973.

881 Pavy, Paul David III. "The Negro in Western Colombia."
Diss. Tulane University, 1967.

882 Piñeda de Gutiérrez, Virginia. Familia y cultura en Colombia.
Bogotá: Universidad de Colombia, 1968.

833 Price, Thomas James. "Saints and Spirits: A Study of Differential Acculturation in Colombian Negro Communities."
Diss. Northwestern University, 1955.

884 Pujol, Nicole. "La raza negra en el Chocó: Antropología físcia."
Revista Colombiana de Antropología, 15 (1970/71), 256-
292.

885 Sanders, Thomas G. "The Blacks of Colombia's Chocó: Race
Culture, and Power in Quibdo," American Universities
Field Staff Reports, 17:2 (1970), 1-7.

886 Sandoval, Alonso de. De Instauranda Aethiopum Salute: El
mundo de la esclavitud negra en America. Bogotá: Em-
presa Nacional, 1956.

887 Sharp, William F. "Forsaken but for Gold: An Economic
Study of Slavery and Mining in the Colombian Choco,
1680-1810." Diss. University of North Carolina, Chapel
Hill, 1970.

888 _____. "Manumission, Libres, and Black Resistance: the
Colombian Choco, 1680-1810." Slavery and Race Relations in Latin America. Ed. Robert B. Toplin. Westport, Conn.: Greenwood Publishing Company, 1974. pp.
80-111.

889 Smith, Lynn T. "The Racial Composition of the Population of Colombia." Journal of Inter-American Studies, 8:2 (April 1966), 213-235.

890 Solaún, Mauricio and Sidney Kronus. Discrimination Without Violence: Miscegenation and Racial Conflict. New York: John Wiley & Sons, 1973.

891 Torres, Giraldo, Ignacia. Los Inconformes: Historia de la rebeldía de las masas en Colombia. Bogotá: Editorial Margen Izquierdo, 1972-1973.

892 Vega, Alipio Valencia. El índio en la independencia. La Paz: Ministerio de Educación, 1961.

893 West, Robert C. Colonial Placer Mining in Colombia. Baton Rouge: Louisiana State University Press, 1952.

894 _____. The Pacific Lowlands of Colombia: A Negroid Area of the American Tropics. Baton Rouge: Louisiana State University Press, 1957.

895 Whittington, James Attison Jr. "Kinship and Family in the Chocó of Colombia: An Afro-American Adaptation." Diss. Tulane University, 1971.

ECUADOR

896 Carvalho Neto, Paulo de. "Bibliografía Afro-Ecuatoriana." Humanitas, 4:2 (1963), 5-19.

897 Cyrus, Stanley. "Racism and the Conditions of Black Communities in Ecuador." Paper presented to the Symposium of the Political Economy of the Black World, U.C.L.A., May 11, 1979.

898 Ecuador. Junta Nacional de Planificación y Coordinación Económica. Sección Estudios Sociales. Listado parcial de la bibliografia social, socio-económica y política del Ecuador: Sección obras generales y sección histórica. Versión preliminar. Quito: J.N.P.C.E., 1972.

899 Estupiñian Tello, Júlio. El negro en Esmeraldas: Apuntes para su estúdio. Quito: Talleres Gráficos Nacionales, 1967.

900 Gold, Robert L. "Negro Colonization Schemes in Ecuador, 1861-1864." Phylon, 30:3 (Fall 1969), 306-316.

901 Megenney, William W. "Problems radicales y culturales en dos piezas de Demêtrio Aguilera Malta." Cuadernos Americanos, 176:3 (May-June 1971), 221-228.

902 Ortiz, Adalberto. El espejo y la ventana. Guayaquil: Editorial Casa de la Cultura Ecuatoriana, Núcleo del Guayas, 1970.

903 _____. "La negritud en la cultura latinoamericana." Expresiones Culturales del Ecuador, 1 (June 1972), 10-18.

904 _____. Tierra son y tambor: Cantares negros y mulatos. Mexico City: Ediciones La Ciagarra, 1945.

905 Peñaherrera de Costales, Piedad, and Costales Samaniego, Alfredo. Coangue, o Historia cultural y social de los negros del Chota y Salinas. Quito: Editorial Llacta, 1959.

906 Rubio Orbe, Gonzalo. Promociones indígenas en América. Quito: Editorial Casa de la Cultura Ecuatoriana, 1957.

907 Vickers, William Taylor. "Cultural Adaptation to Amazonian Habitats: The Siona-Secoya of Eastern Ecuador." Diss. The University of Florida, 1976.

908 Walker, Michael Lee. "The Black Social Identity in Selected Novels of Nelson Estupinan Bass and Adalberto Ortíz." Diss. University of California, Riverside, 1977.

909 Walter, Lynn Ellen. "Interaction and Organization in an Ecuadorian Indian Highland Community." Diss. The University of Wisconsin, Madison, 1976.

BRITISH GUIANA/GUYANA

910 Adamson, Alan H. Sugar Without Slaves: A Political Economy of Guiana 1838-1904. New Haven: Yale University Press, 1972.

911 Bhagwan, Moses. Hitler's Force in Guiana. Georgetown: New Giana Co. Ltd., 1962.

912 Bolingbroke, Henry. A Voyage to the Demerary (1779-1806). Georgetown: Guiana Editions, reprinted c. 1960.

913 Cameron, N. E. The Evolution of the Negro. Georgetown, British Guiana: Argosy Co. Ltd., 1934.

914 Chan, V. O. "The Riots of 1856 in British Guiana." Caribbean Quarterly, 16: 1 (1970), 39-50.

915 Clements, Sir Cecil. The Chinese in British Guiana. Georgetown: Argosy Ltd., 1915.

916 Cruikshank, J. Graham. Black Talk. Demerara, British Guiana: Argosy Press, 1916.

917 Despres, Leo. Cultural Pluralism and Nationalist Politics in British Guiana. Chicago: Rand McNally, 1965.

918 Freeth, Zahra. Run Softly Demerara. London: George Allen and Unwin, 1960.

919 Halperin, Ernst. Racism and Communism in British Guiana. Cambridge, Mass.: M.I.T. Press, 1964.

920 _____. "Racism and Communism in British Guiana." Journal of InterAmerican Studies, 7: 1 (January 1965), 95-134.

921 Jayawardena, Chandra. Conflict and Solidarity in a Guianese Plantation. London: University of London, Athlone Press, 1963.

922 Kahn, M. C. "Bush Negroes of Dutch Guiana." Natural History, 28 (May 1928), 243-252.

923 _____. "Notes on the Saramaccaner Bush Negroes of Dutch Guiana," American Anthropologist, 31 (July 1929), 468-490.

924 Landis, Joseph Boyd. "Race Relations and Politics in Guiana." Diss. Yale University, 1971.

925 Luckhoo, J. A. "The East Indian in British Guiana." Timehri. 6 (1919), n.p.

926 McKenzie, H. I. "Race and Class in Guyana: Bibliography." Study Encounter, 8: 4 (1972), 1-13.

927 Moohr, M. "Economic Impact of Slave Emancipation in British Guiana, 1832-1852." Economic History Review, 25 (November 1972), 588-607.

928 Moore, Brian L. "The Retention of Caste Notions Among the Indian Immigrants to British Guiana During the Nineteenth Century." Comparative Studies in Society and History, 19:1 (January 1977), 96-107.

929 Nath, Dwarka. A History of Indians in British Guiana. London: Nelson, 1950.

930 Omoruyi, Omonhiomwan. "Social Communication and the Plural Society: An Inquiry into the Process of Integration in a Culturally Fragmented Society." Diss. State University of New York at Buffalo, 1971.

931 Price, Richard. "The Guiana Maroons: Changing Perspectives in 'Bush Negro' Studies." Caribbean Studies, 11:4 (January, 1972), 87-105.

932 _____. "Saramaka Emigration and Marriage: A Case Study of Social Change." Southwestern Journal of Anthropology, 26: 2 (Summer 1970), 157-189.

933 Rodway, J. Guiana: British, Dutch and French. London: T. Fisher Unwin, 1912.

934 Ruhomon, Peter. Centenary History of the East Indians in British Guiana, 1838-1938. Georgetown: Guiana Edition No. 10, 1938.

935 Sertima, J. van. Scenes and Sketches of Demerara Life. Demerara: Argosy Press, 1899.

936 Simms, Peter. Trouble in Guyana. London: George Allen & Unwin Ltd., 1966.

937 Smith, Raymond T. The Negro Family in British Guiana. London: Routledge and Kegan Paul, 1956.

938 _____. "Race and Political Conflict in Guiana." Race, 12:4 (April 1974), 415-427.

939 Swan, Michael. British Guiana: The Land of Six Peoples. London: H.M.S.O., 1957.

940 Synnott, Anthony. "Slave Revolts in Guyana and Trinidad: A History and Comparative Analysis." Ms. Sir George Williams University, Montreal, 1971.

941 Vatuk, Ved Prakash. British Guiana. New York: Monthly Review Press, 1963.

942 Williams, Eric E. "Historical Background of British Guiana's Problems." Journal of Negro History, 30 (October 1945), 357-81.

PARAGUAY

943 "Bibliografía: la población en el Paraguay." Revista Paraguaya de Sociologia, 5: 12 (August 1968), 136-140.

944 "Bibliografía sobre la sociedad rural en el Paraguay." Revista Paraguaya de Sociología, 5: 11 (April 1968), 129-134.

945 Carvalho Neto, Paulo de. "Antología del negro paraguayo." Primera Serie, Anales, Organo de la Universidad Central, 91:346 (1962), 37-66.

946 _____. "Contribución al estudio de los negros paraguayos." América Latina. 5 (January-June 1962), 23-40.

947 Kolinski, Charles J. Historical Dictionary of Paraguay.
    Metuchen, N.J.: Scarecrow Press, Inc., 1973.

948 Moscov, Stephen C. Paraguay: An Annotated Bibliography.
    Buffalo: Council on International Studies, State Univer-
    sity of New York at Buffalo, 1972.

949 Plá, Josefina. Hermano negro: La esclavitud en el Paraguay.
    Madrid: Ediciones Paraninfo, 1972.

950 Rivarola, Domingo M. Estudios y datos sobre la población
    en el Paraguay: Bibliografía. Asunción: Centro Para-
    guayo de Estudios Sociológicos, 1970.

951 _____, and G. Heisecke, eds. Población, urbanizacion y
    recursos humanos en el Paraguay. Asunción: n.p.,
    1969.

952 Williams, John Hoyt. "Tevego on the Paraguayan Frontier:
    A Chapter in the Black History of the Americas." Jour-
    nal of Negro History, 56:4 (October 1971), 272-283.

PERU

953 Alisky, Marvin. Historical Dictionary of Peru. Metuchen,
    N.J.: Scarecrow Press, Inc., 1979.

954 Bourque, Susan C. Coming Down the Mountain: The Social
    Worlds of Mayobamba. Ithaca, New York: Cornell Uni-
    versity Press, 1968.

955 Bowser, Frederick P. The African Slave in Colonial Peru:
    1524-1650. Stanford: Stanford University Press, 1974.

956 Campbell, Leon G. "Black Power in Colonial Peru: The
    1779 Tax Rebellion of Lambayeque," Phylon, 33:2 (Sum-
    mer 1972), 140-152.

957 Cushner, Nicholas P. "Slave Morality and Reproduction in
    Haciendas in Colonial Peru." Hispanic American His-
    torical Review, 55:2 (May 1975), 177-199.

958 Dew, Edward M., Jr. "Peasant Organization in Puno, Peru."
    Diss. University of California at Los Angeles, 1966.

959 Dobyns, Henry F. "Estimating Aboriginal American Popula-
    tion: An Appraisal of Technique with New Hemispheric
    Estimate." Current Anthropology, 7: 4 (1966), 395-416.

960 _____. "An Outline of Andean Epidemic History to 1720."
    Bulletin of the History of Medicine, 37: 6 (1963), 493-
    515.

961 Fisher, John. "Royalism, Regionalism, and Rebellion in Co-
     lonial Peru, 1808-1815." Hispanic American Historical
     Review, 59: 2 (May 1979), 232-257.

962 Ford, Thomas R. Man and Land in Peru. Gainesville: Uni-
     versity of Florida Press, 1955.

963 Garcilaso de la Vega, El Inca. Royal Commentaries of the
     Incas and General History of Peru. Austin: University
     of Texas Press, 1966.

964 Gonzales, Michael. "Labor Contracting and Social Change in
     Northern Peru, 1875-1933." Paper presented to the Meet-
     ing of the Committee on Andean Studies, C. L. A. H., San
     Francisco, December 1978.

965 Harth-Terré, Emilio. "El esclavo negro en la sociedad indo-
     peruana." Journal of Inter-American Studies, 3:3 (July
     1961), 297-340.

966 _____. Negros e indios: Un testamento social ignorado
     del Perú colonial. Lima: Editorial Juan Mejia Baca,
     1973.

967 _____, and Alberto Márquez Abanto. "El artesano negro
     en la arquitectura virreinal limeña." Revista del Ar-
     chivo Nacional del Perú 25:1 (1961), 36-430.

968 Herbold, Carl and Steve Stein. Guía bibliográfica para la his-
     toria social y política del Perú en el siglo XX (1895-1960).
     Lima: Instituto de Estudios Peruanos, 1971.

969 Hickman, John M. "The Aymaras of Chinchera, Peru: Per-
     sistence and Change in a Bicultural Context." Diss. Cor-
     nell University, 1963.

970 Lamb, F. Bruce. Wizard of the Upper Amazon. Boston:
     Houghton Mifflin, 1974.

971 Lanning, Edward P. Peru Before the Incas. Englewood
     Cliffs, N. J.: Prentice-Hall, 1967.

972 Lewin, Bolislao. La rebelión de Tupac Amaru. Buenos
     Aires: Hachette, 1957.

973 Lockhart, James. Spanish Peru, 1532-1560. Madison: Uni-
     versity of Wisconsin Press, 1968.

974 Lumbreras, Luis G. The Peoples and Cultures of Ancient
     Peru. Tr. Betty J. Meggers. Washington, D. C.:
     Smithsonian Institution Press, 1978.

975 Mason, J. Alden. The Ancient Civilizations of Peru. Balti-
     more: Penguin Books, 1961.

976 Matos Mar, José and Roger Ravines. Bibliografía peruana de ciencias sociales, 1957-1969; Antropología, ciencia política, economía, educación, lingüística, psicología social, psiquiatría social. Lima: Instituto de Estudios Peruanos, 1971.

977 Metraux, Alfred. The Incas. New York: Vista, 1965.

978 Millones Santagadea, Luis. "Gente negra en el Perú: esclavos y conquistadores." America Indigena, 31 (1971), 595-624.

979 _____. Minorías étnicas en el Perú. Lima: Pontífica Universidad Católica del Perú, 1973.

980 Niera, Hugo. Cuzco: Tierra y muerte. Lima: Populibros Peruanos, 1964.

981 Normano, João F. and A. Gerbi. The Japanese in South America: An Introductory Survey with Special Reference to Peru. New York: n.p., 1943.

982 Salas, Teresa C. and Richard Henry. "Nicomedas Santa Cruz y la Poesía de su Conciencia de Negritud." Cudernos Americanos, 202 (September-October 1975), 182-199.

983 Santa Cruz, Nicomedes. Décimas y poemas. Lima: Campodónico Ediciones, 1971.

984 _____. Ritmos negros del Perú. Buenos Aires: Editorial Losada, 1971.

985 Stein, William W. Life in the Highlands of Peru. Ithaca, New York: Cornell University Press, 1961.

986 Steward, Julian H. and Louis C. Faron. Native Peoples of South America. New York: McGraw-Hill, 1959.

987 Stewart, N. R. "Migration and Settlement in the Peruvian Montana: The Apurimac Valley." Geographical Review, 55: 2 (1965), 143-57.

988 Stewart, W. Chinese Bondage in Peru: A History of the Chinese Coolie in Peru, 1849-1874. Durham, N. C.: Duke University Press, 1951.

989 Tigner, James. "The Ryukyuans in Peru, 1906-1952." The Americas, 35:1 (July 1978), 20-44.

990 United Nations, International Labour Organization. Informe de la misión conjunta de las Naciones Unidas y organismos especializados para el estudio de los problemas de las poblaciones andinas. Geneva: United Nations, 1953.

991 Valcárcel, Daniel. La rebelión de Tupac Amaru. Mexico City: Fondo de Cultura Económica, 1947.

992 Valcárcel Esparza, Carlos. Rebeliones indígenas. Lima, Peru: Editorial PTCM, 1964.

993 Wachtel, Nathan. The Vision of the Vanquished: The Spanish Conquest of Peru Through Indian Eyes, 1530-1570. Tr. Ben and Sian Reynolds. New York: Barnes and Noble, 1977.

994 Wolff, Inge. "Negersklaverei und Negerhandel in Hochperu: 1545-1640." Jahrbuch für Geschichte von Staat, Wirthschaft und Gesellschaft Latinamerikas, 1 (1964), 157-186.

995 Wong, Bernard. "A Comparative Study of the Assimilation of the Chinese in New York City and Lima, Peru." Comparative Studies in Society and History, 20:3 (July 1978), 335-358.

URUGUAY

996 Alisky, Marvin. Bibliography on Uruguay. Montevideo: American International Association, 1969.

997 Carvalho Neto, Paulo de. "The Candombé, a Dramatic Dance from Afro-Uruguayan Folklore." Ethnomusicology, 6:3 (September 1962), 164-174.

998 _____. "La comparsa Lubola del carnaval Montevideo." Archivos Venezolanos de Folklore, 10-11: 7 (1961-1962), 153-185.

999 _____. Estudios afros: Brasil-Paraguay-Uruguay-Ecuador. Caracas: Instituto de Antropologia e Historia, Universidad Central de Venezuela, 1971.

1000 _____. "Investigaciones sociológicas Afro-uruguayas, 1956-1957." Anales, 92: 347 (1963), 35-79.

1001 _____. El negro uruguayo: hasta la abolición. Quito: Editorial Universitaria, 1965.

1002 Holmes, H. A. "Ildefonoso Pereda Valedés y su libro Negros esclavos y negros libres." Revista Iberoamericana, 8 (May 1944), 21-29.

1003 Ortiz Oderigo, Néstor. Calunga, croquis del candombé. Buenos Aires: Eudeba, 1969.

1004 Pereda Valdés, Ildefonso. El negro en el Uruguay. Montevideo: Instituto Histórico y Geográfico del Uruguay, 1965.

1005 _____. Negros esclavos y negros libres. Montevideo: n. p. , 1941.

1006 _____. "Negros esclavos pardos libres y negros libres en Uruguay." Estudios Afrocubanos, 4 (1940), 121-127.

1007 Rama, Carlos M. "Los Afro-uruguayos." Caravelle, 11 (1968), 53-109.

1008 Solari, Aldo E. El desarrollo social del Uruguay en la post-guerra. Montevideo: n. p. , 1967.

1009 _____. Estudios sobre la sociedade uruguaya. Montevideo: Editorial S. A. , 1964.

VENEZUELA

1010 Acosta Saignes, Miguel. Los negros cimarrones de Venezuela. Caracas: n. p. , 1961.

1011 _____. "Sobre la posible existencia de elementos culturales africanos en la Guajira," Archivos Venezolanos de Folklore, 10-11:7 (1961-1962), 279-281.

1012 _____. La trata de esclavos en Venezuela. Caracas: Revista de História, 1961.

1013 _____. Vida de los esclavos en Venezuela. Caracas: Ediciones Hespérides, 1967.

1014 Arcaya, Pedro M. Insurrección de los negros en la serranía de Coro. Caracas: Instituto Panamericano de Geografía y Historia, Comisión de Historia, 1949.

1015 Brito Figueroa, Federico. Las insurrecciones de los esclavos negros en la sociedad colonial Venezuelana. Caracas: Editorial Cantaclaro, 1961.

1016 Cardozo, Lubio. Bibliografía de la literatura indígena venezolana. Mérida: Universidad de los Andes, Centro de Investigaciones Literarias, 1970.

1017 Gallegos, Romulo. Pobre Negro. Buenos Aires: Espasa Calpe, 1961.

1018 Goldman, Irving. The Cubeo: Indians of the Northwest Amazon. Urbana: University of Illinois Press, 1963.

1019 Heaton, Louis E. The Agricultural Development of Venezuela. New York: Praeger, 1969.

1020 Hudson, Randall O. "The Status of the Negro in Northern

South America, 1820-1860." Journal of Negro History, 49 (1964), 225-39.

1021 King, James F. "A Royalist View of the Colored Castes in the Venezuelan War of Independence." Hispanic American Historical Review, 33:4 (November 1953), 526-37.

1022 Lieuwen, Edwin. Venezuela. London: Oxford University Press, 1961.

1023 Lombardi, John V. The Decline and Abolition of Negro Slavery in Venezuela. Westport, Conn.: Negro Universities Press, 1971.

1024 _____. "Los esclavos negros en las guerras venezolanas de la Independencia." Cultura Universitária, 93(October-December 1966), 153-168.

1025 _____. "Manumission, Manumisos, and Aprendizaje in Republican Venezuela." Hispanic American Historical Review, 49:4 (November 1969), 656-678.

1026 Mathiason, John R. "El campesino venezolano: Perspectivas de cambio." Estudios de la politica venezolana: Exploraciones en análisis y sintesis. Ed. Frank Bonilla and José A. Silva Michelena. Cambridge, Mass.: M.I.T. Center for International Studies, 1966.

1027 Pollak-Eltz, Angelina. Cultos Afro-Americanos. Caracas: Universidad Católica Andrés Bello, Instituto de Investigaciones Históricas, 1972.

1028 _____. Vestígios africanos en la cultura del pueblo venezolano. Cuernavaca, Mexico: Centro Intercultural de Documentación, 1971.

1029 "Publicaciones antropológicas sobre Venezuela desde 1967 hasta el presente." Boletín bibliografico de antropología americana, 31 (1968), 53-56.

1030 Ramón y Rivera, Luis Felipe. "El mestizaje de la música Afro-Venezolana." Music in the Americas. Ed. George List and Juan Orrego-Salas. Bloomington: Indiana University Research Center, 1967, pp. 176-204.

1031 _____. La música Afrovenezolana. Caracas: Universidad Central de Venezuela, Ediciones de la Biblioteca, 1971.

1032 Sojo, Juan Pablo. Temas y apuntes Afro-venezolanos. Caracas: Guadernos Literarios de la Asociación de Escritores Venezolanos, 1943.

1033 Wright, Withrop R. "Elitist Attitudes Toward Race in

Twentieth Century Venezuela." Slavery and Race Relations in Latin America. Ed. Robert B. Toplin. Westport, Conn.: Greenwood Publishing Company, 1974, pp. 325-347.

BRAZIL

1034 Aborigines Protection Society of London, Tribes of the Amazon Basin in Brazil. London: APSL, 1973.

1035 Alves, Henrique C. Bibliografia afro-brasileira: estudos sôbre o negro. São Paulo: Edições "H.", 1976.

1036 _____. Nina Rodrígues e o negro do Brasil. São Paulo: Companhis Editôra Nacional, 1962.

1037 Amado, Jorge. Jubiabá. São Paulo: Ed. Martins, 1935.

1038 _____. Tent of Miracles. Tr. Barbara Shelby. New York: Alfred A. Knopf, 1971.

1039 Ayrosa, Plínio. Apontamentos para a bibliografia do lingua Tupí-Guaraní. São Paulo: Faculdade de Filosofia, Ciências e Letras, 1943.

1040 Azevedo, Fernando de. Brazilian Culture. New York: Macmillan, 1950.

1041 Azevedo, Thales de. Cultura e situação racial no Brasil. Rio de Janeiro: Editôra Civilização Brasileira, 1966.

1042 _____. As elites de côr: Un estudo de asençâo social. São Paulo: Companhia Editôra Nacional, 1955.

1043 _____. Democracia racial: Ideologia e realidade. Petrópolis: Ed. Vozes, 1975.

1044 Bailey, Dale S. "Slavery in the Novels of Brazil and the United States." Diss. Indiana University, 1961.

1045 Baldus, Herbert. Bibliografia crítica de etnologia brasileira. São Paulo: n.p., 1954.

1046 Bastide, Roger. Brasil: terra de contrastes. São Paulo: DIFEL, 1959.

1047 _____. O candomblê da Bahia. São Paulo: Companhia Editôra Nacional, 1961.

1048 _____. "The Development of Race Relations in Brazil." Industrialization and Race Relations: A Symposium. Ed. Guy Hunter. London: Oxford University Press, 1965, pp. 9-29.

1049 _____. Estudos Afro-brasileiros. São Paulo: Ed. Perspectiva, 1973.

1050 _____. O negro na imprensa e na literature. São Paulo: Universidade de São Paulo, 1972.

1051 _____. "The Present Status of Afro-American Research in Latin America." Daedalus, 103 (Spring 1974), 111-120.

1052 _____. Sociologia do folclore brasileiro. São Paulo: Editôra Anhembi, 1959.

1053 _____, and Florestan Fernandes, ed. Brancos e negros em São Paulo. 2nd ed., São Paulo: Companhia Editôra Nacional, 1959.

1054 _____, and Pierre van den Berghe. "Stereotypes, Norms, and Interracial Behavior in São Paulo, Brazil.: American Sociological Review, 22 (December 1957), 689-694.

1055 Beiguelman, Paulo. A formação do povo no complexo café-eiro: aspectos políticos. São Paulo: Livraria Pioneira Editôra, 1968.

1056 Beltrão, Luiz. Indio, um mito brasileiro. Petrópolis: Ed. Vozes, 1979.

1057 Bethell, Leslie M. The Abolition of the Brazilian Slave Trade: Britain, Brazil, and the Slave Trade Question, 1807-1869. Cambridge, England: Cambridge University Press, 1970.

1057a _____. "Britain, Portugal and the Suppression of the Brazilian Slave Trade: The Origins of Lord Palmerston's Act of 1839." English Historical Review, 80 (1965), 761-784.

1058 _____. "The Independence of Brazil and the Abolition of Slave Trade: Anglo-Brazilian Relations, 1822-1826." Journal of Latin American Studies, 1: 2 (November 1969), 115-147.

1059 Bicudo, V. L. "Atitudes raciais de prêtos e mulatos em São Paulo." Sociologia, 9:3 (1947), 195-219.

1060 Bilden, Rudiger. "Brazil, Laboratory of Civilization." The Nation, 128 (1929), 71-74.

1061 Blair, Thomas L. "The Negro Worker in Urban Brazil." Crisis, 61 (December 1954), 592-599.

1062 Blomberg, Ralph. Chavante. New York: Taplinger Publishing Company, 1961.

1063 Bodard, Lucien. Green Hell. Massacre of the Brazilian Indians. Tr. Jennifer Monaghan. New York: Outerbridge and Dienstfrey, 1971.

1064 Bojunga, Claúdio. "O brasileiro negro, 90 anos depois." Encontros com a Civilização Brasileira. Rio de Janeiro: Civilização Brasileira, 1978, pp. 175-204.

1065 Bomilcar, Alvaro. O preconceito de raça no Brasil. Rio de Janeiro: n.p., 1916.

1066 Bonardelli, Eugenio. Lo stato di São Paulo e l'emigrazione italiana. Torino: F. Bocca, 1916.

1067 Bonfim, Manoel. A América latina: males de origem. Rio de Janeiro: n.p., c. 1903.

1068 Bonilla, Victor Daniel. Servants of God or Masters of Men? The Story of a Capuchin Mission in Amazonia. Tr. Rosemary Sheed. Baltimore: Penguin Books, 1972.

1069 Borges, João Baptista Pereira. Côr, profissão e mobilidade (o negro e o rádio em São Paulo). São Paulo: Ed. Pionera/Universidade de São Paulo, 1967.

1070 Boxer, Charles R. The Golden Age of Brazil, 1695-1750. Berkeley: University of California Press, 1962.

1071 _____. "Negro Slavery in Brazil: A Portuguese Pamphlet." Race, 5:3 (January 1964), 38-47.

1072 _____. Race Relations in the Portuguese Colonial Empire, 1415-1825. Oxford, England: Clarendon Press, 1963.

1073 Braztel, John F. and Daniel M. Masterson. "O Exemplo: Afro-Brazilian Protest in Pôrto Alegre." The Americas, 33: 4 (April 1977), 58-92.

1074 Brooks, Edwin. "The Brazilian Road to Ethnicide," Contemporary Review, 224 (May 1974), 2-8.

1075 _____. "Frontiers of Ethnic Conflict in the Brazilian Amazon," International Journal of Environmental Studies, 7 (1974), 63-74.

1076 _____. "Twilight of Brazilian Tribes," Geographical Magazine, 45 (January 1973), 304-310.

1077 Burns, E. Bradford. "Manuel Querino's Interpretation of the African Contribution to Brazil." Journal of Negro History, 59: 1 (January 1974), 78-86.

1078 Cardoso, Fernando Henrique. "Colour Prejudice in Brazil." Présence Africaine, 25: 53 (4th Trimestre 1965), 120-128.

1079 _____, and Otávio Ianni. Côr e mobilidade em Florianápolis. São Paulo: Companhia Editôra Nacional, 1960.

1080 Cardozo, Manoel. "Slavery in Brazil as Described by Americans." The Americas, 17: 1 (January 1961), 241-260.

1081 Carneiro, Edison ed. Antologia do negro brasileiro. Rio de Janeiro: Tecnoprint Gráfica, 1967.

1082 _____. Guerras de los Palmares. México: Fondo de Cultura Economica, 1946.

1083 _____. Ladinos e crioulos: estudos sôbre o negro no Brasil. Rio de Janeiro: Editora Civilização Brasileira, 1964.

1084 _____. O quilombo dos Palmares. 2nd ed., São Paulo: Ed. Brasiliana, 1958.

1085 Cascudo, Luis de Câmara. História da alimentação no Brasil. 2 vols. São Paulo: Companhia Editôra Nacional, 1967.

1086 _____. Made in Africa: pesquisas e notas. Rio de Janeiro: Editôra Civilização Brasileira, 1965.

1087 Castro, Jeanne Barrance de. "O Negro na Guarda Nacional Brasileira." Anais do Museu Paulista, 23 (1969), 151-72.

1088 Chabert, Xavier. An Historical Account of the Manners and Customs of the Savage Inhabitants of Brazil. London: C. Baynes, 1822.

1089 Chapman, Charles E. "Palmares: The Negro Numantia." Journal of Negro History, 3: 1 (January 1918), 29-32.

1090 Chiappino, Jean. The Brazilian Indigenous Problem and Policy: The Aripuná Park. Copenhagen: IWGIA, 1974.

1091 Chilcote, Ronald H., ed. Protest and Resistance in Angola and Brazil. Berkeley: University of California Press, 1972.

1092 Clarana, José. "A Letter from Brazil." The Crisis, April 1918, 276-278.

1093 Conrad, Robert. "The Contraband Slave Trade to Brazil, 1831-1845." Hispanic American Historical Review, 49: 4 (November 1969), 617-638.

1094 _____. The Destruction of Brazilian Slavery, 1850-1888. Berkeley: University of California Press, 1972.

1095 _____ . "Neither Slave nor Free: The Emancipados of
Brazil, 1818-1868." Hispanic American Historical Review, 53: 1 (February 1973), 50-70.

1096 _____ . "Nineteenth-Century Brazilian Slavery." Slavery
and Race Relations in Latin America. Ed. Robert B.
Toplin. Westport, Conn.: Greenwood Press, 1974, pp.
146-173.

1097 Corwin, Arthur F. "Afro-Brazilians: Myths and Realities."
Slavery and Race Relations in Latin America. Ed. Robert
Brent Toplin. Westport, Conn.: Greenwood Press, 1974,
pp. 385-438.

1098 Costa Eduardo, Octávio de. The Negro in North Brazil: A
Study in Acculturation. American Ethnological Society
Monograph No. 16, New York, 1940.

1099 Costa Pinto, L. A. O negro no Rio de Janeiro: relações
de raças numa sociedade em mudança. São Paulo: Companhia Editôra Nacional, 1952.

1100 Couceira, Solange Martins. Bibliografia sôbre o negro brasileiro. São Paulo: Escola de Comunicações e Artes,
1971.

1101 Coutinho, Afrânio. "Brazil: Laboratory of Civilization."
Free World, 6 (August 1943), 172-4.

1102 Coutinho, Azevedo. Analise sôbre a justiça do comercio do
resgate dos escravos da Costa da Africa. Paris: n.p.,
1798.

1103 Coutinho, Edilberto. Rondôn: o civilizador da última fronteira. Rio de Janeiro: Civilização Brasileira, 1975.

1104 Couty, Louis. Ebauches sociologiques: Le Brésil en 1884.
Rio de Janeiro: n.p., 1884.

1105 Cowell, Adrian. The Tribe That Hides from Man. London:
Bodley Head, 1974.

1106 Crusoe, Romeu. A maldição de Canaan. Rio de Janeiro:
Ed. Di Giorgio, 1951.

1107 Davis, David Brion. The Problem of Slavery in Western Culture. Ithaca, N.Y.: Cornell University Press, 1966.

1108 Davis, Shelton H. Victims of the Miracle: Development and
the Indians of Brazil. Cambridge, England: Cambridge
University Press, 1977.

1109 Degler, Carl N. Neither Black nor White: Slavery and Race

Relations in Brazil and the United States. New York: Macmillan, 1971.

1110 Delgado de Carvalho, C. "Race as a Sociological Question in Brazil." Rice Institute Pamphlets, 27 (October 1940), 218-41.

1111 Diegues Júnior, Manuel. "Pluralismo étnico e cultural no Brasil contemporâneo." Revista Interamericana de Ciências Sociales, 1:3 (1962), 389-397.

1112 _____. "O quadro social oitenta anos depois da abolição." Cadernos Brasileiros (Rio de Janeiro), 10:47 (May-June 1968), 69-73.

1113 Diggs, Irene. "Zumbi and the Republic of Palmares." Phylon, 14: 1 (1953), 62-69.

1114 Donald, Cleveland Junior. "Equality in Brazil: Confronting Reality." Black World, 22 (November 1972), 23-34.

1115 _____. "Slave Resistance and Abolitionism in Brazil: The Campista Case, 1879-1888." Luso-Brazilian Review, 13: 2 (Winter 1976), 182-193.

1116 Dreller, Gerald. "The Afro-Brazilian: An Expression of Popular Culture in Selected Examples of Bahian Literature." Diss. University of Illinois at Champaign-Urbana, 1974.

1117 Dzidzienyo, Anani. "A Africa vista do Brasil." Afro-Asia, 10-11 (June-December 1970), 79-97.

1118 _____. The Position of Blacks in Brazilian Society. Report no. 7. London: Minority Rights Group, 1971.

1119 Eisenberg, Peter L. "The Consequences of Modernization for Brazil's Sugar Plantations in the Nineteenth Century." Land and Labour in Latin America. Ed. K. Duncan, I. Rutledge, and C. Harding. London: Cambridge University Press, 1977.

1120 _____. "Abolishing Slavery: The Process on Pernambuco's Sugar Plantations." Hispanic American Historical Review, 52:4 (November 1972), 580-597.

1121 _____. "Trabalho livre nos engenhos: Jaboatão na década de 1850." Paper presented to the Sociedade Brasileira para o Progresso de Ciência, São Paulo, July 1977.

1122 Elkins, Stanley. Slavery, A Problem in American Institutional and Intellectual Life. Chicago: University of Chicago Press, 1968.

1123 Ennes, Ernesto. As guerras nos Palmares. São Paulo:
Companhia Editôra Nacional, 1938.

1124 Eduardo, Octavio da Costa. The Negro in Northern Brazil.
New York: J. J. Augustin, 1948.

1125 Fernandes, Florestan. "Beyond Poverty: The Negro and
the Mulatto in Brazil." Slavery and Race Relations in
Latin America. Ed. Robert Brent Toplin, Westport,
Conn.: Greenwood Press, 1974, pp. 277-298.

1126 _____. A integração do negro na sociedade de classes.
2 vols. 3rd ed. São Paulo: Ed. Atica, 1978.

1127 _____. "The Weight of the Past." Daedalus, 96:2
(Spring 1967), 560-579.

1128 Figueiredo, Ariosvaldo. O negro e a violência do branco.
Rio de Janeiro: Ed. José Alvaro, 1977.

1129 Fontaine, Pierre-Michel. "Aspects of Afro-Brazilian Career
Mobility in the Corporate World." Paper presented to
the symposium on "Popular Dimensions of Brazil."
U.C.L.A., Los Angeles, February 2, 1979.

1130 _____. "The Brazilian Economic Model and Afro-Brazilian
Mobility." Paper presented to the Symposium on The Political Economy of the Black World, U.C.L.A., Center
for Afro-American Studies, May 10, 1979.

1131 Fonyat, Bina. Carnaval. Rio de Janeiro: Nova Fronteira,
1978.

1132 Franca, Eurico Nogueira. "The Negro in Brazilian Music."
Afrobeat (Lagos), 1:4 (May 1967), 6-7, 11.

1133 Frazier, E. Franklin. "A Comparison of Negro-White Rela-
tions in Brazil and the United States." On Race Relations:
Selected Writings. Ed. G. Franklin Edwards. Chicago:
University of Chicago Press, 1968, pp. 82-102.

1134 _____. "Negro Family Life in Bahia, Brazil: Influence
of African Culture Patterns." American Sociological Review, 7 (August 1942), 465-78.

1135 Freyre, Gilberto. "Brazil and the International Crisis."
Journal of Negro Education, 10 (July 1941), 510-514.

1136 _____. Em tôrno de alguns túmulos Afro-Cristãos. Salvador: Livraria Progresso, 1951.

1137 _____, comp. Estudos Afro-brasileiros. Trabalhos apre-
sentados ao 1º congresso Afro-Brasileiro reunido do Recife em 1934. Rio de Janeiro: Ariel Editôra, 1935.

230 / Bibliography

1138   . The Gilberto Freyre Reader. Tr. Barbara Shelby. New York: Knopf, 1975.

1139   . The Mansions and the Shanties: The Making of Modern Brazil. New York: Alfred A. Knopf, 1963.

1140   . The Masters and the Slaves: A Study in the Development of Brazilian Civilization. Tr. Samuel Putnam, New York: Alfred A. Knopf, 1946.

1141   . "Misconceptions of Brazil." Foreign Affairs, 40 (April 1962), 453-462.

1142   . "The Negro in Brazilian Culture and Society." Quarterly Journal on Inter-American Relations (Washington) 1(1939), 69-75.

1143   . New World in the Tropics: The Culture of Modern Brazil. New York: Alfred A. Knopf, 1959.

1144   , comp. Novos estudos Afro-brasileiros. Rio de Janeiro: Civilização Brasileira, 1940.

1145   . Order and Progress; Brazil from Monarchy to Republic. New York: Alfred A. Knopf, 1970.

1146   . The Portuguese and the Tropics. Tr. H. D. O'Matthew and F. de Mello Moser. Lisbon: Executive Committee for the Commemoration of the Vth Centenary of the Death of Prince Henry the Navigator, 1961.

1147   . "Slavery, Monarchy, and Modern Brazil." Foreign Affairs, 33 (July 1955), 624-33.

1148 Fuerst, René. "Bibliography on Brazilian Amazonian Indians." Copenhagen: International Workshop on Indigenous Affairs, 1972.

1149 Galey, John. "Industrialist in the Wilderness: Henry Ford's Amazon Venture." Journal of Interamerican Studies and World Affairs, 21:2 (May 1979), 261-289.

1150 Galloway, J. H. "The Last Years of Slavery on the Sugar Plantations of Northwestern Brazil." Hispanic American Historical Review 51:4 (November 1971), 586-605.

1151 Garcia-Zamor, Jean-Claude. "Social Mobility of Negroes in Brazil." Journal of Inter-American Studies and World Affairs, 27:2 (April 1970), 242-254.

1152 Genovese, Eugene D. Roll, Jordan, Roll. The World Slaveholders Made. New York: Random House, 1972.

1153 Gilliam, Angela Marjeanne. "Language Attitudes, Ethnicity

and Class in São Paulo and Salvador da Bahia (Brazil)."
Diss. Union Graduate School, 1975.

1154 Gobineau, J. A. Comte de. "L'emigration au Brésil." Le
Correspondant, 96 [Nouvelle Serie, vol. 60] (July-September 1874).

1155 Gomes, Antônio Osmar. "A vocação musical do mulato."
Revista do Brasil, 2 (April 1939), 33-38.

1156 Gonzalez, Lélia. "The Role of Black Women in Brazilian
Society." Paper presented to the Symposium on The Political Economy of the Black World, U.C.L.A., May 11,
1979.

1157 Gordon, Eugene. An Essay on Race Amalgamation. Pan
American Union: Rio de Janeiro, 1951.

1158 Goulart, José Alípio. Da fuga ao suicídio: aspectos de re-
beldia dos escravos no Brasil. Rio de Janeiro: Conquista, 1972.

1159 _____. Do palmatória ao patíbulo: castigos de escravos
no Brasil. Rio de Janeiro: Conquista, 1971.

1160 Graham, Richard. "Brazilian Slavery Re-Examined: A Review Article." Journal of Social History, 3:4 (Summer
1970), 431-453.

1161 _____. "Causes for the Abolition of Negro Slavery in
Brazil: An Interpretive Essay." Hispanic American
Historical Review, 46:2 (May 1966), 123-137.

1162 Gregor, Thomas. Mehinaku: The Drama of Daily Life in
a Brazilian Indian Village. Chicago: University of Chicago Press, 1978.

1163 Guerreiro Ramos, Alberto. "O problema do negro na sociedade brasileira." Cadernos do Nosso Tempo, 2 (1959),
203-215.

1164 Haberly, David T. "Abolitionism in Brazil: Anti-Slavery
and Anti-Slave." Luso-Brazilian Review, 9:2 (Winter
1972), 30-46.

1165 Hamilton, Russell G. "The Present State of African Cults
in Brazil." Journal of Social History, 3 (Summer 1970),
357-373.

1166 Hanbury-Tenison, Robin. A Question of Survival for the Indians of Brazil. New York: Charles Scribner's Sons,
1973.

1167 Hanke, Lewis. Gilberto Freyre. Vida y Obra, Bibliografia, Antologia. New York: Instituto de las Españas, 1939.

1168 Harris, Marvin. Patterns of Race in the Americas. New York: Columbia University Press, 1956.

1169 _____. "Racial Identity in Brazil." Luso-Brazilian Review, 1:2 (December 1964), 21-28.

1170 _____. "Referential Ambiguity in the Calculus of Brazilian Racial Identity." Southwestern Journal of Anthropology, 26:1 (Spring 1970), 1-14.

1171 _____. Town and Country in Brazil. New York: Columbia University Press, 1966.

1172 _____, and Conrad Kottak. "The Structural Significance of Brazilian Racial Categories." Sociologia, 25: 2 (1963), 203-209.

1173 Hastings, D. "Japanese Emigration and Assimilation in Brazil." International Migration Review, 3: 8 (1969), 32-53.

1174 Hemming, John. Red Gold: The Conquest of the Brazilian Indians. Cambridge, Mass.: Harvard University Press, 1978.

1175 Henshall, J. D. and R. P. Momsen, Jr. A Geography of Brazilian Development. Boulder, Colo.: Westview Press, 1979.

1176 Herskovits, Melville J. "Drums and Drummers in Afro-Brazilian Cult Life." The Musical Quarterly (New York), 30: 4 (1934), 477-92.

1177 _____. "The Negro in Bahia, Brazil: A Problem in Method." American Sociological Review, 8 (August 1943), 394-404.

1178 _____. "Some Economic Aspects of the Afrobahian Candomblé," Miscellanea Paul Rivet, 2 (1958), 227-247.

1179 _____. "Southernmost Outposts of New World Africanisms: The Negro of Pôrto Alegre." American Anthropologist, 45 (October 1943), 495-510.

1180 Holub, Norman. "The Brazilian Sabinada: Revolt of the Negro Masses." Journal of Negro History, 54: 3 (July 1969), 275-283.

1181 Hutchinson, Bertram. "Colour, Social Status and Fertility in Brazil." América Latina, 8:4 (October-December 1965), 3-25.

1182 Hutchinson, Harry William. "Vila Recôncavo: A Brazilian Sugarcane Plantation Community." Diss. Columbia University Press, 1954.

1183 _____. Village and Plantation Life in Northeastern Brazil. Seattle: University of Washington Press, 1957.

1184 Hutter, Lucy Maffei. Imigração italiana em São Paulo: 1880-1889. São Paulo: Instituto de Estudos Brasileiros, 1972.

1185 Ianni, Octávio. As metamorfoses do escravo: apogeu e crise da escravatura no Brasil meridional. São Paulo: DIFEL, 1962.

1186 _____. Raças e classes no Brasil. Rio de Janeiro: Editora Civilização Brasileira, 1966.

1187 Indiana University. Audio-Visual Center. "Brazil: The Vanishing Negro." b/w film, 30 min. Bloomington, Indiana, 1953.

1188 Instituto Brasileiro de Geografia e Estatística. Estudos sôbre a composição de população do Brasil segundo a côr. Rio de Janeiro: Instituto Brasileiro de geografia e Estatístico, 1950.

1189 Jurema, Aderbal. Insurreições negras no Brasil. Recife: Edições Mozart, 1935.

1190 Kalili, Narciso and Odacir de Mattos. "Existe preconceito de côr no Brasil." Realidade (Rio), 2 (1967), 53-55.

1191 Kando, Ata. Slave or Dead. Holland: n.p., 1971.

1192 Karasch, Mary Catherine. "Slave Life in Rio de Janeiro, 1808-1850." Diss. University of Wisconsin, 1972.

1193 Kennedy, James H. "Jorge de Lima: Brazilian Poet." Black World, 22:11 (September 1973), 18-23.

1194 Kent, R. K. "African Revolt in Bahia: 24-25 January 1835." Journal of Social History, 3:4 (Summer 1970), 334-356.

1195 _____. "Palmares: An African State in Brazil." Journal of African History, 6 (1964), 38-47.

1196 Kiemen, Mathias C. The Indian Policy of Portugal in the Amazon Region, 1614-1693. Washington, D.C.: Academy of American Franciscan History, 1954.

1197 _____. "The Status of the Indians in Brazil After 1820." The Americas, 21 (January 1965) 263-273.

1198 Kiernan, James P. "The Manumission of Slaves in Colonial

Brazil: Paraty, 1789-1822." Diss. New York University, 1976.

1199 Kietzman, Dale W. "Indian Survival in Brazil." Diss. University of Southern California, 1972.

1200 Klein, Herbert S. "The Colored Freedmen in Brazilian Slave Society." Journal of Social History, 3:1 (Fall 1969), 30-52.

1201 _____. "The Internal Slave Trade in Nineteenth Century Brazil: A Study of Slave Importations into Rio de Janeiro in 1852." Hispanic American Historical Review, 51:4 (November 1971), 567-585.

1202 _____. "The Trade in African Slaves in Rio de Janeiro, 1795-1811." Journal of African History, 10:4 (1969), 533-549.

1203 Knowlton, Clark. Sírios e libaneses: mobilidade social e espacial. São Paulo: Ed. Anhembi, 1960.

1204 Kottak, Conrad Phillip. "Race Relations in a Bahian Fishing Village." Luso-Brazilian Review, 4 (December 1967), 35-52.

1205 Lacerda, João Baptista. O Congresso Universal das Raças, apreciações e commentários. Rio de Janeiro: n.p., 1911.

1206 _____. "The Métis or Half-Breeds, of Brazil." Papers on Inter-racial Problems Communicated to the First Universal Races Congress held at the University of London, July 26-29, 1911. Ed. G. Spiller. London: Universal Races Congress, 1911, pp. 377-382.

1207 Laërne, C. F. Van Delden. Brazil and Java. London: W. H. Allen, 1885.

1208 Leacock, Seth. "Ceremonial Drinking in an Afro-Brazilian Cult." American Anthropologist, 66:2 (April 1964), 344-354.

1209 _____. "Fun-Loving Deities in an Afro-Brazilian Cult." Anthropological Quarterly, 37:3 (July 1964), 94-109.

1210 _____, and Ruth Leacock. Spirits of the Deep: A Study of an Afro-Brazilian Cult. Garden City, N.Y.: Doubleday, 1972.

1211 Lessa, Origenes. O índio côr-de-rosa. Rio de Janeiro: Editôra Codecri, 1978.

1212 Levine, Robert M. "The First Afro-Brazilian Congress:

Opportunities for the Study of Race in the Brazilian North-east." Race, 15: 2 (October 1973), 185-194.

1213 _____ . Historical Dictionary of Brazil. Metuchen, N. J.: Scarecrow Press, Inc., 1979.

1214 _____ . Pernambuco in the Brazilian Federation, 1889-1937. Stanford: Stanford University Press, 1978.

1215 _____ . "Some Views on Race and Immigration During the Old Republic." The Americas, 28:4 (April 1971), 373-381.

1216 _____ . "Sport & Society: A Case Study of Brazilian Futebol." Paper presented to the Symposium on Popular Culture in Brazil, Los Angeles, U. C. L. A., February 1979.

1217 _____ . The Vargas Regime. New York: Columbia University Press, 1970.

1218 Levi-Strauss, Claude. Tristes Tropiques. Tr. J. Russell. New York: Atheneum, 1963.

1219 Lins e Silva, Augusto. Atualidade de Nina Rodrígues. Rio de Janeiro: Ed. José Olympio, 1945.

1220 Livermore, H. V., ed. Portugal and Brazil: An Introduction. Oxford: Oxford University Press, 1953.

1221 Lobo, H. O negro na vida social brasileira. São Paulo: Panorama Ltda., 1941.

1222 Lowrie, S. H. "O elemento negro na população de São Paulo." Revista do Arguivo Municipal, São Paulo, 4:48 (1938), n. p.

1223 Luz, Nicia Vilela. A Amazônia para os negros americanos: as origens de uma controversia internacional. Rio de Janeiro: Editôra Saga, 1968.

1224 McGregor, Pedro. Jesus of the Spirits. New York: Stein and Day, 1967.

1225 MacLachlan, Colin, M. "African Slave Trade and Economic Development in Amazonia, 1799-1800." Slavery & Race Relations in Latin America. Ed. Robert B. Toplin. West-port, Conn.: Greenwood Publishing Company, 1974, pp. 112-145.

1226 _____ . "The Indian Directorate: Forced Acculturation in Portuguese America (1757-1799)." The Americas, (April 1972), 357-387.

1227 Maeyama, Takashi, et al. The Japanese and Their Descendents in Brazil: An Annotated Bibliography. São Paulo:
Centro de Estudos Nipo-Brasileiros, 1967.

1228 Manchester, Alan K. "Racial Democracy in Brazil." South
Atlantic Quarterly, 64: 1 (Winter 1965), 27-35.

1229 Marais, Ben J. Colour-Unsolved Problem of the West. Capetown: H. Timmins, 1952.

1230 Margulies, Marcos. Iudaica brasiliensis; repertório bibliográfico comentado dos livros relacionados com o judaismo.
Rio de Janeiro: Editôra Documentário, 1974.

1231 Martin, Percy A. "Slavery and Abolition in Brazil." Hispanic American Historical Review, 13:2 (May 1933), 151-
196.

1232 Martuscelli, C. "Uma pesquisa sôbre aceitação de grupos
'raciais' e grupos regionais." Boletim de Psicologia,
3 (1950), 53-73.

1233 Maybury-Lewis, David H. P. "Growth and Change in Brazil
Since 1930." Portugal and Brazil in Transition. Ed.
R. S. Sayers. Minneapolis: University of Minnesota
Press, 1968. pp. 159-173.

1234 _____. The Savage and the Innocent. Boston: Beacon,
1965.

1235 Melo, Verissimo de. "Bambelô: Sobrevivência negra no
Nordeste." Arquivos do Instituto de Anthropologia, 2
(March 1966), 185-190.

1236 Mendonça, Renato. A influência africana no português do
Brasil. 2nd ed. São Paulo: Companhia Editôra Nacional,
1935.

1237 Metall, R. A. and M. Paranhos de Silva. "Equality of Opportunity in a Multiracial Society: Brazil," International
Labour Review, 93 (January-June 1966), n.p.

1238 Miller, Joseph C., comp. Slavery: A Comparative Teaching Bibliography. Waltham, Mass.: African Studies Association, Brandeis University, 1977.

1239 Monk, Abraham. Black and White Race Relations in Brazil.
Buffalo, N.Y.: SUNY/Buffalo Special Studies, #4, 1971.

1240 Montezuma de Carvalho, Joaquim. Entrevista con Gilberto
Freyre. Mexico City: Frente de Afirmación Hispanista,
1975.

1241 Moreira, R. J. "Brancos em bailes de negros." Anhembí, 6 (1956), 274-288.

1242 Morse, Richard M. "The Negro in São Paulo, Brazil." Journal of Negro History, 38 (July 1953), 290-306.

1243 Moser, Bruno. Die schwartze Mutter von São Paulo: Brasilien Heute und Morgen. Koln: Eugen Diederichs Verlag, 1966.

1244 Moura, Clovis. Rebeliões da senzala: quilombos, insurreições, guerrilhas. Rio de Janeiro: Editôra Conquista, 1972.

1245 _____. "Revoltas de escravos em São Paulo." Revista do Arquivo Municipal de Cultura, 181:33 (April 1970), 101-111.

1246 Mulatas. Intro. Jorge Amado. 2nd ed. São Paulo: Ed. Três, 1978.

1247 Nascimento, Abdias de. O genocídio do negro brasileiro: processo de um racismo mascarado. Rio de Janeiro: Paz e Terra, 1978.

1248 _____. "Racial Democracy" in Brazil: Myth or Reality? Ife, Nigeria: University of Ife, 1977.

1249 Nelson, M. V. "Negro in Brazil as Seen Through the Chronicles of Travellers, 1800-1868." Journal of Negro History, 30 (April 1945), 203-18.

1250 Nogueira, O. "Atitudes desfavoráveis de alguns anunciates de São Paulo em relação aos empregados de côr." Sociologia, 4:4 (1942).

1251 Nunes, Maria Luisa. "The Preservation of African Culture in Brazilian Literature: The Novels of Jorge Amado." Luso-Brazilian Review, 10 (June 1973), 86-101.

1252 Oberg, Kalervo. "Race Relations in Brazil." Sociologia, 20:1 (March 1956), 340-353.

1253 Odalia, Nilo. "O ideal de branqueamento da raça na historiografia brasileira." Contexto, 3 (July 1977), 127-136.

1254 Overholt, William H. ed. The Future of Brazil. Boulder, Colorado: Westview Press, 1978.

1255 Parisse, Lucien. "Bibliografía cronológica sôbre a favela do Rio de Janeiro a partir de 1940." América Latina, 12: 3 (July-September 1969), 221-232.

1256 Peixoto, Afrânio. A Esfinge. Rio de Janeiro: Briquet, 1911.

1257 Penn, Dorothy. "We Brazilians Are Becoming One People." Catholic World, 163 (April 1946), 34-40.

1258 Pereira, João Baptista Borges. "Der Neger und die Brasilianische Volksmusik." Staden-Jahrbuch, 16 (1968) 23-31.

1259 _____. "O negro e a comercialização da música popular brasileira." Revista do Instituto de Estudos Brasileiros, 8 (1970), 7-15.

1260 Pierson, Donald. "Diluição da linha de côr na Bahia." Revista do Arquivo Municipal de São Paulo, 139 (1943) 105-127.

1261 _____. "The Negro in Bahia, Brazil." American Sociological Review, 4 (1939), 524-533.

1262 _____. Negroes in Brazil: A Study of Race Contact at Bahia. Carbondale, Illinois: Southern Illinois University Press, 1967.

1263 _____. "Race Relations in Portuguese America." Race Relations in World Perspective. Honolulu: n. p., 1955.

1264 _____. Survey of the Literature on Brazil of Sociological Significance Published up to 1940. Cambridge: Harvard University Press, 1945.

1265 Porter, Dorothy B., comp. Afro-Braziliana: A Working Bibliography. Boston: G. K. Hall, 1978.

1266 _____. "Negro in the Brazilian Abolition Movement." Journal of Negro History, 37 (January 1952), 54-80.

1267 Prado Júnior, Caio. The Colonial Background of Modern Brazil. Tr. Suzette Macedo. Berkeley: University of California Press, 1967.

1268 Preto-Rodas, Richard A. Negritude as a Theme in the Poetry of the Portuguese-Speaking World. Gainesville: University of Florida Humanities Monograph Series, No. 31, 1970.

1269 Primitive People's Fund. Report of a Visit to the Indians of Brazil. London: Primitive People's Fund, 1971.

1270 Putnam, Samuel. "Race and Nation in Brazil." Science and Society, 7:4 (1943), 321-27.

1271 Querino, Manuel. Costumes africanos no Brasil. Rio de
Janeiro, n. p. : 1938.

1272 _____, and E. Bradford Burns. The African Contribution
to Brazilian Civilization. Tempe, Arizona: Center for
Latin American Studies, Arizona State University, 1977.

1273 Rabassa, Gregory. "The Negro in Brazilian Fiction Since
1888." Diss. Columbia University, 1954.

1274 Raeders, Georges. Le Comte de Cobineau au Brésil. Paris:
n. p. , 1934.

1275 Ramos, Arthur. "Acculturation Among the Brazilian Negroes:
Religious Culture in Bahia." Journal of Negro History,
26 (April 1941), 244-50.

1276 _____. A aculturação negra no Brasil. São Paulo: Companhia Editôra Nacional, 1942.

1277 _____. Introdução à antropologia brasileira. 2 vols.
Rio de Janeiro: Edições da Coleção Estudos Brasileiros,
1943-47.

1278 _____. The Negro in Brazil. Washington, D. C. : Association Publishers Inc. , 1939.

1279 _____. "Vila Rica: Profile of a Colonial Brazilian Urban Center." The Americas, 35:4 (April 1979), 495-526.

1280 Rebouças, André Pinto. Agricultura nacional: estudos eco-
nômicos. Rio de Janeiro: n. p. , 1883.

1281 Reeve, Richard Penn. "Race and Social Conflict in a Brazilian Industrial Town." Luso-Brazilian Review, 14 (Winter 1977), 236-253.

1282 Reis, Jaime. "Abolition and the Economics of Slaveholding
in North East Brazil." Boletin de Estudos Latino-Amer-
icanas y del Caribe, 17 (December 1974), 3-20.

1283 Ribeiro, Darcy. Os índios e a civilização. Rio de Janeiro:
Civilização Brasileira, 1970.

1284 Ribeiro, René. "Personality and the Psychosexual Adjust-
ment of Afro-Brazilian Cult Members." Journal de la
Societé des Americanistes (Paris), 58 (1969), 109-120.

1285 _____. "Relations of the Negro with Christianity in Portuguese America." The Americas, 14 (1958), 454-484.

1286 _____. "Situação étnica no nordeste." Sociologia, 15: 3
(August 1953).

1287 Rocha, Manoel Ribeiro. Ethiope resgatado. Lisbon: n.p.,
      1750.

1288 Rodman, Hyman. "On Understanding Lower Class Behavior."
      Social and Economic Studies, 8:4 (December 1959), 441-
      450.

1289 Rodrígues, José Honório. Brazil and Africa. Berkeley:
      University of California Press, 1965.

1290 _____. "The Influence of Africa on Brazil and of Brazil
      on Africa." Journal of African History, 3:1 (1962), 49-
      67.

1291 Rondón, Cândido M. de S. Indios do Brasil. 3 vols. Rio
      de Janeiro: Conselho Nacional de Proteção aos Indios,
      1946.

1292 Rout, Leslie B., Jr. "Brazil: Study in Black, Brown and
      Beige." Negro Digest, 19 (February 1970), 21-23; 65-
      73.

1293 _____. "Race and Slavery in Brazil." The Wilson Quar-
      terly, 1 (August 1976), 73-89.

1294 _____. "Race Relations in Southern Brazil: The Pôrto
      Alegre Experience." Proceedings of the Pacific Coast
      Council on Latin American Studies, 4 (1975), 89-100.

1295/6 _____. "Slight of Hand: Brazilian and American Auth-
      ors Manipulate the Brazilian Racial Situation, 1910-1951."
      The Americas, 29:4 (April 1973), 471-488.

1297 Russell-Wood, A. J. R. "Black and Mulatto Brotherhoods
      in Colonial Brazil: A Study in Collective Behavior."
      Hispanic American Historical Review, 54:4 (November
      1974), 567-602.

1298 _____. "Race and Class in Brazil, 1937-1967." Race,
      10: 2 (October 1968), 185-191.

1299 Rust, Francis. "Wilson Antônio Rosa: An Afro-Brazilian
      Pen Portrait." Contemporary Review, 23 (December
      1973), 318-22.

1300 Sanjek, Roger. "Brazilian Racial Terms: Some Aspects of
      Meaning and Learning." American Anthropologist, 73
      (1971), 1126-1143.

1301 Santana, E. T. Relações entre prêtos e brancos em São
      Paulo. São Paulo: Edição do Autor, 1951.

1302 Sayers, Raymond S. The Negro in Brazilian Literature.
      New York: Hispanic Institute, 1956.

1303 Scarano, Julita. "Black Brotherhoods: Integration or Con-
      tradiction?" Luso-Brazilian Review, 16:1 (Summer 1979),
      1-17.

1304 Schneider, Ronald M. Brazil: Foreign Policy of a Future
      World Power. Boulder, Colorado: Westview Press,
      1977.

1305 Schwartz, Stuart B. "The Manumission of Slaves in Colonial
      Brazil: Bahia, 1684-1745." Hispanic American Historical
      Review, 54:4 (November 1974), 603-635.

1306 Seeger, Anthony and Eduardo Viveiros de Castro. "Pontos
      de vista sôbre os índios brasileiros: um ensaio biblio-
      gráfico." Dados, 17 (1977), 11-35.

1307 Serton, Petrus. Suid Afrika en Brasilie. Capetown: Oxford
      University Press, 1960.

1308 Skidmore, Thomas E. Black into White: Race and Nation-
      ality in Brazilian Thought. New York: Oxford University
      Press, 1974.

1309 _____. "Gilberto Freyre and the Early Brazilian Repub-
      lic: Some Notes on Methodology." Comparative Studies
      in Society and History, 6 (July 1964) 490-505.

1310 _____. "Toward a Comparative Analysis of Race Rela-
      tions Since Abolition in Brazil and the United States,"
      Journal of Latin American Studies, 4 (May 1972), 1-28.

1311 Staley, Austin J. Racial Democracy in Marriage: A Socio-
      logical Analysis of Negro-White Intermarriage in Bra-
      zilian Culture. Ann Arbor: University of Michigan
      Press, 1960.

1312 Staniford, Philip. Pioneers in the Tropics: The Political
      Organization of Japanese in an Immigrant Community of
      Brazil. London: University of London Athlone Press,
      1973.

1313 Stein, Stanley J. "Freyre's Brazil Revisited: A Review of
      New World in the Tropics: The Culture of Modern Brazil."
      Hispanic American Historical Review, 41:1 (February
      1961), 111-113.

1314 Tannenbaum, Frank. Slave and Citizen: The Negro in the
      Americas. New York: Alfred A. Knopf, 1947.

1315 Taylor, Kit Sims. Sugar and the Underdevelopment of North-
      eastern Brazil, 1500-1970. Gainesville: University of
      Florida Press, 1978.

1316 Teatro Experimental do Negro. Testemunhas. Rio de Jan-
      eiro: Ed. GRD, 1966.

1317 Toplin, Robert Brent. "Abolition and the Issue of the Black
      Freedman's Future in Brazil." Slavery and Race Rela-
      tions in Latin America. Ed. Robert B. Toplin. West-
      port, Connecticut: Greenwood Publishing Company, 1974,
      pp. 253-276.

1318 _____. The Abolition of Slavery in Brazil. New York:
      Atheneum, 1972.

1319 _____. "Brazil: Racial Polarization in the Developing
      Giant." Black World, 22:1 (November 1972), 15-22.

1320 _____. "Upheaval, Violence, and the Abolition of Slavery
      in Brazil: The Case of São Paulo." Hispanic American
      Review, 49:4 (November 1969), 639-655.

1321 Turner, Doris J. "Symbols in Two Afro-Brazilian Literary
      Works," Teaching Latin American Studies, Ed. Miriam
      Williford. Gainesville, Fla.: LASA, 1977, pp. 41-61.

1322 Turner, J. Michael. "Reversing the Trend: Afro-Brazilian
      Influences in West Africa," The Thematic Conceptual Ap-
      proach to West African History. Ed. Lathardus Goggins.
      Dubuque, Iowa: n. p. , 1979.

1323 Valente, Waldemar. Sobrevivências daomeanas nos grupos
      de culto Afronordestinos. Recife: Ministerio da Educa-
      ção e Cultura, Instituto Joaquim Nabuco de Pesquisas So-
      ciais, 1964.

1324 Venâncio Filho, Francisco. Euclides da Cunha e seus amigos.
      São Paulo: Companhia Editôra Nacional, 1938.

1325 Verger, Pierre. Bahia and the West African Slave Trade,
      1549-1851. Ibadan, Nigeria: Ibadan University Press,
      1964.

1326 Vianna, Helio. "A abolição de escravidão no Brasil." Re-
      vista de História de América, 60 (July-December 1965),
      69-90.

1327 Vidal, Lux Boelitz. Morte e vida de uma sociedade indigena
      brasileira. São Paulo: HUCITEC, 1977.

1328 Vieira Filho, Domingo, ed. A escravidão negra através de
      anúncio de jornal. São Luis: Depto. de Cultura do Es-
      tado de Maranhão, 1968.

1329 Villas Boas, Orlando and Claudio. "Saving Brazil's Stone
      Age Tribes from Extinction," National Geographic, 134
      (September 1968), 424-444.

1330 _____, and _____. Xingú: The Indians, Their Myths.
Tr. Susana H. Rudge. Ed. Kenneth S. Brecher. New
York: Farrar, Straus and Giroux, 1973.

1331 Viotta da Costa, Emília. Da senzala a colônia. São Paulo:
DIFEL, 1966.

1332 Von Puttkamer, W. Jesco. "Brazil's Kreen-Akarores: Re-
quium for a Tribe?" National Geographic, 147 (February
1975), 254-268.

1333 Wagley, Charles. Amazon Town: A Study of Man in the
Tropics. New York: Columbia University Press, 1964.

1334 _____. Introduction to Brazil. rev. ed. New York:
Columbia University Press, 1971.

1335 _____. Welcome of Tears: The Tapirapé Indians of Central Brazil. London: Oxford University Press, 1977.

1336 _____, and Marvin Harris. Minorities in the New World:
Six Case Studies. New York: Columbia University Press,
1958.

1137 _____, and _____. Race and Class in Rural Brazil.
Paris: UNESCO, 1952.

1338 Warren, Donald, Jr. "The Negro and Religion in Brazil."
Race, 6:3 (January 1965), 199-216.

1339 _____. "Spiritism in Brazil." Journal of Inter-American
Studies, 10:3 (July 1968), 393-405.

1340 Willems, Emílio. "Race Attitudes in Brazil." American
Journal of Sociology, 54 (March 1949), 402-408.

1341 Williams, Mary W. "Treatment of Negro Slaves in Brazilian
Empire: A Comparison with the United States of America." Journal of Negro History, 15 (July 1930), 315-36.

1342 Wycliffe Bible Translators. Brazil's Tribes. Campinas:
Summer Institute of Linguistics, 1967.